Frommer's®

IRREVERENT

guide to

Washington D.C.

6th Edition

By
Tom Price & Susan Crites Price

BICENTENNIAL
1807
WILEY
2007
BICENTENNIAL

Wiley Publishing, Inc.

other titles in the

IRREVERENT GUIDE

series

About the Authors

Tom and Susan Price have lived in and written about Washington, D.C., for more than two decades, Tom focusing on government, politics, business, technology, and education, and Susan on topics of importance to women and families. They coauthored the award-winning *Working Parents Help Book: Practical Advice for Dealing with the Day-to-Day Challenges of Kids and Careers,* which was featured on *Today, Oprah,* and other broadcast and print media. Tom also wrote *Washington, D.C. For Dummies.*

Published by:
Wiley Publishing, Inc.

111 River St.
Hoboken, NJ 07030-5774

ISBN-13: 978-0-470-04729-3
ISBN-10: 0-470-04729-1

Interior design contributed to by Marie Kristine Parial-Leonardo

Editor: Stephen Bassman
Production Editor: Ian Skinnari
Cartographer: Guy Ruggiero
Photo Editor: Richard Fox
Anniversary Logo Design: Richard Pacifico
Production by Wiley Indianapolis Composition Services

For information on our other products and services or to obtain technical support, please contact our Customer Care Department within the U.S. at 800/762-2974, outside the U.S. at 317/572-3993 or fax 317/572-4002.

Wiley also publishes its books in a variety of electronic formats. Some content that appears in print may not be available in electronic formats.

Manufactured in the United States of America

5 4 3 2 1

A Disclaimer

Prices fluctuate in the course of time, and travel information changes under the impact of the varied and volatile factors that influence the travel industry. We therefore suggest that you write or call ahead for confirmation when making your travel plans. Every effort has been made to ensure the accuracy of information throughout this book and the contents of this publication are believed correct at the time of printing. Nevertheless, the publishers cannot accept responsibility for errors or omissions or for changes in details given in this guide or for the consequences of any reliance on the information provided by the same. Assessments of attractions and so forth are based upon the author's own experience and therefore, descriptions given in this guide necessarily contain an element of opinion, which may not reflect the publisher's opinion or dictate a reader's own experience on another occasion. Readers are invited to write to the publisher with ideas, comments, and suggestions for future editions.

Your safety is important to us, however, so we encourage you to stay alert and be aware of your surroundings. Keep a close eye on cameras, purses, and wallets, all favorite targets of thieves and pickpockets.

CONTENTS

INTRODUCTION

It's always been easy to be irreverent about Washington. Thomas Jefferson called the United States' new capital "that Indian swamp in the wilderness." Charles Dickens dubbed it "headquarters of tobacco-tinctured saliva." Civil War–era visitor G. A. Sala described Washington as "a vast practical joke...the most 'bogus' of towns—a shin-plaster in brick and mortar with a delusive frontispiece of marble." According to poet Dylan Thomas, "Washington isn't a city, it's an abstraction." To President Kennedy, it was "a city of Southern efficiency and Northern charm"—which inspired numerous takeoffs about Republican compassion and Democratic frugality, yuppie spontaneity and redneck subtlety, bureaucratic ingenuity and entrepreneurial conscience, liberal piety and conservative angst, Eastern modesty and Midwestern chic, and on into infinity....

Washington Confidential, by Jack Lait and Lee Mortimer, described our town in the '50s as "a made-to-order architectural paradise with the political status of an Indian reservation, inhabited by 800,000 economic parasites; no industries but one, government, and the tradesmen and servants and loafers and scum that feed on the highest average per capita income in the world, where exist the soundest security, the mightiest power, and the most superlative rates of crime, vice, and juvenile delinquency anywhere." (Things are different now, say the cynics. There are only about 550,000 parasites.)

Ah, but still they come. Politicians denounce Washington in the shrillest of tones in frantic efforts to win elections that will let them live here. Journalists compete fervidly for coveted spots in Washington bureaus where they can expose the shocking horrors of politicians running amok. Lawyers...lobbyists...tourists....

Could it be, possibly, because this really is the most powerful city in the world? Because it is the seat of a great democracy, which, it has been said, is the worst possible form of government except for all the others? Because of the free museums, the historical buildings, the ever-improving culture, entertainment, and restaurant offerings? Because watching major-league politics up close can just be a whole lot of fun? All of the above?

This soggy lowland at the convergence of the Potomac and Anacostia rivers became the capital thanks to the kind of big-time insider horse-trading that would later define the Washington way of life. (Until recently, when Democrats and Republicans have moved so far apart they have trouble trading insults!) Two pre-Beltway sharpies, New Yorker Alexander Hamilton and Jefferson the Virginian, brokered the deal. They convinced the South to finally pay off the soldiers who won the Revolutionary War, in return for which they promised the capital would not be one of the big cities of the North—New York, Philadelphia, or (Heaven forbid!) Boston. Thus, Washington was created out of nothing, plopped down in the middle of the new country, nearly in the middle of nowhere, in one of many attempts to reconcile the constantly feuding North and South, which resulted finally, you may recall, in the Civil War.

Washington did not have a natural birth because of coal or iron or a river or a lake or an ocean port. Unlike Pittsburgh or Cleveland or Chicago or New York or any other organic city, Washington was sort of a test-tube baby—invented by politicians and saddled with unnatural DNA that haunts us to this day. Many visitors don't know this, but Congress controls Washington, and Washingtonians do not enjoy the simple rights of citizenship that residents of the 50 states take for granted. We pay federal taxes. When there's a military draft, our children are drafted. But we have no voting representation in Congress. We do get to vote for president. But everything our mayor and council do can be overturned by members of Congress whose knowledge and interests and voting constituents live in California or Maine or Florida or that other Washington. We can't tax commuters. We can't vote to use our own local taxes in ways our federal overseers don't approve. That's why if you look closely at our license plates, you'll see we've adopted a unique city slogan. North

Map 1: D.C. Metropolitan Area

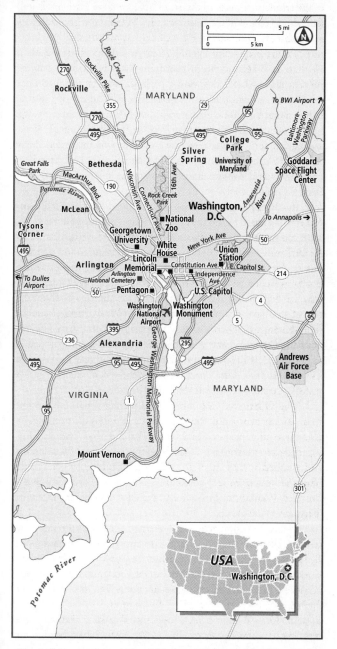

Carolina's plates may proclaim that state to be "First in Flight," Ohio's the "Birthplace of Aviation." (Oooo, let's have a debate.) But, in the capital of the free world, it's "Taxation without Representation."

Unfortunately, we Washingtonians haven't always made it clear that we're capable of governing ourselves. Our longest-serving mayor, Marion S. Barry, Jr., led a corrupt and incompetent government and won himself a jail term by getting videotaped in 1990 ingesting cocaine while in the company of a woman who—how shall we say this?—was not his wife. Following his jail term, the wise voters of Washington awarded Berry one more mayoral term, much to the pleasure of stand-up comedians and congressmen who want to maintain their ultimate control.

By 1995, things got so bad that Congress appointed a financial control board to run the city, and many Washington residents accepted the wisdom of the action. In 1998, we elected Anthony A. Williams—a nerdish, bow-tie-wearing, bean counter—to be our mayor; and he did make a lot of improvements, including convincing Congress that the control board no longer was necessary. Like many big, old cities, however, we still suffer more than our share of urban problems—a handful of truly excellent public schools within a public school system that still lets most of its students down, inadequate public services, a still-too-incompetent bureaucracy, and (the latest burden) the discovery of buried World War I weapons—including components of mustard gas!—in one of our most affluent residential neighborhoods.

The District of Columbia (*dee see* in local parlance) originally spread across a perfect diamond, 10 miles on each side—69 square miles donated by Maryland and 31 by Virginia. D.C. originally was sort of a ministate—or, more accurately, a county. It contained the newly created Washington City, which was to be home to the federal government and site of a capitol and a president's house, and the already thriving river ports of George Town and Alexandria.

George Washington hired Pierre L'Enfant, a Frenchman, to plan the new capital—not surprising since the Marquis de Lafayette, another Frenchman, had helped to win our revolution. L'Enfant's vision—a grid of streets intersected at odd angles by broad avenues and verdant roundabouts—defines the city today.

In 1846, Virginia reclaimed its donation, and now the winding Potomac River marks D.C.'s southwestern border. So, if you live in that former Washington enclave, you get to vote for a representative and two senators who will battle to the death to protect you from the D.C. taxman and to force your political values down the throats of your neighbors to the north. George Town now is Georgetown, Washington's most exclusive residential neighborhood and a popular spot for shopping and nightlife. Alexandria now is one of Virginia's most attractive cities and also a popular spot for shopping and nightlife. Washington City has sort of faded from memory, referred to now most often as D.C.'s "federal core," while many residential and commercial neighborhoods have grown up to fill what was mostly unoccupied land 2 centuries ago. If you see what looks like an old farmhouse, it probably was!

Even more dramatic growth has occurred outside the D.C. borders. Washington today is the hub of a metropolitan area of more than five million, the eighth largest in the United States. It sprawls across Virginia and Maryland suburbs and exurbs and sends commuter tentacles as far as West Virginia and southern Pennsylvania.

Washington also has developed an awkward symbiotic relationship with Baltimore. Because, until 2005, Major League Baseball believed it made more sense to have opening day in Tokyo than to ever play our national pastime in our nation's capital, Washingtonians trekked up I-95 to Baltimore for big-league baseball (not real baseball, of course, but the kind they play in the American League, with hitters who don't field and pitchers who don't hit). Baltimoreans slipped down here for NBA basketball and NHL hockey. Washington returned to the baseball bigs in 2005, when the Montreal Expos moved south and became the Nationals, and we've got a new ballpark in our not-too-distant future. But the Baltimore baseball connection lives on—not just because of residual fandom, but because Major League Baseball exercised its monopoly power to award the Nationals' TV rights to Peter Angelos—the evil lawyer who owns the Orioles—denying the Nats an important source of revenue.

With lots of white-collar jobs, Washington is one of America's most affluent regions. The metropolitan area's $72,000 median family income exceeds that national median of $50,000 by nearly 45%. Nearly 6% of the region's families earn more than $200,000 a year, which is double the national average. In D.C. itself, the median income of $46,000 is not much below the national median. But the city is high on both extremes, with 7% of families in the $200,000-plus bracket and 12.6%—more than double the national average—earning less than $10,000 a year.

Like many inner cities, D.C. has about twice as many black residents (60%) as white (31%), compared with a national population that is 75% white and just 12% black. Sixty percent of the metropolitan area's residents are white, 26% black.

The region is economically strong and becoming more economically diverse. For instance, much of the Internet is managed from northern Virginia, home to America Online and many other cyber-businesses. D.C.'s Maryland suburbs have become a hotbed of biotechnology.

The federal government's presence gives Washington a fascinatingly diverse population as well. Members of Congress, their staffs, the lobbyists who influence them, and the journalists who report about them come from every nook and cranny of America. The Washington region also plays host to diplomats, journalists, and business folks from just about every nation on the globe. As a result, our restaurants serve a wide range of cuisines and our entertainment and cultural institutions are global in scope.

All this diversity makes Washingtonians a fairly tolerant lot, despite the vicious verbal battles that are fought in Congress and on the various radio and television broadcasts that feature Washington denizens shouting at each other from behind their partisan and ideological barricades. Washington is home to an unusually large number of middle-class and wealthy African Americans. D.C.'s gay community is large and vibrant—its most prominent institutions located near Dupont Circle but its members living in homes throughout the city and nearby suburbs.

In most ways, Washingtonians are just like other Americans. Get away from the government buildings and national monuments, and our residential and business neighborhoods look much like anybody else's. Nevertheless, we have to admit that Washington is special—for better and worse—for reasons that are easy to understand.

Politics is to Washington as oil is to Houston, cars are to Detroit, and entertainment is to Los Angeles. Despite D.C.'s growing diversity, a whole bunch of us work for—or around—the government. Even our children soak up the atmosphere. In how many other places would a 4-year-old tell you this joke, as a playmate of our daughter's told us: "I know how to spell Sununu," this little boy said, referring to John Sununu, then chief of staff for the first President Bush. "I just don't know when to stop."

YOU PROBABLY DIDN'T KNOW

What the locals call the place... Seldom "Washington"-too big a mouthful and too easy to confuse with that state out West. More common locutions: "D.C." or "the District."

How to be a "Special Interest"... Americans love to complain that members of Congress cater to special interests instead of taking care of the national interest-and then to demand that *their* senators and representatives bring the bacon home to *their* communities and take care of *them* when *they* need special help. You're like that, too. Or at least you ought to be if you want to get the most out of your Washington visit. Your senators and representative can give you passes to the **Congressional visitors' galleries** so you can watch the action (or, more often, inaction) in the House and Senate chambers. (Spy what's going on in the corner while the C-SPAN cameras are focused on the speaker who probably is addressing a nearly empty room.) Lawmakers also can get you admitted to special

Congressional VIP Tours at many top tourist attractions, including the White House, Capitol, Library of Congress, FBI, Bureau of Engraving and Printing, Kennedy Center for the Performing Arts, and the Supreme Court. Telephone one or more of your legislators and ask for tickets for the VIP tours you want. Also ask if there's any other help they offer to tourists from back home. Lawmakers who tend to get re-elected tend to make nice-nice with their constituents. You might score a private tour of the Capitol. (Really!) You can reach any senator at Tel 202/224-3121, any representative at Tel 202/225-3121. The earlier you call (even several months ahead of your trip), the more likely you are to find some cool deals.

Which attractions require advance planning... Security after the September 11, 2001, terrorist attacks makes long-term planning a must if you want to visit the White House. A limited number of tours are open only to groups of 10 or more who make arrangements through their member of Congress. (To see if this policy has been liberalized, phone the **White House Visitors Office** at Tel 202/456-7041, or check the White House website at www.whitehouse.gov/history/tours.) You can contact your senators or representative up to 6 months before your visit. (See previous paragraph for how.) Early requests also are advised for the Congressional VIP Tours described in the previous paragraph. You can avoid the scramble for tickets to the heavily visited permanent exhibition at the **Holocaust Memorial Museum** by paying $1.75 in advance to Tickets.com (www.tickets.com or Tel 800/400-9373). The only way to tour the **State Department's Diplomatic Reception Rooms** is by making a reservation, preferably at least 90 days in advance. Your best bet is to click the online "Request a Tour" link at reception tours.state.gov, or call Tel 202/647-3241 (TDD line for the deaf is Tel 202/736-4474). You'll need a picture ID for admission. The tour is not recommended for children younger than 12 or for older kids who aren't enthralled by history and art. Tours may be canceled without notice when the reception rooms are required for their primary official use: hosting international pooh-bahs and muckety-mucks. When visiting the **Washington Monument,** you can cut down on your time standing in line and assure your admission by buying time-specific tickets in advance for $2. Call Tel 800/967-2283 between 10am and 10pm Eastern Time.

How to get Redskins tickets... The Redskins are one of the few subjects about which almost everyone in Washington–Democrat/Republican, black/white, male/female-agrees (if you put aside the raging controversy over whether the name "Redskins" itself is a vile racist slur, as the critics contend, or "a tribute to a valorous people," as deceased longtime team owner Jack Kent Cooke was fond of insisting). Almost all Washingtonians are Redskins fans, so it's tough to get tickets, even though the team's constantly expanding FedEx Field now seats more than 90,000! For a single-game ticket, you'll need to buy from a **broker** at a what-the-market-can-gouge price. Google "buy Redskins tickets."

What the president (and everybody else) is doing today... The most comprehensive public listing of official Washington activities is the **"Daybook"** published by *The Washington Times,* the daily newspaper owned by the Unification Church (better known as the Moonies, for their devotion to the Rev. Sun Myung Moon). Here you'll find schedules for the White House, Congress, the Supreme Court, federal agencies, and others. It's also online at www.washingtontimes.com/national/daybook.htm.

How to find out what's really going on with the D.C. government... Local politics can be buried by national politics in the nation's capital, but local political junkies can get at least a partial fix on the local airwaves. Washington's preeminent local political analyst and commentator is probably **Mark Plotkin,** who is both a knowledgeable observer of and a fierce advocate for the District. His *The Politics Program* can be heard at 10am Fridays on *The Washington Post*'s new radio station, WTWP, which unfortunately sends out less-than-ideal signals at 1500 AM and 107.7 FM. If you can't stand WTWP's status, you can watch Plotkin and his guests talk when a videotape of the program is televised by cable's NewsChannel 8 at 1am. It's sort of surreal to watch people in a radio studio, with earphones on their heads and coffee cups in their hands, sometimes fielding phoned-in listener questions from listeners who no longer are listening "live." **Kojo Nnamdi** and **Jonetta Rose Barras** host the *D.C. Politics Hour* at noon Fridays on WAMU, 88.5 FM, the American University station.

Washington's Best Websites

- **FirstGov** (www.firstgov.gov). The federal government's main website. Directories and search engines link to just about everything the federal government puts online and lots of other stuff as well.

- **White House** (www.whitehouse.gov). A wide range of materials from presidential speeches to special stuff for kids. Administration officials answer citizens' questions in an online chat called "Ask the White House."

- **U.S. House of Representatives** (www.house.gov). The Web is one place where the House beats the Senate hands-down. Easy access to information about members, committees, legislation, schedules. There's also a helpful section for tourists called "Visiting D.C."

- **Library of Congress** (www.loc.gov). Ever-growing online access to the world's greatest library. Search the catalog, listen to music, look at paintings, check out Thomas Jefferson's first draft of the Declaration of Independence, and on and on and on.

- **THOMAS** (thomas.loc.gov). Pioneering government website from the Library of Congress. You can search for and read legislation, committee reports, roll calls, the Congressional Record, and other congressional documents.

- **FBI** (www.fbi.gov). Ten Most Wanted list, history of the FBI, enormous amount of information on all kinds of crime and crime fighting. View Osama Bin Laden's Ten Most Wanted poster, on which you're warned that he is "considered armed and extremely dangerous" and you're told of up to $27 million in rewards you could claim for providing information that leads to his capture. You can actually download the poster as a PDF file and make a printout if you'd like some sure-to-start-a-conversation artwork for your wall.

- **CIA** (www.cia.gov). No secrets, but as close to the inside of The Agency as you're likely to get. Take a virtual tour of CIA headquarters. Check out some of The Agency's useful information sources, such as the widely read *World Factbook*.

> - **Washington D.C. Convention and Tourism Corporation** (www.washington.org). Information and services for tourists, meeting planners, and travel professionals. Calendars, maps, hotel reservations, you name it.
> - **The *Washington Post*** (www.washingtonpost.com). One of the world's great newspapers. Reports the top news of the day-including what's happening in D.C. For tourist info, click on the "City Guide" link near the top of the home page.
> - ***Washingtonian*** (www.washingtonian.com). Washington's main magazine. Easy-to-use guides to restaurants, arts, entertainment, and much more.

How to ride an escalator, Washington-style... A *Washington Post* columnist staged a contest a few years ago to come up with a name for people who stand to the left on escalators and block the progress of people who want to walk. The winning entry: "Tourists." You now are forewarned. D.C. escalator etiquette requires that you stand on the right and walk on the left.

How much to fear the parking cops... The Washington city government may have its inefficiencies (to say the least), but one island of Prussian efficiency is its parking police. If you doubt that, try parking in a no-parking zone or at an expired meter. Better yet, park your car along a curb that is to be kept clear during rush hour. The fine is $100, and you'll pay another $100 if your car is towed.

Where to rub (and bend) elbows with politicos... Denizens of the Senate (north) side of the Capitol mourn the passing of **La Colline,** an excellent French restaurant with privacy-protecting seating that was conducive to secret political plotting and confidential reporter-source lunching-when one's newspaper was picking up the tab, that is. In September 2006, it was replaced, at 400 N. Capitol St. NW (Tel 202/296-2021), by **Johnny's Half Shell,** a good seafood restaurant that relocated from Dupont Circle. We'll have to wait to see if it becomes a senatorial hangout. In the meantime, we'll always have **The Monocle,** 107 D St. NE (Tel 202/546-4488), a portrait-festooned nerve center of the Old Boy Network (senators, Supreme Court justices, etc.), which also offers commendable food and attentive service. To check out the New Boy Network (Republican Senate staffers, for example), hit the modern bar at **Bistro Bis,** 15 E St. NW (202/661-2700). Hangouts tend to be more modest on the House side of the Hill. Lots of staffers head for conveniently located **Bullfeathers,** 410 1st St. SE (Tel 202/543-5005), for lunch or happy hour (4-8pm Mon-Sat for drinks, 3:30-6:30pm for food). Staffers and representatives who are into downscale-chic frequent the **Tune Inn,** 331 Pennsylvania Ave. SE (Tel 202/543-2725), where beer and burgers are the consumables of choice.

How to hobnob with Washington society... For information on balls, galas, premieres, fashion shows, house tours, regattas, and charity benefits all over the Washington area, check out the "Benefits" section of the monthly *Washingtonian* magazine.

How not to be a crime victim... Like many big cities, Washington has experienced an increase in crime lately. Crime is still almost unheard of within Metrorail stations and trains. The Mall used to feel safe round the clock, but a couple of well-publicized muggings after dark in 2006 challenged that complacency.

The key to safety remains simple common sense. Don't go wandering about parts of town you know nothing about. At night, stick to the well-lighted streets. If you go partying in Adams-Morgan or the U Street Corridor, don't stay out

● ●

SECURITY CLEARANCE

The level of security in Washington has a lot to do with the latest headlines. As soon as the Persian Gulf War broke out in 1991, security checkpoints quickly popped up in buildings you could previously enter without challenge. Within days of the Oklahoma City bombings in April 1995, the priceless Gutenberg Bible was spirited away from the Library of Congress to parts unknown, and tours of the NASA Goddard Space Flight Center were suspended. Since the attacks of September 11, 2001, tours and public access to government buildings have been suspended or curtailed. You'll have to pass through metal detectors to enter most government buildings, you may not be allowed to carry any but the smallest bag, and the carrying of sharp objects- even small pocket knives-may be prohibited. In addition, some visitor attractions require adults to show a picture ID-a passport or a driver's license with photograph will do the trick. Some places also require your date of birth and Social Security number for security checks.

● ●

past closing time (when drunks hit the streets and sometimes get violent). If Metrorail service has stopped for the night, take a taxi. Know your destination before you get out of the cab. Hold your kids' hands on city streets and sidewalks, on all Metrorail escalators, and on Metrorail platforms. Lock your hotel room door, car doors, and trunk. Don't leave luggage or other items visible in your car when you park it. Lock valuables in a hotel safe deposit box (if not in your room, at the front desk). Keep a tight hold on your pocketbook and camera. Hold onto your purse in a restaurant. Carry your cash and credit cards in a front pocket or a concealed money pouch. Leave the family jewels at home; what you do bring, don't flash. Don't leave a purse or other bag unattended in public. Not only might you lose it to a purse snatcher, you might lose it to law enforcement officials who worry there might be a bomb inside.

The true meaning of "Watergate"... The Watergate scandal that toppled the Nixon presidency was named for the Watergate office building where Nixon supporters tried to bug the Democratic National Committee's offices. In turn, the building was named for nearby steps, east of the Lincoln Memorial, which rose from the Potomac River and once served as the entry point for visitors arriving by water. For several decades following the mid 1930s, concertgoers sat on the steps for performances of the National Symphony Orchestra from a floating band shell that was supplied by the Navy.

Washington's best mystery series... Good mystery novels tell you what goes on beneath the city's surface, and two mystery writers' series are by lifelong insiders. **Margaret Truman,** daughter of "Give 'Em Hell" Harry, writes the Capital Crime Series, so far more than a dozen books on murder in/at/on prominent Washington locations and monuments. Although FDR's son **Elliott Roosevelt** died in 1990, his publisher keeps posthumously releasing thrillers about murders solved by his mother, First Lady Eleanor Roosevelt. **Richard Timothy Conroy,** a one-time diplomat, has written three witty whodunits set in the Smithsonian Institution, of all places *(Mr. Smithson's Bones, The India Exhibition, Old Ways in the New World)*. **Warren Adler's** improbable shamus is Fiona FitzGerald, gorgeous daughter of a U.S. senator, who labors as a D.C. homicide cop in such titles as *The Witch of Watergate* and *Senator Love.*

ODATIONS

1

Basic Stuff

The tourist trade has come roaring back to our nation's capital, with hoteliers reporting occupancy rates at or above pre-9/11 levels. This is great for the local economy—tourism is Washington's second-most-important industry, trailing only government. However, it's not necessarily so good for the tourist, who will find fewer bargains, more no-vacancy signs, and bigger crowds at the attractions. Staying in Cap City, even for a few days, can eat up your tax cut really fast.

Washington has more than 25,000 hotel rooms, ranging from luxurious power palaces frequented by well-heeled lobbyists and political consultants to decent bargain spots popular among not-so-well-heeled political activists and traveling families. The capital is uniquely well endowed with apartment houses built in the first third of the 20th century and later converted into hotels. These converts, available in all price categories, generally offer larger-than-normal rooms with non-cookie-cutter furnishings. They often include kitchens and are situated in what were and are some of the city's prime residential neighborhoods. What Washington lacks are great numbers of good, clean, budget-priced hotels or motels like you may stay at along the highway. You'll find few rooms for under $100 per weekday night. Nevertheless, if you check early for special deals—and again at the last minute—you often can find very nice facilities for less than $150. Thanks to the Washington area's wonderful Metrorail system, you also can find less expensive digs in the suburbs and take the train to town quickly, safely, comfortably (except at rush hour!), and at a modest cost. When inquiring at a suburban hotel, ask how long it will take to walk to the nearest Metro station and if the walk is safe (not only from crime but from busy highways without sidewalks or controlled pedestrian crossings). Some suburban hotels offer shuttle service to Metro stations.

Another thing Washington hotels lack is free parking. Expect to spend $15 to $30 per night most places. On the other hand, because of that great subway system, if you leave your car at home, you can travel around town to your heart's content for a few bucks a day.

Winning the Reservations Game

Hotels are mimicking airlines when it comes to pricing. Yes, there are published rates, but they don't mean a thing when there's vacant space at the inn and the innkeeper slashes his prices to fill his beds.

The best way to get the best rate is to work at it. Check the chain's website, the hotel's website, and a couple of online travel agencies, such as **Expedia.com, Orbitz.com,** or **Travelocity. com.** If you want still more alternatives, try a local hotel booker, such as **Capitol Reservations** (Tel 202/452-1270, 800/847-4832; www.washingtondchotels.com) or **Washington, DC, Accommodations** (Tel 202/289-2220, 800/503-3330; www.dc accommodations.com). For bed-and-breakfast reservations, contact **Bed and Breakfast Accommodations** (Tel 887/893-3233; www.bedandbreakfastdc.com). Online, look for references to packages or discounts. On the phone, ask if there are cheaper rates than the first one quoted. Then ask again. And again. And be sure to mention personal affiliations that might earn you discounts—auto club membership, hotel frequent-sleeper membership, your status as an employee of the government or of a corporation that might have negotiated discounts.

The time of your visit also affects what you'll pay. Peak season runs from mid-March through June, thanks to wonderful weather. School trips are scheduled and families take spring-break vacations while Congress is in session and lobbyists swarm. September through mid-November is the next-busiest time, with Congress in session again and nice weather again attracting vacationers who can get off work in the fall.

July and August make up part of the low season, because Congress usually is in recess and Washingtonians try to flee the hot and humid weather. There's low season in January and February, too. Congress may be back at work for part of that time, but few tourists want to come here during the worst months of Washington's winter. The best deals of all can be found between Thanksgiving and New Year's, when Congress gets away, and tourists stay away.

There's also a "low season" throughout the year on weekends. Business travelers come here during the week, and business-oriented hotels offer great rates to fill their rooms on weekends. This is when you can score luxury or semiluxury accommodations at bargain-basement prices.

Check the travel sections of the *New York Times, Boston Globe, Chicago Tribune,* and *Washington Post* for advertised bargain packages.

Is There a Right Address?

Well, if you're a member of Congress, the right address is Capitol Hill. If you're visiting the White House, the most convenient hotel is downtown. The State Department picked up the nickname "Foggy Bottom" because that's the name of its neighborhood. (And you thought there were other, insulting, reasons.)

Washington's neighborhoods differ, and what they're really like may surprise you if you're suffering from long-distance stereotypes.

In addition to being the Hill upon which the Capitol sits, **Capitol Hill** is an attractive residential neighborhood of brick town houses and a community business district with restaurants, bars, small stores, and a wonderful old market, all frequented by people who live and/or work here. It's also a major tourist draw that sports—in addition to the **Capitol**—the **Supreme Court, Library of Congress, National Postal Museum, Union Station,** and three Metro stops. From near the congressional buildings and Pennsylvania Avenue to about 8th Street SE, this is a vibrant, gentrifying community. Unfortunately, it's close to neighborhoods that aren't so attractive, so crime can be a problem if you wander away from the government/tourist crowds after dark.

Downtown is a large, amorphous area in Northwest D.C. bounded roughly by 10th Street, 22nd Street, Pennsylvania Avenue, and the Dupont Circle neighborhood. You'll encounter office buildings, shops, hotels, sandwich shops, and restaurants galore, and much of the area will remind you of every other downtown business district you've ever ventured into—except, that is, for the **White House** and some other government edifices. Here you can choose from the full gamut of hotel types— luxurious, historic, convention, business, suites, family, B&Bs, and the ultimate bargain **Hostelling International,** which charges as little as $29 per person per night for mostly dormitory-style accommodations. Many of these are a fairly easy walk to the **National Mall** or to one of the many downtown Metro stations.

Penn Quarter is, among other things, a triumph of public relations. D.C. boosters started plastering that name to the area inside 10th Street, 6th Street, Pennsylvania Avenue, and Massachusetts Avenue to give it some cachet. As the placed boomed with restaurants, shops, galleries, and the MCI (now Verizon) Center, the moniker caught on. It's now one of Washington's top nightspots, and it encompasses much of what's left of D.C.'s minuscule **Chinatown.**

Dupont Circle is one of Washington's liveliest and most interesting neighborhoods, best known for boutiques, galleries, restaurants, nightspots, and as the focal point of D.C.'s large, active, and influential gay community. It also can brag about attractive residential side streets, interesting and reasonably priced hotels, and many think tanks and other nonprofit organizations.

The Dupont Circle Metro station provides quick access to the rest of town.

The **Foggy Bottom/West End** neighborhood offers some respite from the noise and bustle of nearby downtown, Georgetown, and Dupont Circle. You'll find row houses lining brick sidewalks on residential blocks that mix uneasily with the academic buildings of ever-growing George Washington University. The **State Department** and **Kennedy Center** guard the south flank of this neighborhood, which is why the area's reasonably priced hotel suites often are occupied by visiting diplomats and performers. (Is that redundant?) Foggy Bottom doesn't have a lot of tourist attractions of its own, but you can stroll to Georgetown, downtown, or Dupont Circle, catch the train at the Foggy Bottom/GWU Metrorail station, or hop a 30-series Metrobus, which traverses Pennsylvania Avenue, M Street, and Wisconsin Avenue.

Georgetown is a nice place to visit and a nice place to live—but you wouldn't want to park here. Washington's oldest neighborhood has no Metrorail service. The 30-series Metrobuses do run on Wisconsin Avenue and M Street, and the Georgetown Metro Connection shuttle buses link the area with the Rosslyn, Dupont Circle, and Foggy Bottom/GWU Metrorail stations. Away from Wisconsin and M, Georgetown is Washington's most exclusive residential neighborhood and home to Georgetown University. JFK lived here before he moved to the White House. The late *Washington Post* publisher Katharine Graham made her home in an enormous mansion at the top of Georgetown's hill. Former secretary of state Madeleine Albright lives here now, as do many other well-known government, political, and media figures. Republicans had fun during the 2004 presidential campaign pointing out that Democratic presidential nominee John Kerry and vice-presidential candidate John Edwards—running as champions of the middle class, working families, and the poor—both made their D.C. homes in ultraexpensive Georgetown. Along and near the main drags, this is a lively, eclectic shopping and entertainment center with numerous restaurants, bars, and stores of all flavors—exclusive, commonplace, and tacky.

North and west of Dupont Circle and Georgetown is a collection of residential neighborhoods known generically as **Upper Northwest.** This is a wonderful place to live, and it's well stocked with good and reasonably priced restaurants, movie theaters, and shopping of all kinds, from **Filene's Basement** and **T.J. Maxx** to **Tiffany** and **Versace.** Unless you're into shopping or film, however, there's not much here to attract tourists beyond the **National Cathedral** and the **National Zoo.**

The Lowdown

Power palaces... If you've got the bread, you can stay with
the powerbrokers in these luxurious hotels that attract folks
with business with the White House, Congress, or free-
spending lobbyists. Public spaces and guest rooms are opu-
lent at the **Willard InterContinental,** which houses the
powerful and influential—and would-be powerful and
influential—practically across the street from the White
House and D.C. government headquarters. The ornate
Willard Room restaurant and polished-mahogany Round
Robin Bar define the traditional stereotypes of how rich
and powerful Washingtonians eat and drink. Similarly,
lobbyists and political activists swarm the public spaces at
the **Renaissance Mayflower Hotel,** which hosted Calvin
Coolidge's inaugural ball the year it opened (1925) and has
been a preferred site for balls, conventions, and other political meetings ever since.

At **Capitol Hill Suites,** it's the government officials
themselves—members of Congress—who take up residence, attracted by special long-term rates. Tourists here
for short-term stays can play at being political insiders.
Guests get access to dining facilities at the Capitol Hill
Club, the GOP social club that's next door to Republican
National Committee headquarters.

Democracy's dowagers... Three of Washington's grand-
est hotels, all near the White House, have a European
ancestor in common: The **Hay-Adams,** the **St. Regis,** and
The Jefferson were built in the 1920s, either as hotels or
apartment buildings, by English immigrant Harry Wardman. Before he lost everything in the stock market crash of
1929, Wardman was responsible for scores of ornate Washington buildings, including the British Embassy. The Hay-
Adams is so named because its prime site, across Lafayette
Square from the White House, once was occupied by the
adjoining homes of John Hay, Lincoln's private secretary
and later a secretary of state, and journalist/scholar/novel-
ist/statesman Henry Adams, author of *Democracy: An
American Novel, The Education of Henry Adams,* and much
else. The St. Regis sits at the nexus of presidential Washington (16th St.) and lawyer/lobbyist Washington (K St.),
while The Jefferson is in the 16th Street Corridor, five
blocks north of the president's mansion—close enough to

be involved in the action but far enough away to harbor strategic retreats.

For conventional thinkers... Lots of organizations hold big meetings in Washington, so Washington has more than its share of humongous convention hotels. If you're one of those bigger-is-better folks—or if you're savvy about look-ing for bargains in humongous hotels when conventioneers aren't filling the rooms—you'll love these big boys. The biggest of the big is the **Wardman Park Marriott,** with nearly 1,500 rooms and suites, including 125 VIP suites, a little bit out of the way, by the Woodley Park–Zoo Metro Station. Before it grew up, its oldest section (built in 1918) was residence for distinguished Washingtonians. Across Calvert Street from the Wardman's back door is another mature giant, the **Omni Shoreham.** A commentary on the Wardman's enormity, the 75-year-old Shoreham has "only" 834 rooms and suites. But it sits on 11 acres of land adja-cent to Rock Creek Park, where guests can walk, run, and bicycle, and it offers a large heated outdoor pool, a for-fee fitness center, and a garden for casual strolling.

A few blocks down Connecticut Avenue but still a tad away from the tourist action, the **Hilton Washington** packs in big gatherings (the White House Correspondents Association dinner, the National Prayer Breakfast) with 1,119 rooms and a ballroom with two zip codes. For size and location, you can't beat the **J.W. Marriott,** an easy walk from the White House, National Press Club, National Mall, theaters, galleries, and Metro stations.

Candidates of character... The **Mansion on O Street** has about 1,480 fewer rooms than the Wardman, but it's got a ton of character that springs from the unbounded imagi-nation of its proprietor, H. H. Leonards. She created her hotel from four adjacent Victorian town houses, and the styles of the rooms and suites range from log cabin (really) to Art Deco and pure whimsy. The **Tabard Inn** also derives from contiguous Victorian town houses in the Dupont Cir-cle neighborhood, but about the only other thing it shares with Leonards's Mansion is a firm commitment to eclecti-cism. The Tabard is warm, charming, European, and not the least bit pretentious. Adhering to this trend of creating hotels of character from adjoining town houses is the antiques-laden **Morrison-Clark Historic Inn and Restau-rant.** The Morrison-Clark exposes Washington's Southern soul with a sweeping veranda and a girdle of greenery. Thursday evenings from spring into fall feature the "Big Easy on the Veranda"—free hors d'oeuvres and cash bar from 5:30 to 7:30pm. (Try the Steel Magnolia, the vodka-and-Cointreau-based house specialty.) Another Morrison—the **Morrison House**—offers 18th-century elegance in Alexandria.

Suite deals... Especially for families, suites can be convenient and frugal. You can have breakfast at your leisure, bring the kids back for midday snacks and naps, make lunch (and dinner, too, if you wish), and have some privacy in separate sleeping quarters at night. A surprising number of all-suite or many-suite hotels offer reasonable rates as well. Be warned that many of these hotels define "suite" liberally—often meaning a large room with kitchen facilities.

In Foggy Bottom, the suite-est part of town, visiting diplomats, performers, and academics mingle at the **George Washington University Inn,** which is convenient to the State Department, Kennedy Center, and (natch) GWU. The university, which owns the place, has laid on a Williamsburg motif befitting the GW teams' nickname (the Colonials). One former U.S. president called **One Washington Circle** "one of the most truly outstanding hotels in the nation." All right, so it was Richard Nixon. But he liked the hotel enough to make an eighth-floor suite his post-Watergate Washington outpost. (Some rooms have a view of the Watergate complex in the distance.) If the Nixon connection doesn't reel you in, this suite hotel is also a magnet for traveling musicians and show folk. Also in Foggy Bottom, the **State Plaza** offers spacious, reasonably priced suites, and **The River Inn** offers ideal suite accommodations to business travelers and great deals to vacationing families during off-peak periods. Despite its name, **Washington Suites Georgetown** actually is on the Foggy Bottom/West End side of Rock Creek, Georgetown's west boundary. That's actually not a bad location, an easy stroll to the Georgetown action and just three blocks from the Foggy Bottom/GWU Metrorail station. And all suites here have a living room with a desk and sofa bed, separate bedroom, two TVs, and kitchen with stove, oven, microwave, refrigerator, dishwasher, and kitchenware.

Georgetown does have suites, including the unimaginatively named **Georgetown Suites,** which scatters a variety of accommodations—all with kitchens—through two buildings in relatively quiet spots south of ever-busy M Street. The State Department has been known to house traveling diplomats here. On M, the **Latham Hotel** offers two-story carriage suites along with other suites that sport heated towel racks and high-speed Internet access. The Latham also has a rooftop swimming pool, on-site exercise center, and free access to a nearby health club. In addition to 10 one-bedroom suites, the **Georgetown Inn** has some adjoining rooms that can be converted to suites for traveling families.

Outside of central D.C., the **Embassy Suites Hotel at the Chevy Chase Pavilion** is modern, efficient, and located in Washington's most exclusive shopping district. For travel to the tourist centers, the hotel sits right on top of the Friendship Heights Metrorail Station.

Rooms with a view... The **Willard Inter-Continental**'s honeymoon suite contains a large, round window that centers on the Washington Monument. Upper-floor rooms on the south side of the **Hay-Adams Hotel** look across Lafayette Square to the White House and the Washington Monument beyond. (Ask if there's any way you can check out the spectacular view from the roof.) Some rooms at the **Four Seasons** and the **Omni Shoreham** offer idyllic visions of Rock Creek Park.

Some of the best hotel views in Washington come not from guest rooms but from two swimming pools and a restaurant. At **Four Points by Sheraton** downtown, the indoor heated pool on the top floor features a panoramic view of Washington. At the **Holiday Inn on the Hill,** it's the outdoor pool on the roof that lets you look around Capitol Hill and to the rest of D.C. in the distance. The Sky Terrace open-air restaurant on the top floor of the **Hotel Washington** has a breathtaking view of the president's mansion. Many of the Washington's guest rooms also look onto the White House and/or the Washington Monument.

Hip in Washington?... Washingtonians may not be naturally hip, but several new or recast hotels are making hipness available to visitors. Some claim hipness through sophisticated cutting-edge design, some through super-trendiness, others through an over-the-top, off-the-wall approach to hospitality. All are courtesy of the Kimpton Group, which specializes in—well—hip boutique hotels.

The **Hotel George**—slyly named for the first president and ideally located near everything on Capitol Hill—greets guests with a sleek and bold decor. Andy Warhol protégé Steve Kaufman's portrait of Washington hangs in every guest room, and other Kaufman works appear in public spaces. Room service is from the on-site Bistro Bis, a good—and hip—French dining spot whose sleek bar is popular with Hill staffers unwinding after a hard day of spending your money.

You expect hip around Dupont Circle, and the most modern version of it is supplied by the **Hotel Madera** and the **Topaz Hotel**. Madera's distinction is personalized service right down to room design, a Kimpton signature. "Cardio rooms" have exercise equipment, "flash rooms" computer with high-speed Internet access, "screening rooms" DVD player and DVDs, and "nosh rooms" kitchenette and grocery-shopping service. At the Topaz you encounter a bit of supertrendy California on the Potomac. Guests are offered complimentary morning "energy potions." The bar's happy hour is called Liquid Therapy, and its signature cocktails include Blue Nirvana, Liquid Yoga, and Tao of Pomegranate.

Hotel Helix, downtown, captured national travel-press attention with its colorful, over-the-top, pop-art references to the '60s and '70s. Interior decorations come in red, orange, pink, purple, mohair, and leather. There's free champagne in the lobby during the nightly "Bubbly Hour." You probably can guess which colors predominate at the renovated **Hotel Rouge**—red accents in the lobby, red lights in the elevator, red silk on the hall walls, and red headboards in the guest rooms along with crimson velvet drapes and deep red carpet. There's a complimentary red-wine-and-beer hour on weekdays and a complimentary Bloody Mary bar on weekends.

Grassroots accommodations... If you're coming to Washington on a grassroots budget, not on a big-time lobbyist's expense account, the least expensive, *reasonable,* place to stay is **Hostelling International**—except, of course, for a friend's or relative's spare room or floor. For as low as $32 per night ($29 for members), you get a bed in a dormitory-style room that sleeps 4 to 12 people. There are a few private family rooms that must be reserved *at least* a month in advance and cost up to $89 or $93, depending on membership. For a little more cash, you can purchase standard hotel accommodations at the **Hotel Harrington** or **Red Roof Inn.** The Harrington, a family-oriented tourist hotel near Pennsylvania Avenue and 11th Street NW, prices its rooms from $99 to $169. Standard rooms at the Red Roof start at about $155. Another bargain option is the charming **Tabard Inn,** which offers rooms for two, sans private bathroom, for as little as $118 and doubles with a private bathroom for $163. Some bed-and-breakfasts offer low-priced accommodations. See two in the B&B section below.

Where the big spenders lay their heads... If your intentions run to big spending rather than budget balancing, Hostelling International probably is not the place for you. For puttin' on the Ritz, you want to head for the **Ritz-Carlton Washington.** Why not reserve a 2,250-square-foot suite with fireplace, dining room, Jacuzzi, and private terrace? Or for a more common touch, get a room on the Club Level, with concierge and special food and beverage service. Also luxurious—and a magnet for rich celebs—is the **Four Seasons Hotel** at the eastern edge of Georgetown. Take high tea. Enjoy the views of Rock Creek Park. Be on the lookout for Tom Hanks, Sheryl Crow, or Nicolas Cage. Don't forget your checkbook or your plutonium MasterCard.

Where to go for foreign affairs... It's hardly surprising that Washington mixes international affairs with political ones. D.C. has several Irish-themed hotels, not because Ireland is such an important world power but because Irish Americans are so important in U.S. politics. The most prominent is the **Phoenix Park Hotel**—on Capitol Hill, of course—named for a park in Dublin. Here, you'll also find the Dubliner pub, a popular watering hole. The Irish Times, another Irish pub, is on the block, too. **Jurys Normandy** and **Jurys Washington** hardly have Irish names, but they are run by Dublin-based Jurys Doyle hotels. Jurys Washington, right on Dupont Circle, is home to Biddy Mulligans, a self-styled Irish pub with a bar brought over from the old country. Beyond their ethnic ties, the Jurys hotels offer comfortable lodging at reasonable prices, sometimes close to $100.

The French-owned **Sofitel Lafayette Square** is named for the square that honors the Frenchman who helped win the American Revolution. What Sofitel calls *art de vivre* and translates as "the art of French living" infuses the place—from the Cafe 15 French restaurant and the French-sounding Le Bar lounge to the French-designed interiors and staff uniforms.

The **Hilton Washington Embassy Row** brags that its Massachusetts Avenue location puts guests within walking distance of more than 100 embassies. It's also a treaty's throw from all the action of Dupont Circle and the convenience of the Dupont Circle Metrorail station.

Where history is in the architecture... Even the hotels have history in Washington, although often not as hotels. The edifice that houses the swanky **Hotel Monaco,** for instance, was built in 1842 and expanded in 1859 as Washington's General Post Office. It later housed the Tariff Commission and didn't become the Monaco until a 3-year renovation was completed in 2002. The Beaux Arts **Churchill Hotel** made it onto the National Trust for Historic Preservation's list of historic hotels by maintaining its "historic integrity, architecture, and ambience." Opened as a luxury apartment building in 1906, the Churchill claimed to provide "every convenience of a high-grade modern hotel, in conjunction with the restful quietude and exclusiveness of a private residence." Now it offers hotel guests large rooms and suites. The **Washington Plaza** might *someday* qualify as a historic property as an example of the 1960s architecture of Morris Lapidus, who perhaps is best known for designing the Fontainebleau in Miami Beach.

When you want breakfast with your bed... Bed-and-breakfasts aren't the first things that come to mind when you contemplate lodging in Washington. But D.C. has quite a few, from the charming and inexpensive to the luxurious and priced that way. The **DC Guest House,** a renovated 1876 mansion, falls into the latter category, with rates ranging from $175 to $300 per night. The guest rooms are large but cozy with eclectic decor, from country manor to urban chic. Two rooms have working fireplaces, most have private bathrooms, and gourmet breakfast is served in an elegant dining room. The four owners collect art, and it's displayed everywhere. Your jaw will drop at the Guest House's strikingly modern renovation. At the 1883 **Swann House,** the jaw-dropping will be in response to the lush restoration of the turreted mansion's early-20th-century grandeur. The innkeepers make you feel like your visiting the home of a very wealthy family at the turn of the 20th century. The entire first floor is common space, and there's a second-floor balcony for sitting.

For those whose budgets don't allow for lifestyles of the rich even if not famous, the **Kalorama Guest House at Woodley Park** offers neat, clean, well-maintained, comfortable, and relatively spacious rooms starting at $55 single and $60 double. Rates here top out at $95 to $135 for a two-room suite with a private bathroom that sleeps up to six. For a touch of elegance, stop by for sherry hour in the late afternoon. At the nearby **Woodley Park Guest House,** you can sit on the front porch and look across the street and up the hill at the gigantic Wardman Park Marriott. People who attend conventions at the Wardman, but who don't like to attend conventions, stay here to escape the crowd. Stay here and hike over to the Wardman to hop on tour buses.

Tough to categorize... Finally come hotels whose claims to fame don't fit easily into other categories. Smaller than the city's humongous convention hotels, the **Capital Hilton** still has sufficient guest rooms and meeting spaces to be a place where things happen—notably the National Spelling Bee (for the nation's most precocious practitioners of orthography). For half a century, this Hilton, just a few blocks from the White House, also hosted the prestigious Gridiron Club dinner (for the capital's most prominent journalists and politicians). But as we go to print the Gridiron is being moved to the **Renaissance Washington,** a hotel that previously was known best for easy access to the new Washington Convention Center and what's left of Chinatown. With its Coeur de Lion restaurant and Blue Bar lounge, the relatively small, elegantly appointed **Henley Park Hotel** is a fine place for romance.

Map 2: Washington, D.C., Accommodations

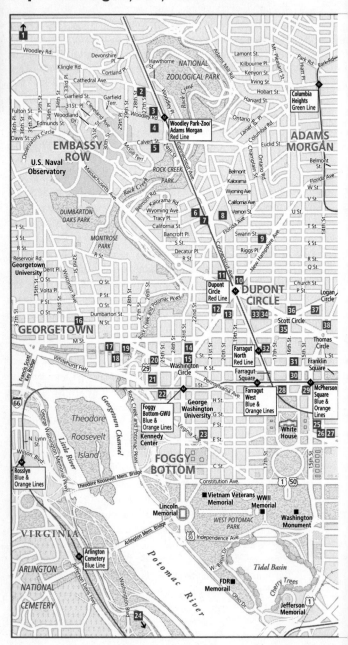

Capitol Hill Suites **51**
Capital Hilton **31**
The Churchill Hotel **7**
DC Guest House **39**
Embassy Suites Hotel at the
  Chevy Chase Pavilion **1**
Four Points by Sheraton **41**
Four Seasons Hotel **19**
Georgetown Inn **16**
Georgetown Suites **18**
George Washington
  University Inn **22**
Hay-Adams Hotel **28**
Henley Park Hotel **43**
Hilton Washington **8**
Hilton Washington
  Embassy Row **11**
Holiday Inn on the Hill **50**
Hostelling International **42**
Hotel George **49**
Hotel Harrington **45**
Hotel Helix **37**
Hotel Madera **13**
Hotel Monaco **46**
Hotel Rouge **36**
Hotel Washington **25**
The Jefferson **35**
Jurys Normandy **6**
Jurys Washington **10**
J.W. Marriott Hotel **26**

Kalorama Guest House at
  Woodley Park **2**
Latham Hotel **17**
The Mansion on O Street **12**
Morrison-Clark Historic Inn
  and Restaurant **40**
Morrison House **24**
Omni Shoreham **5**
One Washington Circle **15**
Phoenix Park Hotel **48**
Red Roof Inn **47**
Renaissance Mayflower
  Hotel **32**
Renaissance Washington **44**
Ritz-Carlton Washington **14**
The River Inn **21**
St. Regis **30**
Sofitel Lafayette Square **29**
State Plaza **23**
Swann House **9**
Tabard Inn **33**
Topaz Hotel **34**
Wardman Park Marriott
  Hotel **4**
Washington Plaza **38**
Washington Suites
  Georgetown **20**
Willard Inter-Continental
  Washington **27**
Woodley Park Guest House **3**

The Index

See Map 2 on the previous page for all Accommodations listings.

$$$$$	more than $400
$$$$	$301–$400
$$$	$201–$300
$$	$100–$200
$	less than $100

Price ratings are based on the lowest price quoted for a standard double room in high season. Unless otherwise noted, rooms have air-conditioning, phones, private bathrooms, and TVs.

The following abbreviations are used for credit cards:

AE	American Express
DC	Diners Club
DISC	Discover
MC	MasterCard
V	Visa

Capitol Hill Suites (p. 20) CAPITOL HILL Key attractions here are location at the heart of Capitol Hill and access to dining facilities at the Republican Party's Capitol Hill Club. The hotel is two blocks from the Capitol Grounds and across the street from the Library of Congress's Madison Building. All rooms have kitchenettes and there's a free continental breakfast.... *Tel 202/543-6000 (866/716-8114). Fax 202/547-2608. www.capitolhillsuites.com. 200 C St. SE, 20003. Capitol South Metro. 152 rooms. AE, DC, DISC, MC, V. $$$*

Capital Hilton (p. 27) DOWNTOWN Less than two blocks from Metro and three blocks from the White House, this upscale convention and business hotel is noted for convenience, a wide range of tourist and business services, a large health club and spa, and a ballroom to host events.... *Tel 202/393-1000 (800/445-8667). Fax 202/639-5784. www.hilton.com. 1001 16th St. NW, 20036. Farragut N. or McPherson Sq. Metro. 544 rooms. AE, DC, DISC, MC, V. $$$$$*

The Churchill Hotel (p. 26) DUPONT CIRCLE Listed as one of the National Trust for Historic Preservation's Historic Hotels of America, the Churchill offers large guest rooms as well as junior and deluxe suites. International travelers account for much of the clientele. There's an in-house fitness center. The Chartwell Grill serves three meals a day.... *Tel 202/797-2000 (800/424-2464). Fax 202/462-0944. www.thechurchillhotel.com. 1914 Connecticut Ave. NW, 20009. Dupont Circle Metro. 144 rooms. AE, DC, DISC, MC, V. $$$*

DC Guest House (p. 26) DOWNTOWN One block from D.C.'s new convention center, this 19th-century mansion offers large guest rooms and a warm, comfortable ambience. Antiques mixed with modern furnishings, original art, and African artifacts reflect the personal tastes of the four friends-cum-innkeepers who lovingly restored and furnished this historic home near Logan Circle. A gourmet breakfast is included.... *Tel 202/332-2502. Fax 202/332-6013. www.dcguesthouse.com. 1337 10th St. NW, 20001. Mt. Vernon Sq. Metro. 6 rooms. AE, MC, V. $$*

Embassy Suites Hotel at the Chevy Chase Pavilion (p. 23) UPPER NORTHWEST This hotel is convenient to Washington's most exclusive shopping district on the Maryland-D.C. border. There are lots of nearby restaurants and an on-site Metro station with a 10-minute ride to Dupont Circle and 14 minutes to Metro Center. The two-room suites come with free breakfast, complimentary cocktails at the manager's reception, and free use of the indoor pool, whirlpool, sauna, and fitness center.... *Tel 202/362-9300 (800/362-2779). Fax 202/686-3405. www.embassy-suites.com. 4300 Military Rd. NW, 20015. Friendship Heights Metro. 198 suites. AE, DC, DISC, MC, V. $$$*

Four Points by Sheraton (p. 23) DOWNTOWN When you're not taking in the view from the top-floor pool, you can play with your in-room high-speed Internet access or work out in the fitness center. For sleeping accommodations, you can choose from several room configurations plus a couple of suites.... *Tel 202/289-7600 (888/481-7191). Fax 202/349-2215. www.fourpoints washingtondc.com. 1201 K St. NW, 20005. Metro Center Metro. 265 rooms. AE, DC, DISC, MC, V. $$$*

Four Seasons Hotel (p. 23) GEORGETOWN This is one of Washington's most luxurious hotels (try the 3,300-sq.-ft. Presidential Suite), one of its most kid-friendly hotels, and a magnet for celebrities. The rooms are tastefully furnished, and many overlook Rock Creek Park or the C&O Canal. The spa and fitness center inspire calorie burning by adults, and there are numerous children's services to keep kids from getting antsy.... *Tel 202/342-0444 (800/819-5053). Fax 202/944-2076. www.fourseasons.com. 2800 Pennsylvania Ave. NW, 20007. Foggy Bottom/GWU Metro. 196 rooms. AE, DC, DISC, MC, V. $$$$$*

Georgetown Inn (p. 23) GEORGETOWN If you want to stay in Georgetown, you can't beat this address. Double-paned windows insulate street-side rooms from the raucous Wisconsin Avenue late-night scene. The hotel offers one-bedroom suites and adjoining rooms that can be converted to suites.... *Tel 202/333-8900 (800/368-5922). Fax 202/333-8308. www.georgetowncollection. com. 1310 Wisconsin Ave. NW, 20007. Take Georgetown Connection Rte. 1 shuttle bus from Foggy Bottom/GWU Metrorail Station or take a 30-series Metrobus. 96 rooms. AE, DC, DISC, MC, V. $$$$*

Georgetown Suites (p. 22) GEORGETOWN This two-building hotel south of M Street offers studio, one-bedroom, two-bedroom, town-house, and penthouse suites, all with kitchens. Guests get free continental breakfast, Internet access, and use of an exercise center. The building on 30th Street is quieter.... *Tel 202/298-7800 (800/348-7203). Fax 202/348-7203. www.georgetownsuites. com. 1111 30th St. and 1000 29th St. NW, 20007. Take Georgetown Connection Rte. 1 shuttle bus from Foggy Bottom/GWU Metrorail Station or a 30-series Metrobus. 220 rooms. AE, DC, DISC, MC, V. $$*

George Washington University Inn (p. 22) FOGGY BOTTOM/ WEST END Located on a quiet, residential street in Foggy Bottom, the GWU Inn offers spacious rooms with fridges, microwaves, and coffeemakers. There also are 31 suites, many with kitchenettes. Free access to a Bally Total Fitness center is included. Deep discounts are often available.... *Tel 202/337-6620 (800/426-4455). Fax 202/298-7499. www.gwuinn.com. 824 New Hampshire Ave. NW, 20037. Foggy Bottom/GWU Metro. 95 rooms. AE, DC, MC, V. $$$$$*

Hay-Adams Hotel (p. 20) DOWNTOWN This is the best-situated hotel in Washington, directly across Lafayette Square from the White House. It's also one of the most luxurious, renovated to the tune of $18 million in 2002 and offering all the amenities desired by traveling business executives with plump expense accounts.... *Tel 202/638-6600 (800/853-6807). Fax 202/638-2716. www.hayadams.com. 1 Lafayette Sq. NW, 16th and H sts., 20006. McPherson Sq. Metro. 145 rooms, including 20 suites. AE, DC, DISC, MC, V. $$$$$*

Henley Park Hotel (p. 27) PENN QUARTER The staff at this relatively small, Tudor-style hotel provides attentive service and makes a point to get to know regular guests. The on-site Coeur de Lion restaurant, with even more-attentive maitre d's, is a favorite for romantic dinners, and the Blue Bar is a comfortable spot for listening to a pianist from about 8pm on Thursday, Friday, and Saturday evenings.... *Tel 202/638-5200 (800/222-8474). Fax 202/638-6740. www.henleypark.com. 926 Massachusetts Ave. NW, 20001. Mount Vernon Sq. Metro. 96 rooms, including a few suites. AE, DC, DISC, MC, V. $$$*

Hilton Washington (p. 21) DUPONT CIRCLE Known by local practitioners of dark humor as "The Killer Hilton" because John Hinckley shot President Reagan here, this curving mid-1960s structure is the type of hostelry that "boutique" and "Euro-style" hotels position themselves against. With the big size come a heated outdoor pool, a children's pool, a large fitness center, and tennis courts. It's a bit out of the way, but at least the walk to Dupont Circle is downhill.... *Tel 202/483-3000 (800/445-8667). Fax 202/232-0438. www.hilton.com. 1919 Connecticut Ave. NW, 20009. Dupont Circle Metro. 1,119 rooms, including 41 suites. AE, DC, DISC, MC, V. $$$$*

Hilton Washington Embassy Row (p. 26) DUPONT CIRCLE Come here for prime location, rooftop pool with drinks, and 21st Century hotel amenities. Discounts as low as $110 can be found at non-peak times.... *Tel 202/265-1600 (800/445-8667). Fax 202/328-7526. www.hilton.com. 2015 Massachusetts Ave. NW, 20036. Dupont Circle Metro. 193 rooms. AE, DC, DISC, MC, V. $$$$$*

Holiday Inn on the Hill (p. 23) CAPITOL HILL A $10-million renovation completed in 2003 makes this a much more attractive—and more expensive—spot. The staff wears jet-black-and-cobalt-blue uniforms, and the facilities are decorated in a similarly striking way. Standard rooms now come with one king bed and easy chair or sofa, or two queen beds with an easy chair. The prime location hasn't changed, of course—about two blocks from the Capitol and Union Station. The outdoor pool on the roof, with a great view of the area, is still open in summer, too. Deep discounts are often available with advance reservations.... *Tel 202/638-1616 (800/638-1116). Fax 202/638-0707. www.hionthehilldc.com. 415 New Jersey Ave. NW, 20001. Union Station Metro. 347 rooms. AE, DC, DISC, MC, V. $$$*

Hostelling International (p. 24) DOWNTOWN These dormitory-style rooms sleep 4 to 12 people at $32 per person per night ($29 for Hostelling members). The bathroom's down the hall. But, for your money, you get free continental breakfast, high-speed internet access, and access to a theater-style TV room with a 60-inch television screen, a kitchen, dining room, luggage storage, lockers, coin-operated laundry, and expert staff for touring advice and special events. If you want one of the few private family rooms, reserve *at least* a month in advance and pay $89 or $93 per room.... *Tel 202/737-2333. Fax 202/737-1508. www.hiwashingtondc.org. 1009 11th St. NW, 20001. Metro Center Metro. 300 beds. MC, V. $*

Hotel George (p. 24) CAPITOL HILL This bright, energetic Capitol Hill hotel, one of Washington's hippest, is a welcome antidote to D.C.'s ubiquitous traditional decor and federal architecture. Cleverly fitted guest rooms have an open, streamlined feel. Bistro Bis chef Jeffrey Buben's restaurant serves updated French bistro classics. All this is one block from Union Station, about three from the Capitol, and a reasonable stroll from the other sights on the Hill.... *Tel 202/347-4200 (800/576-8331). Fax 202/347-0359 www.hotelgeorge.com. 15 E St. NW, 20001. Union Station Metro. 139 rooms. AE, DC, DISC, MC, V. $$$$$*

Hotel Harrington (p. 25) DOWNTOWN An easy walk from many attractions, the Harrington may be the best housing bargain in town. It's not fancy by anyone's imagination. But it's got rooms starting at $99, extra-large rooms that sleep up to six, and two-room family accommodations that include a compact fridge. In fact, if you need it, you can get a fridge put into many of the rooms.... *Tel 202/628-8140 (800/424-8532). Hotel fax 202/347-3924. Fax for guests 202/393-2311. www.hotel-harrington.com. 436 11th St. NW, 20004. Metro Center Metro. 242 rooms. AE, DC, DISC, MC, V. $*

Hotel Helix (p. 24) DOWNTOWN *Elle* called Helix a "tongue-in-cheek '60s acid trip." *Travel + Leisure* described it as a "palace devoted to kitsch Americana." Whatever *you* call it, it's striking, fun, and doesn't take itself seriously. The entry drive sparkles. Interiors are wildly decorated. Four specialty guest rooms are equipped with plasma TVs, high-end stereos, and lava lamps. Oh, and the rooms are large and comfortable with all the expected 21st-century amenities.... *Tel 202/462-9001 (800/706-1202). Fax 202/332-3519. www.hotelhelix.com. 1430 Rhode Island Ave. NW, 20005. Farragut N. or McPherson Sq. Metro. 160 rooms, 18 suites. AE, DC, DISC, MC, V. $$$$*

Hotel Madera (p. 24) DUPONT CIRCLE A strikingly attractive boutique hotel near Dupont Circle, the Madera offers personalized service right down to the kind of amenities you'd like in your room. All guests get free overnight shoeshines and are invited to the complimentary "wine hour" each evening. Rooms are sometimes available for as low as $129.... *Tel 202/296-7600 (800/430-1202). Fax 202/293-2476. www.hotelmadera.com. 1310 New Hampshire Ave. NW, 20036. Dupont Circle Metro. 82 rooms. AE, DC, DISC, MC, V. $$$$*

Hotel Monaco (p. 26) PENN QUARTER Opened in 2002 after a 3-year rehabilitation, this swanky boutique hotel is housed in a National Landmark, the original General Post Office Building. The exterior sports marble Corinthian columns; the interior is a whimsical jumble of 19th- and turn-of-the-21st-century elements. The guest rooms are colorful and spacious, with workspaces, cordless phones, and high-speed Internet access. Lest you forget you're in the nation's capital, each room is guarded by a bust of Thomas Jefferson.... *Tel 202/628-7177 (800/649-1202). Fax 202/628-7277. www.monaco-dc.com. 700 F St. NW, 20004 Gallery Place–Chinatown Metro. 184 rooms and suites. AE, DC, DISC, MC, V. $$$$*

Hotel Rouge (p. 24) DUPONT CIRCLE The superhip Rouge carries its red theme all the way through happy hours with free red drinks. Rooms are spacious and comfortable and come with a few more than the usual amenities. You sometimes can find rooms for $125.... *Tel 202/232-8000. (800/738-1202). Fax 202/667-9827. www.rougehotel.com. 1315 16th St. NW, 20036. Dupont Circle Metro. 137 rooms. AE, DC, DISC, MC, V. $$$$*

Hotel Washington (p. 23) DOWNTOWN It's the hotel closest to the White House and, opened in 1913, the oldest continuously operating hotel in town. The lobby is comfortable and has a good people-watching bar at one end. The rooms, some with Mall/Monument views, have classy two-poster beds and lace curtains. There is a fitness center, and you can get discounts on weekends, holidays, and when Congress not it session.... *Tel 202/638-5900 (877/512-6314). Fax 202/638-1594. www. hotelwashington.com. 515 15th St. NW, 20004. Metro Center or McPherson Sq. Metro. 315 rooms, 26 suites. AE, DC, MC, V. $$$*

The Jefferson (p. 20) DOWNTOWN A superb, intimate hotel with excellent 24-hour service. A third of the rooms are suites, some with wood-burning fireplaces. Antiques, original art, and historical documents are scattered among the rooms and public spaces. There's a 24-hour fitness center on-site, along with access to a private health club across the street.... *Tel 202/347-2200 (866/270-8118). Fax 202/331-7982. www.thejeffersonwashingtondc. com. 1200 16th St. NW, 20036. Farragut N. Metro. 100 rooms. AE, DC, DISC, MC, V. $$$$*

Jurys Normandy (p. 25) DUPONT CIRCLE A bargain by Washington standards, this small hotel is a bit out of the way but situated in a neighborhood of exclusive homes and diplomatic residences. The rooms are comfortable, and you may run into traveling diplomats at the Tuesday-evening wine-and-cheese reception. Stroll about five blocks to Dupont Circle or Adams Morgan for some of D.C.'s most vibrant shopping and nightlife.... *Tel 202/483-1350 (800/424-3729). Fax 202/387-8241. www.jurys-washingtondc-hotels.com. 2118 Wyoming Ave. NW, 20008. Dupont Circle Metro. 75 rooms. AE, DC, DISC, MC, V. $$$*

Jurys Washington (p. 25) DUPONT CIRCLE Located at 1 o'clock on Dupont Circle, this Jurys hotel is patronized by organizations holding meetings in the area because of location and reasonable rates (when discounted). The rooms are large and comfortable and equipped with high-speed Internet access. It also has 24-hour room service, a business center, and an exercise room.... *Tel 202/483-6000 (800/424-3729). Fax 202/328-3265. www.jurys-washingtondc-hotels.com. 1500 New Hampshire Ave. NW, 20036. Dupont Circle Metro. 314 rooms. AE, DC, DISC, MC, V. $$$$*

J.W. Marriott Hotel (p. 21) DOWNTOWN This gigantic convention/meeting hotel offers full services for business and vacation travelers and a central location. There are a large indoor pool, fitness center with sauna and whirlpool, two restaurants, and 24-hour room service. The adjacent Shops at National Place contain several quick-eating places. Rates can dip below $200.... *Tel 202/393-2000 (888/236-2427). Fax 202/626-6991. www.marriott.com. 1331 Pennsylvania Ave. NW, 20004. Metro Center Metro. 738 rooms. AE, DC, DISC, MC, V. $$$$$*

Kalorama Guest House at Woodley Park (p. 27) UPPER NORTHWEST This 18-room B&B encompasses two early-20th-century houses on a relatively quiet residential street just off Connecticut Avenue and a three- to four-block walk from the Woodley Park-Zoo Metrorail Station.... *Tel 202/328-0860. Fax 202/328-8730. www.kaloramaguesthouse.com. 2700 Cathedral Ave. NW, 20008. Woodley Park–Zoo Metro. 18 rooms. AE, DC, DISC, MC, V. $*

Latham Hotel (p. 23) GEORGETOWN In Georgetown's commercial heart, the 10-story Latham offers both rooms and suites on bustling M Street. The hotel is home to Michel Richard's acclaimed Citronelle restaurant, which is the high-class source of the hotel's room service.... *Tel 202/726-5000 (888/876-0001). Fax 202/337-4250. www.thelatham.com. 3000 M St. NW, 20007. Take Georgetown Connection Rte. 2 shuttle bus from Dupont Circle or Rosslyn Metrorail station, or a 30-series Metrobus. 142 rooms. AE, DC, DISC, MC, V. $$$*

The Mansion on O Street (p. 21) DUPONT CIRCLE It's just about impossible to describe this Dupont Circle B&B. Luxurious rooms are decorated in eclectic fashion. Everything in the place—antiques, artwork, clothing—is for sale. The distinctive nature of each of the 18 rooms and suites is dramatized by the range of room rates—from $250 to $850 per night. That includes breakfast and use of an outdoor pool.... *Tel 202/496-2000. Fax 202/833-8333. www.omansion.com. 2020 O St. NW, 20036. Dupont Circle Metro. 18 rooms and suites. AE, DC, DISC, MC, V. $$$*

Morrison-Clark Historic Inn and Restaurant (p. 21) DOWNTOWN Listed on the National Register of Historic Places, this inn incorporates the 1864 Victorian mansions of the Morrison and Clark families. Rooms are individually decorated. Furnishings include period antiques. Some rooms on Massachusetts Avenue have porches and character, but inner courtyard rooms are quieter and cozy. Rates include continental breakfast.... *Tel 202/898-1200 (800/222-8474). Fax 202/289-8576. www.morrisonclark. com. 1015 L St. NW, 20001. Mount Vernon Sq. Metro. 54 rooms. AE, DC, DISC, MC, V. $$$*

Morrison House (p. 22) ALEXANDRIA If you want to spend the night in Alexandria, this study in 18th-century elegance will make you feel pampered in a very understated way. Smallish rooms with four-poster beds are modulated with up-to-date touches such as hair dryers, TVs, and bathroom phones. On-site Elysium is a unique, expensive, good restaurant where the chef discusses your likes and dislikes with you before preparing your meal.... *Tel 703/838-8000 (866/834-6628). Fax 703/684-6283. www.morrisonhouse.com. 116 S. Alfred St., Alexandria, VA 22314. Take DASH shuttle bus from King St. Metro. 45 rooms. AE, DC, DISC, MC, V. $$$$*

Omni Shoreham (p. 21) UPPER NORTHWEST Another large, ornate hotel that routinely hosts inaugural balls, conventions, and political gatherings of all kinds. The rooms are extra-large. Because it's a full-service convention hotel, the Omni has a restaurant, snack shop, lounge, and another bar and restaurant pool-side, plus 24-hour room service. Not a prime tourist location, but it's only a short walk from the Metro.... *Tel 202/234-0700 (888/444-6664). Fax 202/265-7972. www.omnihotels.com. 2500 Calvert St. NW, 20008. Woodley Park–Zoo Metro. 834 rooms. AE, DC, DISC, MC, V. $$$$$*

One Washington Circle (p. 22) FOGGY BOTTOM/WEST END Popular with business travelers and families, this all-suites hotel was renovated in 2002. Choose from five classes of suites, most with kitchens and balconies. Unique morning touch: Every unit is supplied with coffee beans and a grinder. There's an outdoor pool and fitness facilities. Deep discounts, to the low $100s, are sometimes available.... *Tel 202/872-1680 (800/424-9671). Fax 202/887-4989. www.thecirclehotel.com. 1 Washington Circle NW, at New Hampshire Ave., 20037. Foggy Bottom/ GWU Metro. 151 suites. AE, DC, DISC, MC, V. $$$$$*

Phoenix Park Hotel (p. 25) CAPITOL HILL This hotel's Dubliner pub serves as a hub of Irish cheer on Capitol Hill, one block from Union Station and about four from the Capitol. Rooms are small but comfortable. Some suites have balconies and working fireplaces. Discounts of below $150 are sometimes available.... *Tel 202/638-6900 (800/824-5419). Fax 202/393-3236. www. phoenixparkhotel.com. 520 N. Capitol St. NW, 20001. Union Station Metro. 143 rooms, 6 suites. AE, DC, DISC, MC, V. $$$$$*

Red Roof Inn (p. 25) CHINATOWN This 10-story hotel near Verizon Center and the Penn Quarter arts/entertainment district does not at first glance resemble your typical Red Roof Inn. However, it does have your standard highway motel amenities (two double beds in many rooms, free local phone calls, TV), plus an exercise facility and sauna. Business travelers can request a king room with a large desk and speakerphone.... *Tel 202/289-5959 (800/733-7663). Fax 202/289-0754. www.redroof.com. 500 H St. NW, 20001. Gallery Place–Chinatown Metro. 195 rooms. AE, DC, DISC, MC, V. $*

Renaissance Mayflower Hotel (p. 20) DOWNTOWN The newly renovated rooms are luxurious. The Connecticut Avenue location is ideal, midway between Dupont Circle and the White House, right atop the Farragut North Metrorail Station. Discounted rates sometimes drop below $200.... *Tel 202/347-3000 (800/228-7697). Fax 202/776-9182. www.marriott.com. 1127 Connecticut Ave. NW, 20036. Farragut N. Metro. 583 rooms, 74 suites. AE, DC, DISC, MC, V. $$$$$*

Renaissance Washington (p. 27) DOWNTOWN A convenient choice if you have business at the Washington Convention Center or a hankering for Chinese food in nearby Chinatown. Rooms have all the expected amenities. The hotel offers a pool, exercise room, restaurant, coffee shop, and bar. Sometimes rooms are offered for less than $200.... *Tel 202/898-9000 (800/228-7697). Fax 202/289-0947. www.marriott.com. 999 9th St. NW, 20001. Mt. Vernon Sq. Metro. 807 rooms, 13 suites. AE, DC, DISC, MC, V. $$$$$*

Ritz-Carlton Washington (p. 25) WEST END In this luxurious hotel, even the standard rooms come with marble in the bathrooms, goose-down pillows, and your basic 21st-century communication amenities. Guests have access to the 100,000-square-foot Sports Club/LA next door. Frequent guests can opt for "luggage-less" travel—leave your clothes in your room and the hotel will launder, dry clean, press, and store them, and then place them in your room when you return.... *Tel 202/835-0500 (800/241-3333). Fax 202/835-1588. www.ritzcarlton.com. 1150 22nd St. NW, 20037. Foggy Bottom/George Washington University Metro. 300 rooms. AE, DC, DISC, MC, V. $$$$$*

The River Inn (p. 22) FOGGY BOTTOM/WEST END The amenities make this Foggy Bottom all-suite boutique attractive to business travelers: large desk, good lighting, and a wireless Internet connection in every unit. Also available are a sofa bed, full kitchen, coffee beans and grinder, free *Washington Post,* and a free shoeshine on weekdays. "Potomac Suites" have separate bedrooms, sitting areas, and dining/meeting niches. For families, off-peak rates below $120 are hard to beat.... *Tel 202/337-7600 (800/424-2741). Fax 202/337-6520. www.theriverinn.com. 924 25th St. NW, 20037. Foggy Bottom/George Washington University Metro. 126 suites. AE, DC, MC, V. $$$$*

St. Regis (p. 20) Routinely rated in best-hotels lists, the St. Regis was built in the style of an Italian Renaissance palace. Antiques are encountered throughout the hotel. The rooms are luxurious. The service is attentive. The Library Lounge is one of the most inviting bars in Washington, with dark-paneled walls, bookshelves, and a working fireplace.... *Tel 202/638-2626 (888/625-5144). Fax 202/638-4231. www.stregis.com. 923 16th St. NW, 20006. McPherson Sq. Metro. 193 rooms. AE, DC, DISC, MC, V. $$$*

Sofitel Lafayette Square (p. 26) DOWNTOWN Cheerful, airy rooms with beige tones and lots of light greet you at this Sofitel near Lafayette Square and the White House. Opened in 2002 in a renovated 1928 office building, the hotel's French owners aimed for a decor that melds 1920s Art Deco with a contemporary style. Bathrooms have separate tubs and showers.... *Tel 202/730-8800 (800/763-4835). Fax 202/730-8500. www.sofitel.com. 806 15th St. NW, 20005. McPherson Sq. Metro. 220 rooms, 17 suites. AE, MC, V. $$$$*

State Plaza (p. 22) FOGGY BOTTOM This hotel is great for visiting diplomats, performers, scholars, and families who like the location as well as the convenience and economy of preparing some meals in their suite's kitchen.... *Tel 202/861-8200 (800/424-2859). www.stateplaza.com. 2117 E St. NW, 20037. Foggy Bottom/George Washington University Metro. 228 rooms. AE, DC, DISC, MC, V. $$*

Swann House (p. 27) DUPONT CIRCLE Rooms and suites in this spectacular B&B come with some eye-popping amenities. A couple of them have fireplaces and/or Jacuzzis. One has a private balcony (with a less-than-spectacular view). One bathroom has a high-domed ceiling, an enormous bathtub, and a gigantic rain shower. Swann House's in-ground pool is a rarity in the Dupont Circle neighborhood.... *Tel 202/265-4414. Fax 202/265-6755. www.swannhouse.com. 1808 New Hampshire Ave. NW, 20009. Dupont Circle Metro. 8 rooms. AE, DISC, MC, V. $$*

Tabard Inn (p. 25) DUPONT CIRCLE This hotel supplies old European comfort, charm and eccentricity (including 11 rooms with shared bathrooms). Comprised of three contiguous Victorian town houses, this small hotel offers rooms in a variety of configurations and prices. Also included are free continental breakfast in the Tabard's excellent restaurant and free admission to the nearby Capital YMCA.... *Tel 202/785-1277. Fax 202/785-6173. www.tabardinn.com. 1739 N St. NW, 20036. Dupont Circle Metro. 40 rooms. AE, DC, DISC, MC, V. $$*

Topaz Hotel (p. 24) DUPONT CIRCLE The supertrendy California flair here includes staff in sunburst tunics and furnishings accented with silk, mohair, velvet, and leather. Some guest rooms are special "energy rooms" or "yoga rooms," with appropriate accoutrements for exercise or yoga. The spacious, comfortable guest rooms are brightly decorated. The lobby flows into the equally trendy Topaz Bar. Off-peak rates can fall to $125.... *Tel 202/393-3000 (800/775-1202). Fax 202/785-9581. www. topazhotel.com. 1733 N St. NW, 20036. Dupont Circle Metro. 99 rooms. AE, DC, MC, V. $$$$*

Wardman Park Marriott Hotel (p. 21) UPPER NORTHWEST Washington's largest hotel, a mega–convention venue, serves up two outdoor swimming pools, fitness center, restaurant, pub, bar, deli, its own Starbucks, many suites (some with balconies), and easy access to the Metro.... *Tel 202/328-2000 (888/236-2427). Fax 202/234-0015. www.marriott.com. 2660 Woodley Rd. NW, 20008. Woodley Park–Zoo Metro. 1,340 rooms, 125 suites. AE, DC, DISC, MC, V. $$$$*

Washington Plaza (p. 26) DOWNTOWN The large outdoor pool at this 1960s hotel accommodates poolside dining and drinking as well as watersports. There's a fitness center, and guests get a free *Washington Post* Monday through Saturday. Rooms have the standard amenities, but you pay for wireless Internet access. Promotions can cut rates to $149.... *Tel 202/842-1300 (800/ 424-1140). Fax 202/371-9602. www.washingtonplazahotel.com. 10 Thomas Circle NW, at Massachusetts Ave. and 14th St., 20005. McPherson Sq. Metro. 314 rooms. AE, DC, DISC, MC, V. $$$*

Washington Suites Georgetown (p. 22) FOGGY BOTTOM/WEST END On the edge of Georgetown and Foggy Bottom, this all-suites facility is a bargain, with deals as low as $149 a night. Check out the list of freebies: cookies at check-in, reception Tuesday evening, *Washington Post* Monday through Friday, continental breakfast daily, high-speed Internet access, and an exercise room. Each suite has two TVs, and there's a coin-operated laundry on-site.... *Tel 202/333-8060 (877/736-2500). www. washingtonsuitesgeorgetown.com. 2500 Pennsylvania Ave. NW, 20037. Foggy Bottom/George Washington University Metro. 124 suites. AE, DISC, MC, V. $$$*

Willard InterContinental Washington (p. 20) DOWNTOWN Long-time power palace near the White House, the Willard reeks of history and is a favorite haunt of business executives and lobbyists with generous expense accounts. The Federal, Victorian, and Edwardian decor in the luxurious rooms cunningly conceals 21st-century amenities.... *Tel 202/628-9100 (888/424-6835). Fax 202/637-7326. www.washington.intercontinental.com. 1401*

Pennsylvania Ave. NW, 20004. Metro Center Metro. 294 rooms, 40 suites. AE, DC, DISC, MC, V. $$$$$

Woodley Park Guest House (p. 27) UPPER NORTHWEST Rooms here range from tiny to moderately small, and some share bathrooms. But they're comfortable, modern (renovated in 2001), close to the Metro, and they can be had for as little as $125. It's a good place to stay if you're an artist, as all the artwork on the walls was purchased from hotel guests.... *Tel 202/667-0218 (866/667-0218). Fax 202/6671080. woodleyparkguesthouse. com. 2647 Woodley Rd NW, 20008. Woodley Park–Zoo Metro. 18 rooms. AE, MC, V. $$*

Basic Stuff

One upon a time, Washington was a self-admitted culinary backwater. But that's gone the way of the horse-drawn streetcar and congressional bipartisanship. Nowadays it seems like a new—good—restaurant opens every week. And even hotel eateries have become places where Washingtonians (not just exhausted travelers) choose to dine.

There is no "Washington cuisine," the way one thinks of Boston seafood or Chicago steaks. But—perhaps even better—just about everybody else's cuisine has taken up residence here. Because every nook and cranny in America is represented in Congress, most American regional cooking finds its way into Washington restaurants. Because Washington is the capital of the world, much of the world's culinary achievements eventually show up here as well.

What with lobbyists, political operatives, and journalists constantly on the prowl, Washington probably hosts more expense-account meals than most other towns. As a result, we enjoy a steady increase in the number of dining establishments that figure they can charge an arm and a leg for a claw or a tail. Unless you hail from New York or San Francisco, you'll probably be taken aback by your tab. Luckily, there are plenty of alternatives to white tablecloths and silver, even though the soup and sandwiches probably will cost you more than you pay back home. Despite their reputation as big-spending wasters of taxpayers' dollars, most Washingtonians are working stiffs just like most Pittsburghers. They may toil on Capitol Hill or at the Internal Revenue Service, but they still prefer a cheap, quick lunch. There are lots of coffee shops to meet that demand. And, if you're so inclined, you'll have no problem spotting whichever fast-food megachain tickles your taste buds.

Only in D.C.

Because Washington lacks its own cuisine, we've had to borrow from others. The most-borrowed are crab-centric concoctions that spill down from Baltimore and over from Maryland's Eastern Shore. Crab cakes—crabmeat mixed with egg, milk, scallions, breading, and seasoning—are served in sandwiches or platters in many restaurants, whatever their other specialties. Hard-shelled crabs are served by the bucket and consumed during lengthy ceremonies involving mallets, picks, and paring knives on paper-covered tabletops. More restaurants serve softshell crabs, which are the same animal, caught when it's shed its old shell and hasn't had time to grow a new one. You can eat soft-shells with standard-issue knife and fork.

Side dishes at breakfast sometimes bring another borrowed flavor, such as Southern grits (Washington once was considered a Southern town) or scrapple, a fried meat-and-cornmeal mush, down from Pennsylvania Dutch country. D.C.'s only original food appears to be the half-smoke, a mild, hot-dog-like sausage sold on every street corner, found in every grocery store, and a specialty at the Washington eating institution **Ben's Chili Bowl.** There's nothing special about half-smokes, they just don't seem to be sold anywhere else.

How to Dress

Washington is filled with folks who work in business suits and business dresses, so you'll find that attire common in restaurants. But Washington doesn't have much of a dress code. You'll have to look hard for an eating spot that bars entry to a man without a coat and tie or a woman in shorts. In fact, you can wear jeans and pretty informal shirts almost anywhere, though you may feel conspicuously underdressed at better restaurants. And because many Washingtonians work long hours during the day and attend formal affairs at night, you never have to worry about overdressing. Feel free to take the subway if you're wearing a tux or evening gown to a fancy event. Locals do.

When to Eat

Few restaurants start serving breakfast before 7am, and few keep serving dinner after 11pm. If you arrive for lunch by noon, you'll probably beat the crowds. Or you can hold off till about 1:30pm. The lady who gets too hungry for dinner at 8 would be quite comfortable here. Washingtonians go to dinner *before* the show, not after.

Where to Smoke

The D.C. government enacted a broad smoking ban in 2006 that was to take full effect at the beginning of 2007. It banned smoking in restaurant dining rooms immediately. It extended to bars and the bar areas of restaurants in 2007. Smoking could continue in cigar and hookah bars and outdoor areas such as sidewalk cafes. The ban also covers offices and apartment-building lobbies. You can smoke in your hotel room. Establishments, of course, are free to impose stricter limitations of their own.

Where the Chefs Are

Among the most interesting things about Washington's top chefs today are the rise of women in a profession that has been so dominated by men and the chefs' cultivation of local farmers as sources of fresh ingredients.

Jamie Leeds won Washington fame as chef at 15 ria. In mid-2005 she opened her own spot, a few blocks from Dupont Circle, which she named **Hank's Oyster Bar,** after her father, who took her fishing, and after the food in which the restaurant specializes. She shops for produce at the Dupont Circle farmers' market and has developed relationships with oyster farmers, so she knows what she gets is good and fresh. Interestingly, she brought along her "Meat and Two" specials from 15 ria—comfort food, such as roast chicken or pork chops, with your choice of two sides. Ann Cashion brings a cosmopolitan background to **Cashion's Eat Place** in Adams Morgan. A Mississippi native, Cashion has, like her restaurant, Southern roots. But she's also cooked in Italy, France, and California, and that experience is evident in her menu. Cashion chefs additionally at Johnny's Half Shell, a seafood house she owns with John Fulchino.

The busiest chef in D.C. right now is the Spanish-born **Jose Andres,** who rides herd on six excellent dining spots: Mediterranean Zaytinya, Latin American Cafe Atlantico, and Spanish Jaleo—all in Penn Quarter—two more Jaleos in the suburbs, and Oyamel, a Mexican restaurant in Arlington (225 Crystal Dr.; Tel 703/413-2288; www.oyamel.com). His dream of creating at least one more, where he could prepare the finest meals without worrying so much about the cost, is fulfilled in part at the inventive Minibar, a six-seat restaurant within a restaurant at Atlantico.

Finally, no review of D.C.'s top chefs could be complete without mention of **Yannick Cam,** a veteran of restaurants in his native France as well as New York. Cam captured Washington's imagination at the highly regarded Le Pavillon, which closed in 1990. After several other ventures, Cam thrilled Washington gastronomes when he joined Michael Klein, his Le Pavillon partner, in opening Le Paradou in Penn Quarter. Here Cam serves up an elite French dining experience with prices to match.

Street Food

D.C.'s ubiquitous food carts are cheap and convenient, but they're woefully bland and predictable. The exception to the rule occurs during special events. Japanese food takes up residence along D.C. streets during the National Cherry Blossom Festival in late March and early April. You can cop free samples along Pennsylvania Avenue during the National Capital Barbecue Battle in June. Traditional foods from featured nations and states can be had on the Mall during the Smithsonian Folklife Festival in late June and early July. Washington restaurants sell their wares from stands set up along Pennsylvania Avenue during the Taste of D.C. in October.

Info, Info, Info

The *Washington Post* (www.washingtonpost.com) and *Washingtonian* magazine (www.washingtonian.com) provide useful current listings. At the top of the *Post* site's home page, click on City Guide for a list of attractions, lodging, dining, and entertainment, including *Post* critics' reviews. At the top of the *Washingtonian* site, you'll find links to restaurant reviews and info about arts and entertainment. The Vegetarian Resource Group posts descriptions of vegetarian-friendly restaurants on its website, www.vrg.org.

The Lowdown

First-family sightings... Washington restaurateurs still miss Bill Clinton, the most dining-out president in history, and are grateful that Senator Hillary brings him back to town from time to time. During his 8 years at the White House, Clinton often embarked to sample whatever Washington's eating establishments had to offer, from McDonald's to such upscale eateries as **Galileo** and **Kinkead's.** President Bush the First was known to step out from time to time, too, but he seemed to like old familiar places, especially the Peking Gourmet Inn in suburban Falls Church, Virginia. Jeffrey's, said to be one of George the Second's favorite haunts back in Austin, moved to D.C. and opened a branch. Unfortunately, it didn't last long. Like father, like son, George II has been known to frequent the Peking Gourmet, and he and first lady Laura Bush have visited the **Cactus Cantina** Tex-Mex spot in Upper Northwest. Every president since Harry Truman has had at least one meal at **Martin's Tavern** in Georgetown. Truman, Jack Kennedy, Lyndon Johnson, and Richard Nixon were Martin's regulars during their years in Congress.

Congressional hangouts... In his whodunit *Murder in the Senate,* no less an inside source than former senator William S. Cohen labeled **The Monocle** "a watering hole for lobbyists, members, and Hill staffers...a place to discuss matters off the record." Standing near the Senate office buildings, this off-campus clubhouse for lawmakers serves a traditional American menu. Representatives occasionally wander into **Bullfeathers** for a drink or a bite on the House side of the Hill. House aides do it all the time.

Seats of power... There are plenty of off-the-Hill restaurants where pols, journalists, and deep-pocketed lobbyists give their expense accounts a beating. Everyone who is anyone dines at **The Palm** near Dupont Circle. At **The Prime Rib** downtown, well-dressed lobbyists know their fellow diners and their waiters will be well dressed as well. Male guests must wear jackets and ties, and male waiters work in tuxedos. **Morton's** is still a place for important meetings and important meat, though former House Ways and Means Committee Chairman Dan Rostenkowski— jailed for mail fraud—no longer holds court at the table that once bore a plaque marking "Rosty's Rotunda."

Decision makers for international organizations congregate at **Taberna del Alabardero** downtown, which also is popular with visiting Spanish royalty. When White House staffers are let loose, they're apt to wind up at **The Occidental** or the **Old Ebbitt Grill** nearby. The restaurants draw nearby bureaucrats as well. On Occidental's walls, the framed photos of everybody who was ever anybody let you know it's been feeding the powerful and the famous for a century on the same site (though in different buildings). Opt for the downstairs room for its mahogany bar and stronger in-crowd vibes. The nerve center of local power is **Georgia Brown's** downtown, which boasts "nouveau soul food" and one of the most-integrated dining rooms in Washington. When the local powers are in a more down-home mood, they're apt to head for **Ben's Chili Bowl** at U and 12th streets.

Historic surroundings... The 1962 Cuban Missile Crisis was resolved in part in secret meetings at the Yenching Palace, (3524 Connecticut Ave., at Porter St. NW; Tel 202/362-8200), a Chinese restaurant not far from the National Zoo. Unfortunately, while adequate, it is not worth the trip unless you happen to be hungry and in the neighborhood. For history and good food, the best bet is **Poste,** the restaurant at the Hotel Monaco in Penn Quarter. Lots of history has passed through this building, opened in 1842 as Washington's General Post Office, which was expanded in 1859, and later housed the Tariff Commission.

Election winners... Everybody who's anybody in the D.C. dining biz belongs to the Restaurant Association of Metropolitan Washington (motto: "fighting for the right to eat, drink, and be merry"). Anybody who likes to dine pays attention to the association's annual "Rammy" awards. **Ristorante Tosca,** a fine downtown Italian restaurant, scored as 2005's "Fine Dining Restaurant of the Year." **Johnny's Half Shell,** an informal seafood spot moving to bigger digs on Capitol Hill, was named "Informal Dining Restaurant of the Year." Fabio Trabocchi of suburban Maestro (1700 Tysons Blvd, McLean, VA; Tel 703/821-1515) won "Chef of the Year." And **Kinkead's** downtown, long regarded as one of D.C.'s very best seafood houses, was honored for its dough as well when Chris Kujala was crowned "Pastry Chef of the Year."

Kid pleasers... Skip the fast-food chains and take your children to local restaurants that are loud and festive and serve tasty (and sloppy?) food. Places like the bustling, brightly decorated **Austin Grill** in Penn Quarter and just above Georgetown. Children and grown-ups alike enjoy the tasty Tex-Mex dishes. Or head for Dupont Circle's **Sette Osteria,** a modern, airy, attractive restaurant that's full of hard surfaces (bare tables, bare walls, tile floors), and lots of hustle, bustle, and noise. Pizza, pasta, and high chairs raise the kid-friendly quotient. Give the kids a real treat of authentic Neapolitan pizza at **2Amys** in Upper Northwest or **Pizzeria Paradiso** near Dupont Circle and in Georgetown.

Youngsters also find lots of appealing dishes at the **Old Ebbitt Grill** near the White House, from very good burgers to finger food on the appetizer menu. And there are plenty of sophisticated dishes for the grownups. D.C. parents take their children to **Sequoia,** on the Georgetown waterfront, because the restaurant's noisy, the food's good, there's a nice view, and you can sit outside in good weather.

Vegging out... Most restaurants now include at least one vegetarian item on the menu. If you don't like to even be in the presence of meat, head over to Georgetown's **Amma Indian Vegetarian Kitchen,** which serves up exactly what its name suggests and does so at bargain-basement prices. Practically next door, the **Harmony Cafe**'s attractive dining room can please vegetarians and omnivores at the same table. Most of its Asian dishes come in vegetarian versions, a testament to the ability of soy to mimic other foods. **Taberna del Alabardero** downtown, the only U.S. branch of a Spanish chain, offers a separate vegetarian menu, including vegan items. At **Zaytinya**—a dramatically attractive and hip Mediterranean restaurant in Penn Quarter—70% of the small meze dishes (think Mediterranean tapas) are vegetarian. Similarly, vegetarian and vegan items can be found among the Turkish meze at **Meyhane** on Capitol Hill. **The Tombs** in Georgetown conjures up a veggie burger that's nearly as fat and juicy as a real hamburger. Other spots noted for placing some good vegetarian offerings on their menus include **Firehook Bakery, Restaurant Nora, Asia Nora,** and the **Red Sage Border Cafe,** which has created an eight-vegetable chili.

For committed carnivores... Because of its A-list of politically powerful patrons, **The Palm** near Dupont Circle is Washington's most famous steakhouse, even though it's actually part of a chain that started in New York. **Morton's**—with restaurants downtown, in Georgetown, and in four suburbs—fetches top dollar for its aged steaks, each of which could feed a small village. For the atmosphere of a 1940s supper club, stroll into **The Prime Rib** downtown and order prime rib. Gentlemen must wear jackets and ties.

Something fishy... It's not hard to find good seafood in this town, although you'll often find yourself paying more than you might expect. **Kinkead's** downtown is one of Washington's very best restaurants. **Sea Catch** hides in a courtyard below M Street in Georgetown, but you'll find excellent food and great views once you get there. Floor-to-ceiling windows overlook the C&O Canal. In nice weather you can dine on a terrace above the canal. In cold weather, fireplaces warm two of the dining rooms. The menu changes frequently at pricey French **Gerard's Place** downtown. Consider yourself extremely lucky if you happen in when the offerings include lobster with ginger, lime, and sauterne. If you go to **The Oceanaire Seafood Room,** note the name of the restaurant, and don't take your cues from Ghazi Yawar—the interim president of Iraq who came to Washington for Ronald Reagan's funeral in mid-2004—who dined at the downtown restaurant, and ordered steak. For Chinese seafood, head to **Tony Cheng's Seafood Restaurant** in Chinatown and peruse what's swimming in the tank. Those fish are not pets.

DINING

Nouveau Southern... What happens to food when an old Southern city full of Southern politicians collides with the 21st century? Can you say "Nouveau Southern cuisine"? No? Well, maybe you'd like to eat it. When Bill Clinton moved up from Arkansas, Jeffrey Buben brought what he calls "American cuisine with a Southern accent" to downtown's **Vidalia,** named for the onion. Look for the five-onion soup. **Georgia Brown's** downtown once described its unique cuisine as "Nouveau Soul Food." That means dishes such as fried green tomatoes stuffed with herbed cream cheese and served on green tomato relish with lemon-cayenne mayonnaise and watercress. Yum. (Really!) Rahman Harper's dishes at **B. Smith's** in Union Station are rooted in Cajun, Creole, and traditional Southern cooking. The house special is Swamp Thing, mixed seafood over greens in a mustard-based seafood sauce. Throwing a Washington-area flavor into the mix, Harper created Chesapeake Bay Surf & Turf, which is fried chicken and crab cakes.

Asian delights... Washington doesn't have much of a Chinatown, though the Friendship Archway at 7th and H streets NW is an interesting sight. But you'll have no trouble finding Asian cooking, which seems to be peddled on every corner throughout the city. In Chinatown itself, people frequent the **Lei Garden** for dim sum at lunch every day and for good Chinese cooking all the time. The dining room is light and airy, with floor-to-ceiling windows, faux skylights, white tablecloths, white china, and hanging plants. Nearby, **Eat First** and **Full Kee** don't draw patrons with their decor— both have plain dining rooms. But both serve top-notch food and are among a handful of places where you can get a good meal after midnight. Also nearby (remember, this Chinatown is small), Tony Cheng offers a variety of dining experiences. Seafood obviously is the specialty at **Tony**

Cheng's Seafood Restaurant, which actually serves a full range of standard Chinese foods upstairs. On the first floor, **Tony Cheng's Mongolian Restaurant** lets you pick your ingredients then choose your cooking method—grilled by the chefs or cooked by you in a hot pot of boiling stock at your table. Outside of Chinatown (just above Dupont Circle, to be precise), **City Lights of China** serves up a large and varied menu that's noted for Peking duck and crisp-fried Cornish hen.

Thai restaurants have proliferated in Washington. One, **Busara,** just above Georgetown, feels sleek and hip, with modern art on the walls and nightclubish-blue lighting in an otherwise dimly lighted room. For food you've probably not tried before, check out **Malaysia Kopitiam** near Dupont Circle. Malaysian cuisine shares a lot with Chinese, Thai, and Indian cooking. Malaysia Kopitiam's menu contains descriptions and photos to help you decide what to eat. From the subcontinent comes **Rasika,** the "Modern Indian" restaurant with the well-traveled chef. Vikram Sunderam is a native of India who cooked at London's Bombay Brasserie before moving to the U.S. capital.

If your party doesn't want to confine itself to one Asian cuisine, pick a Pan-Asian or Asian-influenced kitchen, such as **Asia Nora** or **Nooshi.** At Nora, the focus is on healthful, organic foods that chef/owner Nora Pouillon calls "fusion cuisine." Nooshi was a popular noodles joint—called Oodles Noodles—that added sushi and changed its name.

La cuisine française... Right-wing Republicans' hate-hate relationship with France had no perceptible impact on French dining in this nation's capital—even in the shadow of the GOP-controlled Capitol itself. For those of you who like France and enjoy pretending you're there when you're not, Capitol Hill's **Montmartre** and Dupont Circle's **Bistro Du Coin** will put you in a fine mood. Both are noisy, bustling, crowded, and send you French waitresses speaking fractured *anglais.* The sign over Montmartre's door, the sidewalk cafe, the ceiling fans, and the unisex restrooms seal the deal. At Du Coin, it's the long, high-ceilinged, brightly lit room with wooden tables covered by butcher paper, caned chairs, and French signs and prints on the walls. As for the food: Have you ever had a bum meal in France?

Just below M Street in Georgetown, **Café La Ruche** will put you in mind of a neighborhood hangout in Paris or perhaps in a small town in the French countryside. You can eat downright cheaply here from a menu focused on soups, salads, sandwiches, quiches, and other light fare. Desserts—the most expensive $5.25—are impossible to turn down. At the extreme other end of *la cuisine française* is **Le Paradou,** where superstar chef Yannick Cam performs in Penn Quarter. If you've got $110 to spend on a six-course tasting menu—or $145 for nine—this is the place for you. The gorgeous dining rooms won't necessarily make you feel like you're in France, but the exquisite food will make you feel you've just eaten one of the best meals of your life.

On the cutting edge of Washington's French cuisine stands **Gerard's Place.** This jewel box of a restaurant downtown is a favorite of French diplomats. **Bistro Bis,** on the Hill, serves up a modern American spin on classic French bistro and brasserie fare. The zinc bar and its sleek surroundings are popular with congressional aides. Chef Michel Richard serves what he calls "French/California cuisine" at his highly regarded **Michel Richard Citronelle** in Georgetown. **Marcel's,** in Foggy Bottom/West End, offers wonderful "French cuisine with a Flemish flair."

Palazzi italiani... Top-of-the-line **Galileo** has gravity-defying prices, but Chef Roberto Donna is capable of producing world-class Italian meals of gravity-defying quality. Laboratorio del Galileo, Donna's "cooking suite" and private dining area, can be even better and is always even more expensive. Dining at **Teatro Goldoni** downtown is as much about the show as the food, which is traditional Venetian cuisine updated and tweaked with ideas from other countries. You can watch the chefs work in their glass-enclosed kitchen, count the Venetian masks hanging on the wall, chuckle at the barbershop-pole-striped pillars, and marvel when the red-vested waiters bring your salad on a plate the size of Sicily and your soup in a bowl as deep as the Mediterranean. A clue to **Ristorante Tosca**'s quality is chef/owner Cesare Lanfranconi's training at Galileo. Lanfranconi serves contemporary northern Italian meals on white tablecloths in a simple, elegant room. Among his offerings are tasting menus that range from $60 to $95 to a $32 pretheater tasting. **Obelisk,** a small cafe near Dupont Circle, offers a fixed-price menu with a few superb selections each evening.

Poca casa italiana... The peasants must eat, too, and Roberto Donna wants to include them among those he serves. In the bar area of his multifaceted **Galileo** restaurant, Donna has opened what he calls Osteria del Galileo and Galileo Al Bar. At dinner, Osteria offers appetizers, pastas, main courses, side dishes, and desserts—nothing priced higher than $12. Al Bar serves lunch, also at modest cost.

Pizza has always epitomized economic Italian dining, and **Pizzeria Paradiso** and **2Amys** bake up true Neapolitan pizza in wood-fired ovens. In addition to the pies, Paradiso serves desserts, salads, and focaccia sandwiches near Dupont Circle and in Georgetown. Similarly, 2Amys, near the National Cathedral, offers desserts, salads, and a growing selection of small side dishes such as meatballs, fried rice balls stuffed with cheese, and deviled eggs with pesto sauce. The latest entry to the best-pizza competition is **Matchbox** in Chinatown. It, too, bakes in a wood-burning oven, but what comes out is traditional New York pizza. Matchbox has a full menu of appetizers, salads, entrees, and sandwiches, as well as a wide range of domestic and international beers. You'll find good pizza from a wood-fired oven and a full Italian menu at **Sette Osteria** in Dupont Circle. By fairly early in the evening, young professionals crowd three-deep at the bar, standing, drinking, chatting, glancing at the large-screen TVs, and juggling their pizza slices. Beware that these spots don't take reservations, so long lines are likely at peak meal times.

Don't sweat the little things (eat them)... Nearly every cuisine in town seems to offer its version of little dishes you share with your dining companions in a festive environment. Often (though not always!) this is a terrific way to sample high-quality food at a fairly low price. King of little things in Washington right now is Jose Andres, chef at previously mentioned **Zaytinya, Cafe Atlantico, Jaleo,** and Oyamel in Arlington (225 Crystal Dr.; Tel 703/413-2288; ww.oyamel.com). Jaleo, serving tapas, was Andres's first venture into little things—which makes sense, since he hails from Spain. At this lively, colorful restaurant, you can order main courses. But the fun is in the tapas, such as chorizo sausage with garlic mashed potatoes; spinach with pine nuts, apples, and raisins; or red bell pepper stuffed with crabmeat. At Zaytinya—a stunning modern room with soaring floor-to-ceiling windows—Andres dishes out his versions of meze, tapping especially the traditions of Lebanon, Turkey, and Greece. At Cafe Atlantico, Andres commandeered a small space for Minibar, a six-seat counter where he serves little things that defy classification. The $95 tasting menu might surprise you with potato mousse with caviar and vanilla oil; scallops and sea urchin with frozen mango soup; or a dollop of foie gras surrounded by cotton candy! For Turkish meze, climb Capitol Hill to **Meyhane.**

Another way to sample small dishes is by taking traditional afternoon tea at **Teaism.** Daily from 2:30 to 5:30pm, this Penn Quarter restaurant offers both the traditional British-style tea, with little sandwiches, scones, truffles and other goodies, and an Asian tea with rice balls, tofu and more truffles. Fondue has made a comeback at **The Melting Pot** near Dupont Circle (and in several suburbs), where you dip little things into hot cheeses, broths, and (for dessert) melted chocolate. The "Lovers Lane" section of the restaurant features dimly lit booths for two. Elsewhere, large tables accommodate a dozen or more for sharing a bigger selection of meats, fowl, seafood, vegetables, and fruits. Make a meal of Italian nuggets at **2Amys** Neapolitan pizzeria near the National Cathedral.

Beyond the Beltway... Two establishments that regularly make Washington's best-restaurants lists lie beyond—and way beyond—the Capital Beltway. Enthusiasts contend that dining at the **Inn at Little Washington** is a life-changing experience. It almost has to be to justify driving 70 miles one-way to the edge of Virginia's Blue Ridge Mountains, paying way more than $100 for each diner, and spending several hundred more for a room if you don't want to finish your evening with the drive back home. For your money, you'll be treated to an exquisite meal prepared from the products of local farms—or perhaps Chesapeake Bay crab or Maine lobster. Closer to home, L'Auberge Chez François serves traditional Alsatian food in a romantic Alsatian-style country inn at Great Falls, Virginia. You may need to reserve a month in advance to dine on the likes of game; seafood in puff pastry; or a platter of sausage, pork, duck, foie gras, and pheasant on a bed of sauer-kraut—finished with a Grand Marnier soufflé.

Alfresco... Because of Washington's semi-Southern climate, you can find restaurants that will feed you outdoors from Easter till Thanksgiving. At **Sequoia,** along the Potomac in Georgetown's Washington Harbour complex, there's more to watch than the river. This area has become a major human meat market with nonstop cocktail parties under way every pleasant evening at the various outdoor bars. The river walk is a fine place to spot strollers—and skaters and bicyclists—of all kinds. In nice weather, **Meyhane,** the Turkish restaurant, throws its floor-to-ceiling windows open and welcomes the Capitol Hill sidewalk inside.

The **Tabard Inn** serves food and drinks in its inner-courtyard garden, well-shielded from the bustle of its Dupont Circle neighborhood. **Sea Catch** offers a relaxing view of the C&O Canal south of Georgetown's M Street. **Zaytinya** serves its fine cooking on an outdoor terrace when the weather's nice. And **Le Paradou'**s sidewalk tables provide a means to enjoy superior French cooking at less lofty prices. **Circle Bistro** in Foggy Bottom offers barbe-cues on the deck by the pool of One Washington Circle Hotel from 4 to 10pm weekends in the summer.

The soul of black Washington... Now in its seventh decade, the **Florida Avenue Grill** is a classic corner diner, known for Southern-style food, heavy on the four G's—grits, greens, gravy, and grease—and friendly waitresses too familiar with the regulars to take any lip. Since 1958, nearby **Ben's Chili Bowl** has been a late-night hangout for African-American entertainers, civil rights activists, and students from nearby Howard University. Like the Grill, it's also a breakfast institution. When black Washingtoni-ans go upscale, two of their favorite dining spots are **Georgia Brown's** downtown and **B. Smith's** in Union Station. Both root their innovative American cooking in the foods of the South.

When romance is in the air... The soft light, warm decor, plush seats, candles on the tables, and soft music seeping in from the bar make **Coeur de Lion** in Penn Quarter an ideal spot to pop the question, light a new fire, or rekindle a long romance. Part of this Henley Park Hotel restaurant is in an old courtyard now topped by a glass ceiling. The tables are well spaced, and there's a corner nook where a couple can sit side by side and feel special and removed from the rest of the room. Lots of diners return here frequently, and maitre d' Ralph Fredericks seems to know (and fuss over) everyone, so this probably is not the spot for a secret rendezvous. After dinner you can adjourn to the adjacent Blue Bar, where a pianist entertains from about 8 on Thursday, Friday, and Saturday evenings. The bar has nooks and crannies conducive to intimate imbibing.

For countryside romance, take a drive through the northern Virginia hills to **L'Auberge Chez François,** where a table by the fireplace or on the garden-side terrace creates the perfect ambience. Back in Georgetown, snare the table by the fire in **Sea Catch**'s front dining room—the one with stone walls, wood paneling, beamed ceiling, and floor-to-ceiling windows overlooking the C&O Canal. At **The Melting Pot** fondue house in Dupont Circle, one dimly lit section of booths-for-two is called Lovers' Lane.

Ya gotta have a gimmick... When a good meal alone isn't enough to satisfy your hunger, Washington has a gaggle of restaurants happy to entertain you in ways that extend beyond serving fine food. The granddaddy of gastronomical gimmicks here is the downtown Moroccan restaurant **Marrakesh,** which perfectly evokes an American fantasy of *Casablanca* and *The Arabian Nights.* In a developing but not-yet-gentrified part of town, you knock on a closed door to be admitted, and then slip through a heavy curtain into a large, dimly lighted dining room that's decorated with multicolored, intricately patterned tapestries. You sit on cushions around a low table upon which food is served communally for you to eat with your hands, except for when you're watching the periodic belly dance. This is most fun with a group. At **Zola,** next to the International Spy Museum in Penn Quarter, the gimmick is—no mystery—spies. Declassified intelligence documents are on display in this Modern American restaurant, as are blowups of frames from noir films. The waiters dress in black. James Bond would feel at home in a big, comfortable, red-velvet booth beside a mirrored wall with a frosted peep hole that lets him spy on the next dining room or the kitchen.

The gimmick at **Firefly** is, well, fireflies, which are supposed to conjure up sweet memories of summer nights spent lounging in the backyard with family and friends. You can't miss the "firefly tree," a floor-to-ceiling birch trunk dangling candle-lighted copper lanterns from its branches. The Dupont Circle restaurant—noisy when crowded—serves Contemporary American dishes that often are based on comfort-food staples such as pot roast, short ribs, or roasted chicken. Nearby, **Mimi's American Bistro** serves up singing waiters with your American food. The decor here is essentially backstage theater, with very dark walls and tables. At **Busboys and Poets** in the U Street Corridor, the focus would seem to be on poetry. But this is a restaurant, bookstore, theater, bar, coffee house and Internet café rolled into one.

At the **Brickskeller** and the **Capitol City Brewing Company,** the gimmicks are in the beer. That's more than 1,000 varieties at the Brickskeller, according to the Dupont Circle restaurant's latest count. With brick walls, checkered tablecloths, Janis Joplin on the jukebox, and beer bottles and cans serving as the major decorative elements, the Brickskeller feels like your classic college pub. It's got a pretty classic pub menu, too. At Capitol City (it's their name and they'll spell it the way they want to), the emphasis is on a handful of beers brewed on-site. The D.C. brewpubs are big and strikingly attractive, with the sparkling brewing machinery on central display. They're also historic, the Capitol Hill pub residing in the old post office and the downtown pub in the old bus station. (Two others are in Baltimore and the VA suburbs.) The menu is typical of these types of modern restaurant/bars that cater to young singles, dates, and families with kids in tow.

Great Georgetown hangouts... The original **Clyde's** on M Street in Georgetown dates back to 1963 and claims to be the inspiration for the Starland Vocal Band's 1976 hit "Afternoon Delight." Clyde's was renovated in 1996 and no longer has the feel of a comfortable old shoe. But it still has its saloonlike atmosphere, and the food's probably better—and certainly more ambitious—than it was 4 decades ago. A couple blocks east on M Street, **Garrett's** really is a well-worn old tavern with vintage Dylan on the jukebox and a secret tucked into a corner of the second floor; go up the stairs just east of the first-floor bar, ignore the two bars on the second floor, and step into a very attractive little dining room with large windows and a glass roof.

The granddaddy of Georgetown hangouts, **Martin's Tavern** was opened in 1933 by William S. Martin, who emigrated from Ireland. Inside you'll find wooden booths, tables, Tiffany lamps, and a mahogany bar. The narrow sidewalk cafe is great for eating and Georgetowner-watching in nice weather. Over the years regulars here have included Jack and Jackie Kennedy, Richard Nixon, Harry Truman, Lyndon Johnson, and Sam Rayburn. Students, faculty, and neighborhood residents frequent **The Tombs,** a basement pub on the edge of the Georgetown University campus, where the food is much better than you might expect at a college pub.

Cheap eats... On Connecticut Avenue just south of Dupont Circle, **Luna Grill & Diner** is exactly what its name proclaims and then a bit more. The blue-plate specials run to pork chops and fried chicken, but there also are Green Plate Specials for vegetarians, and you can buy breakfast all day. **Booeymonger** is a popular deli in Georgetown, Upper Northwest, Bethesda, and northern Virginia. Open early to late, with full breakfasts in the morning. **Firehook Bakery,** with six D.C. locations and two in the suburbs, fixes scrumptious made-from-scratch soups and inventive sandwiches served on house-baked breads. The Firehooks also bake breakfast and dessert pastries and serve and sell locally roasted Quartermaine coffee and beans.

Caffeine scenes... Yes, the plague of West Coast coffeehouses has descended on nearly every Washington street corner. But there are spots for a spot that comes with local flavor. The aforementioned **Firehook Bakery** shops are a good for-instance. **Kramerbooks & Afterwords Cafe,** at Dupont Circle, has been serving food, coffee, and other beverages while selling books from early morning to late night since long before the national chains figured that might be a good idea.

Map 3: Washington, D.C., Dining

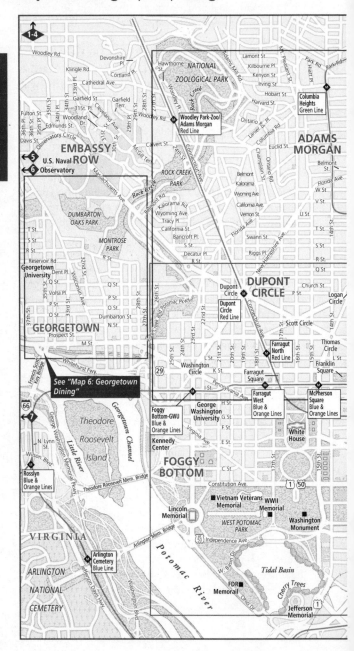

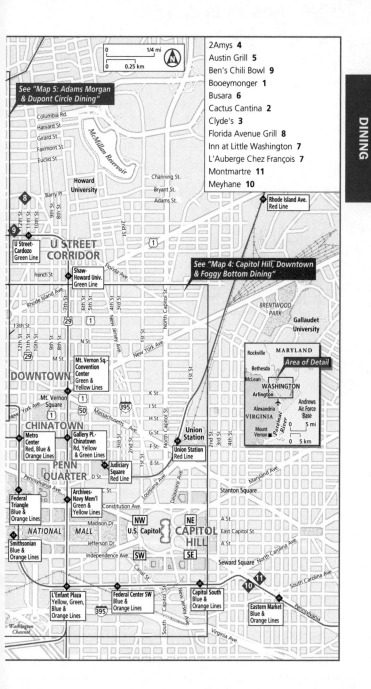

DINING

2Amys **4**
Austin Grill **5**
Ben's Chili Bowl **9**
Booeymonger **1**
Busara **6**
Cactus Cantina **2**
Clyde's **3**
Florida Avenue Grill **8**
Inn at Little Washington **7**
L'Auberge Chez François **7**
Montmartre **11**
Meyhane **10**

See "Map 5: Adams Morgan & Dupont Circle Dining"

See "Map 4: Capitol Hill, Downtown & Foggy Bottom Dining"

Columbia Rd.
Harvard St.
Girard St.
Fairmont St.
Euclid St.
Barry Pl.

McMillan Reservoir

Howard University

Channing St.
Bryant St.
Adams St.

Rhode Island Ave.
Red Line

U STREET CORRIDOR

U Street-Cardozo
Green Line

French St.

Shaw-Howard Univ.
Green Line

Florida Ave.

BRENTWOOD PARK

Gallaudet University

Rhode Island Ave.

7th St.
6th St.
5th St.
4th St.
3rd St.
New Jersey Ave.
North Capitol St.
1st St.

N St.

29

MARYLAND
Rockville
Bethesda
McLean
Arlington
VIRGINIA
Alexandria
Mount Vernon

WASHINGTON
Area of Detail

Andrews Air Force Base

Potomac River

0   5 mi
0   5 km

13th St.
12th St.
11th St.
10th St.
9th St.
8th St.

29

M St.

DOWNTOWN

Mt. Vernon Sq.-Convention Center
Green & Yellow Lines

Mt. Vernon Square

1

New York Ave.

New York Ave.

50

Massachusetts Ave.

395

K St.
I St.
H St.
G St.
F St.

CHINATOWN

Metro Center
Red, Blue & Orange Lines

Gallery Pl.-Chinatown
Rd, Yellow & Green Lines

Union Station

Union Station
Red Line

PENN QUARTER

Pennsylvania Ave.

Archives-Navy Mem'l
Green & Yellow Lines

Judiciary Square
Red Line

D St.

C St.

Stanton Square

Maryland Ave.

Federal Triangle
Blue & Orange Lines

Constitution Ave.

Madison Dr.

NATIONAL MALL

Smithsonian
Blue & Orange Lines

Jefferson Dr.

Independence Ave.

NW

NE

U.S. Capitol

SW

SE

CAPITOL HILL

East Capitol St.

A St.

A St.

Seward Square

North Carolina Ave.

South Carolina Ave.

Louisiana Ave.

Delaware Ave.

Canal St.

L'Enfant Plaza
Yellow, Green, Blue & Orange Lines

395

Federal Center SW
Blue & Orange Lines

Capitol South
Blue & Orange Lines

Eastern Market
Blue & Orange Lines

Pennsylvania Ave.

Washington Channel

South Capitol St.

New Jersey Ave.

Virginia Ave.

0   1/4 mi
0   0.25 km

Map 4: Capitol Hill, Downtown & Foggy Bottom Dining

DINING

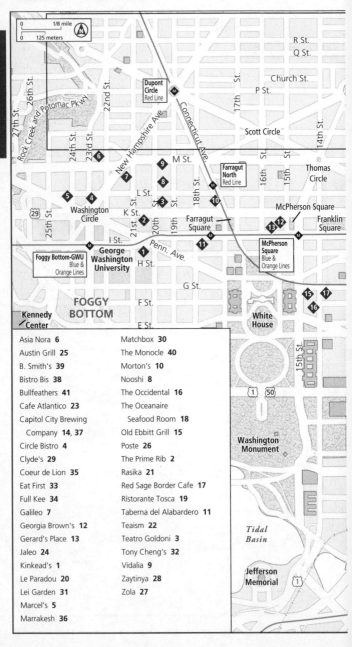

Asia Nora **6**	Matchbox **30**
Austin Grill **25**	The Monocle **40**
B. Smith's **39**	Morton's **10**
Bistro Bis **38**	Nooshi **8**
Bullfeathers **41**	The Occidental **16**
Cafe Atlantico **23**	The Oceanaire
Capitol City Brewing	Seafood Room **18**
Company **14, 37**	Old Ebbitt Grill **15**
Circle Bistro **4**	Poste **26**
Clyde's **29**	The Prime Rib **2**
Coeur de Lion **35**	Rasika **21**
Eat First **33**	Red Sage Border Cafe **17**
Full Kee **34**	Ristorante Tosca **19**
Galileo **7**	Taberna del Alabardero **11**
Georgia Brown's **12**	Teaism **22**
Gerard's Place **13**	Teatro Goldoni **3**
Jaleo **24**	Tony Cheng's **32**
Kinkead's **1**	Vidalia **9**
Le Paradou **20**	Zaytinya **28**
Lei Garden **31**	Zola **27**
Marcel's **5**	
Marrakesh **36**	

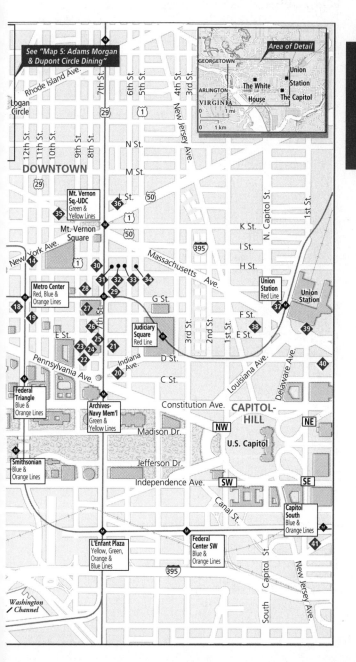

Map 5: Adams Morgan & Dupont Circle Dining

Bistro Du Coin **11**

Brickskeller **4**

Busboys & Poets **19**

Cashion's Eat Place **13**

City Lights of China **12**

Firefly **2**

Firehook Bakery **8**

Hank's Oyster Bar **18**

Kramerbooks &
   Afterwords Cafe **7**

Luna Grill & Diner **14**

Malaysia Kopitiam **17**

The Melting Pot **1**

Mimi's American Bistro **3**

Obelisk **5**

The Palm **16**

Pizzeria Paradiso **6**

Restaurant Nora **10**

Sette Osteria **9**

Tabard Inn **15**

Map 6: Georgetown Dining

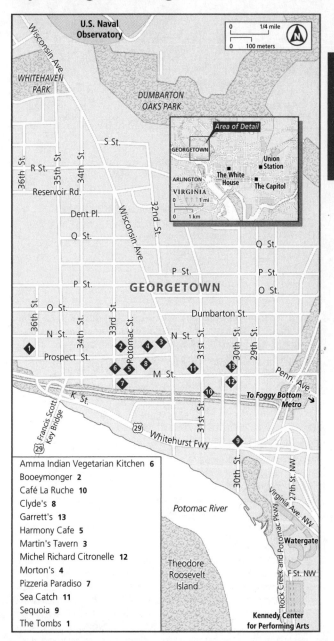

U.S. Naval Observatory

WHITEHAVEN PARK

DUMBARTON OAKS PARK

0 — 1/4 mile
0 — 100 meters

Area of Detail

GEORGETOWN

Union Station

ARLINGTON
The White House

VIRGINIA
The Capitol

0 — 1 mi
0 — 1 km

Wisconsin Ave.

S St.

R St.
36th St.
35th St.
34th St.

Reservoir Rd.

Dent Pl.

Wisconsin Ave.

32nd St.

Q St.

Q St.

P St.

P St.

P St.

O St.

GEORGETOWN

O St.
36th St.
34th St.
33rd St.
Potomac St.
N St.

Dumbarton St.

N St.

31st St.
30th St.
29th St.

Prospect St.

M St.

Penn. Ave.

To Foggy Bottom Metro

K St.

Francis Scott Key Bridge

29

29

Whitehurst Fwy

31st St.

30th St.

Rock Creek and Potomac Pkwy.

Virginia Ave. NW

27th St. NW

Watergate

F St. NW

Potomac River

Theodore Roosevelt Island

Kennedy Center for Performing Arts

Amma Indian Vegetarian Kitchen **6**
Booeymonger **2**
Café La Ruche **10**
Clyde's **8**
Garrett's **13**
Harmony Cafe **5**
Martin's Tavern **3**
Michel Richard Citronelle **12**
Morton's **4**
Pizzeria Paradiso **7**
Sea Catch **11**
Sequoia **9**
The Tombs **1**

The Index

$$$$$	over $40
$$$$	$31–$40
$$$	$21–$30
$$	$12–$20
$	under $12

Ratings reflect the average price of entrees at dinner.

The following abbreviations are used for credit cards:

AE	American Express
DC	Diners Club
DISC	Discover
MC	MasterCard
V	Visa

Amma Indian Vegetarian Kitchen (p. 50) GEORGETOWN *INDIAN/VEGETARIAN* If you're new to Indian cuisine, try one of the house specials, which will give you tastes of several items.... *Tel 202/625-6652. 3291 M St. NW, near 33rd St. Take Georgetown Connection shuttle bus Rte. 2 from Dupont Circle or Rosslyn Metrorail Station. Reservations accepted. AE, MC, V. Mon–Fri 11:30am–2:30pm; Mon–Thurs 5:30–10pm; Fri 5:30–10:30pm; Sat 11:30am–10:30pm; Sun 11:30am–4pm.* $

See Map 6 on p. 65.

Asia Nora (p. 50) FOGGY BOTTOM/WEST END *ASIAN/ORGANIC* Organic Modern American cooking with Asian touches, served in a beautiful dining room with soft chairs.... *Tel 202/797-4860. www.noras.com. 2213 M St. NW, at 22nd St. Foggy Bottom/GWU Metro. Reservations recommended. AE, MC, V. Mon–Thurs 5:30–10pm; Fri–Sat 5:30–10:30pm.* $$$

See Map 4 on p. 62.

Austin Grill (p. 49) PENN QUARTER/UPPER NORTHWEST *SOUTHWESTERN* Good-time places with good Tex-Mex food. The original, above Georgetown, is small and funky; the others are new, spacious, and gaily decorated.... *Penn Quarter: Tel 202/393-3776; www.austingrill.com; 750 E St. NW, between 7th and 8th sts.; Gallery Place Metro; Sun 11am–9:30pm, Mon–Thurs 11am–10pm, Fri–Sat 11am–11pm. Upper Northwest: Tel 202/337-8080; 2404 Wisconsin Ave. NW, near 37th and Calvert sts.; 30-series Metrobus lines; Sun 11am–10:30pm, Mon 11:30am–10:30pm, Tues–Thurs 11:30am–11pm, Fri 11:30am–midnight, Sat 11am–midnight.*

Also in Bethesda and Silver Spring, MD, and Alexandria and Springfield, VA. AE, DC, DISC, MC, V. $$

See Map 3 on p. 60.

Ben's Chili Bowl (p. 48) U STREET CORRIDOR *AMERICAN* Ben and Virginia Ali opened this neighborhood lunch counter in 1958, endured riots and Metrorail construction, and created an institution that their children now run.... *Tel 202/667-0909. www.benschilibowl.com. 1213 U St. NW, between 12th and 13th sts. U St./Cardozo Metro. No credit cards. Mon–Thurs 6am–2am; Fri–Sat 6am–4am; Sun noon–8pm.* $

See Map 3 on p. 60.

Bistro Bis (p. 53) CAPITOL HILL *MODERN BISTRO* Bis has eye-catching decor, comfortable seating, and an excellent menu that changes frequently. Hang out—or eat—in the bar area and you can eavesdrop on congressional staffers dissecting who did what to whom that day.... *Tel 202/661-2700. www.bistrobis.com. 15 E St. NW, west of N. Capitol St. Union Station Metro. Reservations recommended. AE, DC, DISC, MC, V. Daily 7–10am and 5:30–10:30pm; Mon–Fri 11:30am–2:30pm.* $$$

See Map 4 on p. 62.

Bistro Du Coin (p. 52) DUPONT CIRCLE *FRENCH* Much of the menu is French comfort food—what Mom would cook if Mom were French. *Tel 202/234-6969. www.bistrotducoin.com. 1738 Connecticut Ave. NW, between R and S sts. Dupont Circle Metro. AE, DC, DISC, MC, V. Sun 11am–11pm; Mon–Wed 11:30am–11pm; Thurs–Fri 11:30am–1am; Sat 11am–1am.* $$

See Map 5 on p. 64.

Booeymonger (p. 59) GEORGETOWN/UPPER NORTHWEST *AMERICAN* Informal deli with full breakfast in the morning and lots of sandwiches, salads, and sides the rest of the day. Especially good: the roast beef Manhattan and the veggie Pita Pan.... *Georgetown: Tel 202/333-4810; www.booeymonger.com; 3265 Prospect St. NW, at Potomac St.; take Georgetown Connection shuttle bus from Dupont Circle, Foggy/GWU, or Rosslyn Metrorail Station, or ride 30-series Metrobus; daily 8am–midnight. Upper Northwest: Tel 202/686-5805; 5252 Wisconsin Ave. NW, at Jenifer St.; Friendship Heights Metro; daily 7:30am–1am. Also in Bethesda, MD, and northern VA. AE, MC, V.* $

See Map 3 on p. 60.
See Map 6 on p. 65.

Brickskeller (p. 58) DUPONT CIRCLE *AMERICAN* The food's surprisingly good at this 1,000-variety beer joint. The fish and chips are crispy and tasty. If you don't like secondhand smoke, avoid the bar.... *Tel 202/293-1885. www.thebrickskeller.com. 1523 22nd St. NW, between P and Q sts. Dupont Circle Metro. AE, DC, DISC, MC, V. Mon–Thurs 11:30am–2am; Fri 11:30am–3am; Sat 6pm–3am; Sun 6pm–2am.* $

See Map 5 on p. 64.

B. Smith's (p. 51) CAPITOL HILL *SOUTHERN* Located in the soaring, ornate President's Room at Union Station, B. Smith's is a striking—if noisy—place to dine. Jazz on Friday and Saturday nights.... *Tel 202/289-6188. www.bsmith.com. In Union Station, 50 Massachusetts Ave. NE, at 1st St. Union Station Metro. Reservations recommended. AE, DC, DISC, MC, V. Mon–Fri 11:30am–3pm; Sat noon–3pm; Mon–Thurs 5–9pm; Fri–Sat 5–10pm; Sun 11:30am–9pm. $$$*

See Map 4 on p. 62.

Bullfeathers (p. 48) CAPITOL HILL *AMERICAN* Handy to House office buildings, this place teems with congressional staffers, journalists, and other Hill hangers-on at lunch and in the evening when Congress is in session.... *Tel 202/543-5005. www.bullfeatherscapitolhill.com. 410 1st St. SE, between D and E sts. Capitol South Metro. AE, DC, DISC, MC, V. Mon–Sat 11:30am–midnight. $$*

See Map 4 on p. 62.

Busara (p. 52) UPPER NORTHWEST *THAI* This strikingly good-looking restaurant with excellent food offers a nine-item vegetarian menu among the scads of dishes containing various combinations of meat, fowl, and seafood.... *Tel 202/337-2340. www.busara.com. 2340 Wisconsin Ave. NW, south of Calvert St. 30-series Metrobus lines. Reservations recommended. AE, DC, DISC, MC, V. Mon–Fri 11am–3pm; Sat–Sun 11am–4pm; Sun–Thurs 5–10:30pm; Fri–Sat 5–11pm. Also in northern VA. $$*

See Map 3 on p. 60.

Busboys and Poets (p. 58) U STREET CORRIDOR *AMERICAN* Enjoy salads, sandwiches, pizzas, burgers, meatloaf, catfish and more while Ralph Nader gives a reading. The restaurant serves good food and an eclectic collection of entertainment (not just readings).... *Tel 202/387-7638. www.busboysandpoets.com. 2021 14th St. NW, between U and V streets. U Street Metro. AE, DC, DISC, MC, V. Mon–Thur 10am-midnight; Fri-Sun 10am-2am. $*

See Map 5 on p. 64.

Cactus Cantina (p. 47) UPPER NORTHWEST *SOUTHWESTERN* This large and lively Tex-Mex restaurant with outdoor seating is so much fun, it attracted a presidential party in 2003. You can follow the lead of Texans George W. and Laura Bush and order cheese enchiladas (him) or fajitas (her).... *Tel 202/686-7222. www.cactuscantina.com. 3300 Wisconsin Ave. NW, at Macomb St. 30-series Metrobus lines. AE, DC, DISC, MC, V. Mon–Thurs 11am–11pm; Fri–Sat 11am–midnight; Sun 10:30am–11pm. $$*

See Map 3 on p. 60.

Cafe Atlantico (p. 54) PENN QUARTER *LATIN AMERICAN* From the creative minds of chefs Jose Andres and Katsuya Fukushima come innovative treats building on the cuisines of the Caribbean, Central America, and South America. On the second

floor of this lively, colorful, three-tiered house, Andres serves small treats that defy categorization from a $95 tasting menu.... Tel 202/393-0812. www.cafeatlantico.com. 405 8th St. NW, between D and E sts. Archives–Navy Memorial Metro. Reservations recommended. AE, DC, DISC, MC, V. Daily 11:30am–2:30pm; Sun–Thurs 5–10pm; Fri–Sat 5–11pm. $$$

See Map 4 on p. 62.

Café La Ruche (p. 53) GEORGETOWN *FRENCH* A simple place with simple food. Start with onion soup, and then move on to salade niçoise or quiche. Finish with the fruit tart. The $11 weekend brunch from 10am to 3pm may be the best food deal in town.... Tel 202/965-2684. www.cafelaruche.com. 1039 31st St. NW, between M and K sts. Take Georgetown Connection shuttle bus from Dupont Circle, Foggy/GWU, or Rosslyn Metrorail Station, or ride 30-series Metrobus. AE, DC, DISC, MC, V. Mon–Fri 11:30am–midnight, Sat–Sun 10am–midnight. $

See Map 6 on p. 65.

Capitol City Brewing Company (p. 58) CAPITOL HILL/DOWNTOWN *AMERICAN* You can get a "flight" of several small glasses to sample the brewers' wares. Among the best pub fare: burgers, chili, crab-and-corn chowder.... Capitol Hill: Tel 202/842-2337; www.capcitybrew.com; 2 Massachusetts Ave. NE, between N. Capitol St. and Union Station, in the old Post Office; Union Station Metro; Mon–Sat 11am–midnight, Sun 11am–11pm. Downtown: Tel 202/628-2222; 1100 New York Ave. NW, at 11th and H sts. Metro Center Metro; Sun–Thurs 11am–11pm, Fri–Sat 11am–midnight. AE, DC, MC, V. $

See Map 4 on p. 62.

Cashion's Eat Place (p. 46) ADAMS MORGAN *AMERICAN* The seasonal menu changes daily and emphasizes fresh ingredients.... Tel 202/797-1819. www.cashionseatplace.com. 1819 Columbia Rd. NW, near Biltmore St. Take 98 Metrobus from Woodley Park–Zoo Metrorail Station. Reservations recommended. MC, V. Tues 5:30–10pm; Wed–Sat 5:30–11pm; Sun 11:30am–2:30pm (brunch) and 5:30–10pm. $$$

See Map 5 on p. 64.

Circle Bistro (p. 56) FOGGY BOTTOM/WEST END *AMERICAN/MEDITERRANEAN* Choice seems unlimited at this excellent restaurant: breakfast, lunch, dinner, Sunday brunch, pretheater dinner, seasonal fixed-price dinners, bar happy hour, bar food, drinks by the pool. Don't skip dessert.... Tel 202/293-5390. www.circlebistro.com. 1 Washington Circle NW, at 23rd St. and New Hampshire Ave. Foggy Bottom/George Washington University Metro. AE, DC, DISC, MC, V. Mon–Thurs 7–10am; Fri–Sun 8–10:30am; daily 11:30am–2:30pm; Sun–Thurs 5–10pm; Fri–Sat 5–11pm. $$$

See Map 4 on p. 62.

DINING

THE INDEX

City Lights of China (p. 52) DUPONT CIRCLE *CHINESE* This popular restaurant's expansion gives diners a choice between the original subterranean rooms hiding away from the Dupont Circle bustle and new rooms with picture windows that look out on the street and sidewalk action. The food, of course, remains great.... *Tel 202/265-6688. www.citylightsofchina.com. 1731 Connecticut Ave. NW, between R and S sts. Dupont Circle Metro. Reservations recommended. AE, DC, DISC, MC, V. Mon–Fri 11:30am–10:30pm; Sat noon–11pm; Sun noon–10:30pm. $$*

See Map 5 on p. 64.

Clyde's (p. 58) GEORGETOWN/PENN QUARTER/UPPER NORTHWEST *AMERICAN* Clyde's evolved from neighborhood tavern to local chain in part because it gets fresh produce from local farmers.... *Georgetown: Tel 202/333-9180; www.clydes.com; 3236 M St. NW, between Wisconsin Ave. and Potomac St.; take Georgetown Connection shuttle bus from Dupont Circle, Foggy/GWU, or Rosslyn Metrorail Station, or ride 30-series Metrobus; reservations recommended; Mon–Thurs 11:30am–midnight, Fri 11:30am–1am, Sat 10am–1am, Sun 9am–midnight. Penn Quarter: Tel 202/349-3700; 707 7th St. NW, between G and H sts.; Gallery Place/Chinatown Metro; reservations recommended; Mon–Fri 11am–1am, Sat–Sun 10am–1am. Upper Northwest: Tel 301/ 951-9600; 70 Wisconsin Circle, in Chevy Chase Shopping Center at 5441 Wisconsin Ave., just north of the D.C./MD border; Friendship Heights Metro; reservations recommended; Mon–Sat 11am–12:30am, Sun 10am–12:30am. AE, DC, DISC, MC, V. Additional locations in suburban VA and MD. $$*

See Map 3 on p. 60.
See Map 4 on p. 62.
See Map 6 on p. 65.

Coeur de Lion (p. 56) PENN QUARTER *MODERN AMERICAN* Many regulars return specifically for the attention lavished by maitre d' Ralph Fredericks, which some first-timers find over-the-top. The simplest cooking is best here.... *Tel 202/638-5200. www.henleypark.com. 926 Massachusetts Ave. NW, west of 9th St., in the Henley Park Hotel. Mount Vernon Sq. Metro. Reservations recommended. AE, DC, DISC, MC, V. Daily 7–10:30am and 6–10pm; Mon–Sat 11am–2:30pm; Sun 11:30am–2:30pm. $$$*

See Map 4 on p. 62.

Eat First (p. 51) CHINATOWN *CHINESE* Nothing fancy here. Just good, inexpensive Chinese food.... *Tel 202/289-1703. 609 H St. NW, between 6th and 7th sts. Gallery Place–Chinatown Metro. Reservations accepted. AE, MC, V. Sun–Thurs 10:30am–2am; Fri–Sat 10:30am–3am. $$*

See Map 4 on p. 62.

Firefly (p. 58) DUPONT CIRCLE *CONTEMPORARY AMERICAN* The braised short ribs with roasted vegetables—which taste, really, as if Grandma might have made them—may be the best dish here. The apple tart with ice cream is pretty darn good, too....

Tel 202/861-1310. www.firefly-dc.com. 1310 _____
Ave. NW, north of N St. at the Hotel Madera. Dupo___
Reservations recommended. AE, DC, DISC, M____
7–10am, 11:30am–2:30pm, and 5:30–10:30pm;
and 5–10pm; Sun 8–10am, 11am–2:30pm (brun__
10pm. $$$

See Map ___ ___ __.

Firehook Bakery (p. 50) CITYWIDE AMERICAN You can pick from a wide variety of breads here. Also a great place for a quick sandwich, pastry, cookie, or cup of locally roasted coffee.... Tel 202/588-9296. www.firehook.com. 1909 Q St. NW, at Connecticut Ave. Dupont Circle Metro. AE, DC, MC, V. Mon–Sat 6:30am–9pm; Sun 7am–7pm. For other locations, call 703/ 263-2253. $

See Map 5 on p. 64.

Florida Avenue Grill (p. 56) U STREET CORRIDOR AMERICAN Breakfast here is a Washington institution. Try the pancakes, French toast, omelets, or biscuits and gravy. Regulars also swear by the corn muffins and fried apples.... Tel 202/265-1586. 1100 Florida Ave. NW, at 11th St. U St./Cardozo Metro. AE, DC, DISC, MC, V. Tues–Sat 8am–9pm; Sun 8am–4:30pm. $

See Map 3 on p. 60.

Full Kee (p. 51) CHINATOWN CHINESE Locals flock here for shrimp dumpling soup, crispy roast duckling, or fresh seafood. A late-night favorite with local chefs.... Tel 202/371-2233. 509 H St. NW, between 5th and 6th sts. Gallery Place–Chinatown Metro. No credit cards. Daily 11am–2am. $

See Map 4 on p. 62.

Galileo (p. 47) DOWNTOWN ITALIAN Chef Roberto Donna essentially runs three (he says four) restaurants here. The main dining room serves Italian haute cuisine; Laboratorio del Galileo, Donna's private kitchen/dining room, soars even higher; the bar area serves food mere mortals can afford. *Note:* Galileo was scheduled to close for renovations from late 2006 until late summer 2007... Tel 202/293-7191. www.galileodc.com. 1110 21st St. NW, between L and M sts. Farragut N. Metro. Reservations recommended at Galileo, required at Laboratorio, not accepted at bar. AE, DC, DISC, MC, V. Mon–Fri 11:30am–2:15pm; Mon–Thurs 5:30–10pm; Fri–Sat 5:30–10:30pm; Sun 5–10pm. $–$$$$$

See Map 4 on p. 62.

Garrett's (p. 58) GEORGETOWN AMERICAN You can pick from a large selection of soups, salads, pastas, burgers, sandwiches, appetizers, and finger food, or go for flakey, tasty chicken potpie with so much gravy it's served with a spoon.... Tel 202/333-1033. www.garrettsdc.com. 3003 M St. NW, at 30th St. Take Georgetown Connection shuttle bus from Dupont Circle, Foggy

Bottom/GWU, or Rosslyn Metrorail Station, or ride 30-series Metrobus. AE, DC, DISC, MC, V. Mon–Thurs 11:30am–1:30am; Fri–Sat noon–2:30am; Sun noon–1:30am. $$

See Map 6 on p. 65.

Georgia Brown's (p. 48) DOWNTOWN *SOUTHERN* The waiter immediately brings biscuits and corn bread. Side dishes include grits, black-eyed peas, and collard greens. But this is a modern, upscale, Southern restaurant, so you can have your greens alongside shrimp stuffed with crab cakes. Also serves excellent vegetarian dishes.... *Tel 202/393-4499. www.gbrowns.com. 950 15th St. NW, between I and K sts. McPherson Sq. Metro. Reservations recommended. AE, DC, DISC, MC, V. Mon–Fri 11:30am–10:30pm; Sat 5:30–10:30pm; Sun 10am–2:15pm (brunch) and 5:30–9pm.* $$$

See Map 4 on p. 62.

Gerard's Place (p. 50) DOWNTOWN *FRENCH* Chef Gerard Pangaud starts with French classics, then makes them his own. The pricey poached lobster is his best-known dish. He recently added a three-course dinner for $59. The five-course dinner stays on the menu at $85. The best way to sample Pangaud's skills without taking out a second mortgage remains going for the $30 fixed-price lunch.... *Tel 202/737-4445. 915 15th St. NW, between I and K sts. McPherson Sq. Metro. Reservations recommended. AE, DC, MC, V. Mon–Thurs 11:30am–2:30pm and 5:30–9pm; Fri 11:30am–2pm and 5:30–9:30pm; Sat 5:30–9:30pm.* $$$$

See Map 4 on p. 62.

Hank's Oyster Bar (p. 46) DUPONT CIRCLE *SEAFOOD* Just about everything chef Jamie Leeds touches turns out great. Some of the best here are the fried calamari and popcorn shrimp, crab cakes, onion rings, and, of course, oysters—raw and fried. This small, informal, neighborhood spot is popular and doesn't take reservations, so be prepared to wait for a table at peak meal times.... *Tel 202/462-4265. www.hanksdc.com. 1624 Q St. NW, between 16th and 17th sts. Dupont Circle Metro. AE, MC, V. Sun–Tues 5:30–10pm; Wed–Sat 5:30–11pm; Sat–Sun 11am–3pm.* $$

See Map 5 on p. 64.

Harmony Cafe (p. 50) GEORGETOWN *ASIAN* At this monument to vegetarian-carnivore detente, have your Asian salad with flesh or without. Try the grilled shiitake mushrooms appetizer. If you don't see what you want, the menu advises, "Ask for it."... *Tel 202/338-3881. 3287½ M St. NW, near 33rd St. Take Georgetown Connection shuttle bus Rte. 2 from Dupont Circle or Rosslyn Metrorail Station. DISC, MC, V. Mon–Sat 1130am–11pm; Sun 5–11pm.* $

See Map 6 on p. 65.

Inn at Little Washington (p. 55) VIRGINIA *MODERN AMERICAN*
Simply one of the best—and most expensive—restaurants anywhere near Washington. Spend the night and you might be able to
have yourselves a thousand-dollar evening. Book way in
advance.... *Tel 540/675-3800. www.theinnatlittlewashington.com.
Middle St. at Main St., Washington, VA, 70 miles from Washington,
D.C. Reservations essential. AE MC, V. Mon–Thurs 6–9:15pm; Fri
5:30–9:15pm; Sat 5:15–9:30pm; Sun 4–8:15pm. $$$$$*

See Map 3 on p. 60.

Jaleo (p. 54) PENN QUARTER *SPANISH* A great place to party
before and/or after attending a nearby theater. The more who
share the tapas, the more the fun.... *Tel 202/628-7949.
www.jaleo.com. 480 7th St. NW, at E St. Gallery Place–Chinatown
Metro. AE, DC, DISC, MC, V. Sun–Mon 11:30am–10pm; Tues–Thurs
11:30am–11:30pm; Fri–Sat 11:30am–midnight. Also in Bethesda,
MD, and northern VA. $$*

See Map 4 on p. 62.

Kinkead's (p. 47) DOWNTOWN *SEAFOOD* Lots of dishes worth
ordering here: Try fried clams followed by pumpkin-seed-crusted
salmon with a crab, shrimp, corn, and chili ragout; or cod served
with Crab Imperial, ham spoon bread, sweet potato puree, and a
mustard cream sauce.... *Tel 202/296-7700. www.kinkead.com.
2000 Pennsylvania Ave. NW, between 20th and 21st sts. Foggy
Bottom/GWU Metro. Reservations recommended. AE, DC, DISC,
MC, V. Sun–Thurs 11:30am–10pm; Fri 11:30am–10:30pm; Sat
5:30–10:30pm. $$$$*

See Map 4 on p. 62.

Kramerbooks & Afterwords Cafe (p. 59) DUPONT CIRCLE *AMER-
ICAN* A great place to pick up a book, a quick bite, and a date—
or a full meal with drinks for that matter. Insomniac readers,
note this cafe doesn't close on Friday and Saturday nights. Live
music Wednesday through Saturday nights.... *Tel 202/387-
1462. www.kramers.com. 1517 Connecticut Ave. NW, just above
Dupont Circle. Dupont Circle Metro. Reservations accepted for
parties of 6 or more. AE, DISC, MC, V. Mon–Thurs 7:30am–1am;
weekends 7:30am Fri to 1am Mon. $$*

See Map 5 on p. 64.

L'Auberge Chez François (p. 57) VIRGINIA *ALSATIAN FRENCH*
Locals flock to this charming hideaway in the Virginia countryside
when they have something to celebrate.... *Tel 703/759-3800.
www.laubergechezfrancois.com. 332 Springvale Rd., Great Falls,
VA. Reservations required. AE, DC, DISC, MC, V. Tues–Sat 5:30–
9:30pm; Sun 1:30–8pm. $$$$*

See Map 3 on p. 60.

(p. 51) CHINATOWN *CHINESE* Dim sum served from carts at lunch is a highlight here, along with such dishes ry spicy boiled beef and Yu-Shion chicken.... Tel 202/216-5. 629 H St. NW, at 7th St. Gallery Place–Chinatown Metro. DC, MC, V. Mon–Thurs 11:30am–11pm; Fri–Sat 11:30am–midnight; Sun 11:30am–10:30pm. $$

See Map 4 on p. 62.

Le Paradou (p. 53) PENN QUARTER *CONTEMPORARY FRENCH* Chef Yannick Cam spares no effort or expense in offering the finest French dining experience. Entrees start at $29. Tasting menus are $110 and $145. Save a bit by coming at lunch or eating in the bar or the sidewalk cafe.... Tel 202/347-6780. www.leparadou.net. 678 Indiana Ave. NW, between 6th and 7th sts. Archives–Navy Memorial Metro. Reservations recommended. AE, DC, DISC, MC, V. Mon–Fri 11:45am–2:15pm; Mon–Thurs 5:30–10pm; Fri–Sat 5:15–10pm. $$$$$

See Map 4 on p. 62.

Luna Grill & Diner (p. 59) DUPONT CIRCLE *AMERICAN* No New Age twists here. This really *is* comfort food. How about meatloaf, mashed potatoes, and gravy for $9.95?... Tel 202/835-2280. www.lunagrillanddiner.com. 1301 Connecticut Ave. NW, at N St. Dupont Circle Metro. AE, DISC, MC, V. Mon–Thurs 8am–10:30pm; Fri 8am–midnight; Sat 10am–midnight; Sun 10am–10pm. Also in VA. $

See Map 5 on p. 64.

Malaysia Kopitiam (p. 52) DUPONT CIRCLE *MALAYSIAN* Check out the specials on the chalkboard as you step down from the sidewalk into this unusual restaurant near Dupont Circle. The decor is subtle tiki bar. The food is similar to Chinese, Thai, and Indian cuisines. Ask the helpful waiters to explain what you don't understand.... Tel 202/833-6232. 1827 M St. NW, between 18th and 19th sts. Farragut N. Metro. AE, DISC, MC, V. Mon–Thurs 11:30am–10pm; Fri–Sat 1130am–11pm; Sun noon–10pm. $$

See Map 5 on p. 64.

Marcel's (p. 53) FOGGY BOTTOM/WEST END *FRENCH* Unquestionably one of D.C.'s best restaurants. Going to Kennedy Center? For $48, Marcel's will feed you between 5:30 and 7pm, send you to the show in a limo, and then return you to the restaurant for dessert.... Tel 202/296-1166. www.marcelsdc.com. 2401 Pennsylvania Ave. NW, at 24th St. Foggy Bottom/George Washington University Metro. Reservations recommended. AE, MC, V. Mon–Thurs 5:30–10pm; Fri–Sat 5:30–11pm; Sun 5:30–9:30pm. $$$$

See Map 4 on p. 62.

Marrakesh (p. 57) DOWNTOWN *MOROCCAN* A great place to bring a party of fun-loving friends who can get their grins from sitting on pillows, eating with their fingers, and watching a belly

dancer. The seven-course meal is $29.... Tel 202/3
marrakeshwashington.com. 617 New York Ave. NW
and 7th sts. Mount Vernon Sq. Metro. Reservations
credit cards. Daily 6–11pm. $$$

See Ma

Martin's Tavern (p. 47) GEORGETOWN *AMERICAN* A tru
tution, this corner tavern has served every kind of Washington-
ian—from peasants to presidents—since 1933. This is the kind
of place where you order corned beef and cabbage, fish and chips,
or Brunswick stew. Or the burger. Or breakfast, which is served
until 4pm every day. Tel 202/333-7370. www.martins-tavern.com.
1264 Wisconsin Ave. NW, at N St. Take Georgetown Connection
shuttle bus from Dupont Circle, Foggy Bottom/GWU, or Rosslyn
Metrorail Station, or ride 30-series Metrobus. Reservations recom-
mended. AE, DC, DISC, MC, V. Mon–Thurs 10am–11pm; Fri
10am–12:30am, Sat 8am–12:30am; Sun 8am–11pm. $$

See Map 6 on p. 65.

Matchbox (p. 54) CHINATOWN *PIZZA/ECLECTIC* Excellent thin-
crust, New York–style pizza is the main attraction, although this
is a full-service restaurant with a menu running from burgers to
grilled salmon in citrus beurre-blanc sauce with sautéed aspara-
gus and mozzarella potato polpette.... Tel 202/289-4441. www.
matchboxdc.com. 713 H St. NW, at 7th St. Gallery Place–Chinatown Metro. Reservations not accepted. AE, MC, V. Mon–Fri
11am–10pm or later; Sat noon–11pm or later. $$

See Map 4 on p. 62.

The Melting Pot (p. 55) DUPONT CIRCLE *FONDUE* Another place
for a big group to come for fun—or for dates to dip each other's
strawberries at the booths for two.... Tel 202/857-0777. www.
meltingpot.com. 1220 19th St. NW, between M and N sts. Dupont
Circle Metro. Reservations suggested. AE, MC, V. Mon–Thurs
5–10pm; Fri 5pm–midnight; Sat 4pm–midnight; Sun 4–9pm. $$

See Map 5 on p. 64.

Meyhane (p. 50) CAPITOL HILL *TURKISH* This lively, noisy, informal
dining room gives off the vibe of a popular neighborhood cafe.
The room is long and narrow and is painted in bright red, sky
blue, and white. Ceiling fans turn languidly overhead. Try the zuc-
chini fritters—light with a crispy crust and a rich taste. The lamb
shish is another good choice. Tel 202/544-4753. 633 Pennsylvania Ave. SE, between 6th and 7th sts. Eastern Market Metro. AE,
MC, V. Mon–Fri 5–10pm; Tues–Wed and Fri noon–3pm; Sat
noon–11pm; Sun noon–10pm. $

See Map 3 on p. 60.

Michel Richard Citronelle (p. 53) GEORGETOWN *FRENCH/CALI-
FORNIA* What seems very un-Californian here is the require-
ment that men don jackets at dinner. The dress code does go
with the tab: fixed-price meals from $85 to $150 and a chef's

table from $275. The food is superb. If you dine in the bar, you can pick entrees from $16 to $35.... *Tel 202/625-2150. www. citronelledc.com. 3000 M St. NW, at 30th St., in the Latham Hotel. Take Georgetown Connection shuttle bus from Dupont Circle, Foggy Bottom/GWU, or Rosslyn Metrorail Station, or ride 30-series Metrobus. Reservations required. AE, DC, MC, V. Daily 6:30–10:30am; Mon–Thurs 6–10pm; Fri–Sat 6–10:30pm; Sun 6–9:30pm. $$$$$*

See Map 6 on p. 65.

Mimi's American Bistro (p. 58) DUPONT CIRCLE *AMERICAN* The singing waiters make this a fun place. Mimi offers several nightly specials and several vegetarian items. For the frugally inclined, sandwiches are available from lunch through dinner.... *Tel 202/464-6464. www.mimisdc.com. 2120 P St. NW, between 21st and 22nd sts. Dupont Circle Metro. Reservations suggested. AE, DC, DISC, MC, V. Mon–Thurs 11:30am–11pm; Fri–Sat 11:30am–midnight; Sun 11am–midnight. $$*

See Map 5 on p. 64.

The Monocle (p. 48) CAPITOL HILL *AMERICAN* A longtime hangout for senators and those who would influence them, The Monocle is known for the food and drink senators and lobbyists are traditionally thought to consume—martinis, steaks, chops, crab, and, at lunch, good hamburgers.... *Tel 202/546-4488. www.the monocle.com. 107 D St. NE, between 1st and 2nd sts. Union Station Metro. Reservations suggested. AE, DC, DISC, MC, V. Mon–Fri 11:30am–midnight. Closed the 2 weeks before Labor Day. $$$*

See Map 4 on p. 62.

Montmartre (p. 52) CAPITOL HILL *FRENCH* A taste of Paris on Capitol Hill. Start with the endive salad with walnuts and bleu cheese, finish with the spectacular berry tart. In the middle? Well, how about something homey, such as cod on a bed of garlic mashed potatoes?... *Tel 202/544-1244. 327 7th St. SE, between Pennsylvania Ave. and C St. Eastern Market Metro. Reservations recommended. AE, DC, MC, V. Tues–Sun 11:30am–2:30pm; Tues–Thurs 5:30–10pm; Fri–Sat 5:30–10:30pm; Sun 5:30–9pm. $$*

See Map 3 on p. 60.

Morton's (p. 48) DOWNTOWN/GEORGETOWN *STEAKHOUSE* Prime aged beef for larger-than-life appetites with larger-than-life expense accounts.... *Downtown: Tel 202/955-5997; www. mortons.com; 1050 Connecticut Ave. NW, between K and L sts.; Farragut N. Metro; reservations recommended; Mon–Fri 11:30am–11pm, Sat 5:30–11pm, Sun 5:30–10pm. Georgetown: Tel 202/342-6258; 3251 Prospect St. NW, between Potomac St. and Wisconsin Ave.; take Georgetown Connection shuttle bus from Dupont Circle, Foggy Bottom/GWU, or Rosslyn Metrorail Station, or ride 30-series Metrobus; Mon–Sat 5:30–11pm, Sun 5–10pm. Also locations in VA and MD. AE, DC, MC, V. $$$$*

See Map 4 on p. 62.
See Map 6 on p. 65.

Nooshi (p. 52) DOWNTOWN *PAN ASIAN* Formerly Oodles Noodles, Nooshi still has the inventive array of Pan-Asian noodle dishes, such as *mee goreng* (a spicy marriage of Malaysian and Indian-style noodles with vegetables), as well as dishes sans noodles, such as chicken with basil. The sushi menu is large and reasonably priced. Go early, especially at lunch when office workers grab all the tables.... *Tel 202/293-3138. 1120 19th St. NW, between L and M sts. Farragut N. Metro. AE, DC, DISC MC, V. Mon–Sat 11:30am–11pm; Sun 4:30–10pm.* $$

See Map 4 on p. 62.

Obelisk (p. 54) DUPONT CIRCLE *ITALIAN* Local cognoscenti book up the $60 five-course dinner in this small, superb dining room. Savor handmade pasta, fresh ingredients, and a terrific Italian wine list. See if you can score the table at the window overlooking P Street.... *Tel 202/872-1180. 2029 P St. NW, between 20th and 21st sts. Dupont Circle Metro. Reservations recommended. DC, MC, V. Tues–Sat 6–10pm.* $$$$$

See Map 5 on p. 64.

The Occidental (p. 48) DOWNTOWN *AMERICAN* Rodney Scruggs started working here as a teenager, moved on to several other venues, then returned recently as executive chef. Two blocks from the White House, this power palace's menu still has lobster and steak, plus she-crab soup, pan-seared jumbo shrimp, and a lamb salad.... *Tel 202/783-1475. www.occidentaldc.com. 1475 Pennsylvania Ave. NW, between 14th and 15th sts. Metro Center Metro. Reservations recommended. AE, DC, MC, V. Mon–Sat 11:30am–3pm; Mon–Thurs 5–10pm; Fri–Sat 5–10:30pm; Sun 5–9:30pm.* $$$$

See Map 4 on p. 62.

The Oceanaire Seafood Room (p. 51) DOWNTOWN *SEAFOOD* Excellent seafood and a festive atmosphere in surroundings designed with a 1930s ocean liner in mind. Larger parties find this a fun place to dine. Top choices: oysters, crab cakes, and just about any fried or broiled fresh fish.... *Tel 202/347-2277. www.theoceanaire.com. 1201 F St. NW, at 12th St. Metro Center Metro. Reservations recommended. AE, DISC, MC, V. Mon–Thurs 11:30am–10pm; Fri 11:30am–11pm; Sat 5–11pm; Sun 5–9pm.* $$$

See Map 4 on p. 62.

Old Ebbitt Grill (p. 48) DOWNTOWN *AMERICAN* Old Ebbitt traces its history to 1856 and moved its artifacts into the current location in 1983. This new Old Ebbitt is large, comfortable, and conducive to conducting business, flirting with dates, or entertaining kids. Many regulars come for the bar food—and the raw bar—but the diverse menu changes daily according to what's fresh and in season from local farmers.... *Tel 202/ 347-4800. www.ebbitt.com. 675 15th St. NW, between F and G* sts. Metro Center Metro. Reservations recommended. AE, DC, DISC, MC, V. Mon–Fri 7:30am–1am; Sat–Sun 8:30am–1am. $$

See Map 4 on p. 62.

The Palm (p. 48) DUPONT CIRCLE *STEAKHOUSE* Come here for steak and views of the rich and powerful. Lobster, fried onions, and creamed spinach are good, too.... *Tel 202/293-9091. www.thepalm.com. 1225 19th St. NW, between M and N sts. Dupont Circle Metro. Reservations recommended. AE, DC, MC, V. Mon–Fri 11:45am–10:30pm; Sat 5:30–10:30pm; Sun 5:30–9:30pm.* $$$$

See Map 5 on p. 64.

Pizzeria Paradiso (p. 49) DUPONT CIRCLE/GEORGETOWN *PIZZA/ITALIAN* Real Neapolitan pizza, plus desserts, salads, and focaccia-bread sandwiches. New in the lower level of the Georgetown location: Birreria Paradiso, where you can choose from 80 bottled beers and 16 on tap to accompany your food.... *Dupont Circle: Tel 202/223-1245; www.eatyourpizza.com; 2029 P St. NW, between 20th and 21st sts.; Dupont Circle Metro; Mon–Thurs 11:30am–11pm, Sat 11:30am–midnight, Sun noon–10pm. Georgetown: Tel 202/337-1245; 3282 M St. NW, between Potomac and 33rd sts.; take Georgetown Connection shuttle bus from Dupont Circle, Foggy Bottom/GWU, or Rosslyn Metrorail Station, or ride 30-series Metrobus. Same hours. DC, MC, V.* $

See Map 5 on p. 64.
See Map 6 on p. 65.

Poste (p. 49) PENN QUARTER *MODERN AMERICAN* This dining room is a feast for the eye as well as the tongue. Chef Robert Weland showcases fresh local products in his Modern American dishes: wild mushroom consommé, arugula salad, lemon roasted chicken, and apple tart with ice cream and pecan caramel sauce. Seasonal tasting menu for $55.... *Tel 202/783-6060. www.postebrasserie.com. 555 8th Street NW, between E and F sts. Archives/Navy Memorial or Gallery Place–Chinatown Metro. Reservations recommended. AE, DC, DISC, MC, V. Mon–Fri 7–10am and 11:30am–2:30pm; Sat–Sun 9am–4pm; Mon–Thurs 5–10pm; Fri–Sat 5–10:30pm; Sun 5–9pm.* $$$

See Map 4 on p. 62.

The Prime Rib (p. 50) DOWNTOWN *STEAKHOUSE/AMERICAN* Step off a boring block of office buildings and pretend you're acting in a 1940s flick that has important scenes set in a classy supper club. The maitre d' will loan a jacket and tie to any man who stumbles in without one. You're not required to order the superb prime rib, but it's senseless not to.... *Tel 202/466-8811. www.theprimerib.com. 2020 K St. NW, between 20th and 21st sts. Farragut W. Metro. Reservations recommended. AE, DC, MC, V. Mon–Fri 11:30am–3pm; Mon–Thurs 5–11pm; Fri–Sat 5–11:30pm.* $$$$

See Map 4 on p. 62.

Rasika (p. 52) PENN QUARTER *INDIAN* If you think you don't like the food of India, this may be the restaurant that changes your mind. Executive Chef Vikram Sunderam's "modern Indian cuisine" is quite pleasing to the Western palate. You can order a multicourse meal here or graze among Rasika's small-plate offerings. Not to be missed: deep-fried baby-spinach salad, tandoori black cod, apple jalebi for dessert. *Tel 202/637-1222. www.rasikarestaurant.com. 633 D St. NW, between 6th and 7th sts. Archives–Navy Memorial Metro. Reservations recommended. AE, DC, DISC, MC, V. Mon–Fri 11:30am–2:30pm; Mon–Thurs 5:30–10:30pm; Fri–Sat 5:30–11pm. $$*

See Map 4 on p. 62.

Red Sage Border Cafe (p. 50) DOWNTOWN *SOUTHWESTERN* Good food (and margaritas) at moderate prices.... *Tel 202/638-4444. www.redsage.com. 605 14th St. NW, at F St. Metro Center Metro. Reservations not accepted. AE, DC, DISC, MC, V. Mon–Sat 11:30am–11pm; Sun 4:30–10pm. $$*

See Map 4 on p. 62.

Restaurant Nora (p. 50) DUPONT CIRCLE *NEW AMERICAN/ ORGANIC* Washington's most politically correct restaurant: organic food, triple-filtered water, coffee from small organic cooperatives, uniforms of organic yarn, and wine from winemakers who don't use chemicals. High-quality food comes with high prices.... *Tel 202/462-5143. www.noras.com. 2132 Florida Ave. NW, at R St. Dupont Circle Metro. AE, MC, V. Mon–Thurs 5:30–10pm; Fri–Sat 5:30–10:30pm. $$$$*

See Map 5 on p. 64.

Ristorante Tosca (p. 49) DOWNTOWN *ITALIAN* Excellent contemporary northern Italian food in an elegant, quiet room. Chef Cesare Lanfranconi offers tasting menus for $60 and $95, as well as a three-course pretheater menu from 5:30 to 7pm for $32. All items are available a la carte.... *Tel 202/367-1990. www.toscadc.com. 1112 F St. NW, between 11th and 12th sts. Metro Center Metro. Reservations recommended. AE, DC, MC, V. Mon–Fri 11:30am–2:30pm; Mon–Thurs 5:30–10:30pm; Fri–Sat 5:30–11pm. $$$$*

See Map 4 on p. 62.

Sea Catch (p. 50) GEORGETOWN *SEAFOOD* If they're on the menu, try the salad of grapefruit, avocado, and crushed hazelnuts over mixed greens and the main course of crab cakes. Don't skip dessert.... *Tel 202/337-8855. www.seacatchrestaurant. com. 1054 31st St. NW, south of M St. at the C&O Canal. Take Georgetown Connection shuttle bus from Dupont Circle, Foggy Bottom/GWU, or Rosslyn Metrorail Station, or ride 30-series Metrobus. Reservations recommended. AE, DC, DISC, MC, V. Mon–Sat noon–3pm and 5:30–10pm; Sun 11am–3pm (brunch) and 5:30–9pm. $$$*

See Map 6 on p. 65.

DINING

THE INDEX

Sequoia (p. 49) GEORGETOWN *AMERICAN* Attractive though noisy restaurant on Georgetown's waterfront offers good food with good views, indoors and outdoors, day and night. After dark, nearby trees sparkle with hundreds of white lights.... *Tel 202/944-4200. www.arkrestaurants.com. 3000 K St. NW, at 30th St. in Washington Harbour complex. Take Georgetown Connection Rte. 1 shuttle bus from Foggy Bottom/GWU Metrorail Station, or ride 30-series Metrobus. AE, DC, DISC, MC, V. Mon–Thurs 11:30am–11pm; Fri–Sat 11:30am–midnight; Sun 10:30am–11pm. $$*

See Map 6 on p. 65.

Sette Osteria (p. 49) DUPONT CIRCLE *ITALIAN* Come early or late to this popular hangout or be prepared to wait for a table. Sette's pizzas boast a thin, chewy crust under excellent toppings. Or try the cavatelli pasta with mild Italian sausage, or gnocchi with a tomato-mozzarella-basil sauce.... *Tel 202/483-3070. www.setteosteria.com. 1666 Connecticut Ave. NW, at R St. Dupont Circle Metro. Reservations not accepted. AE, DC, DISC, MC, V. Mon–Thurs 11:30am–1am; Fri–Sat 11:30am–2am; Sun 11:30am–midnight. $$*

See Map 5 on p. 64.

Tabard Inn (p. 56) DUPONT CIRCLE *MODERN AMERICAN* Excellent seasonal cooking prevails at this colorful old inn scattered about three adjoining town houses.... *Tel 202/833-2668. www.tabardinn. com. 1739 N St. NW, between 17th and 18th sts. Dupont Circle Metro. Reservations recommended. AE, DISC, MC, V. Mon–Fri 7–10am; Sat–Sun 8–9:30am; Mon–Sat 11:30am–2:30pm; Sun 10:30am–2:30pm; Sun–Thurs 6–9:30pm; Fri–Sat 6–10pm. $$$*

See Map 5 on p. 64.

Taberna del Alabardero (p. 48) DOWNTOWN *SPANISH* A dignified dining destination for those who wish to celebrate grandly with sophisticated Spanish food. Paella is a top choice here. Or graze on tapas. Vegetarians and vegans find options as well. Chef Santi Zabaleta offers a $78 tasting menu. The dress code has been relaxed to "business casual."... *Tel 202/429-2200. www.alabardero.com. 1776 I St. NW (enter on 18th St. between I and H sts). Farragut W. Metro. Reservations recommended. AE, DC, DISC, MC, V. Mon–Fri 11:30am–2:30pm; Mon–Sat 5:30–10:30pm. $$$$*

See Map 4 on p. 62.

Teaism (p. 55) PENN QUARTER *ASIAN FUSION* Come here for traditional tea from 2:30-5:30pm daily, or order a la carte. You'll find both Asian and traditional American cooking, full breakfast in morning, and many options for lunch and dinner, including beer, wine, sake and cocktails. Most under $0; afternoon tea is $20.... *Tel 202/638-6010. www.teaism.com. 400 8th St. NW, at D St. Archives/Navy Memorial Metro. AE, MC, V. Mon–Fri 7:30am–10pm; Sat-Sun 9:30am-9pm. $*

See Map 4 on p. 62.

Teatro Goldoni (p. 53) DOWNTOWN *ITALIAN* Grab these excellent dishes if you see them on the changing menu: the Teatro Caesar salad; orecchiette pasta with sausage; and risotto with lobster, roasted tomatoes, truffle oil, and basil.... *Tel 202/955-9494. www.teatrogoldoni.com. 1909 K St. NW, between 19th and 20th sts. Farragut W. Metro. Reservations recommended. AE, DC, DISC, MC, V. Mon–Fri 11:30am–2pm; Mon–Thurs 5:30–10pm; Fri–Sat 5–11pm. $$$*

See Map 4 on p. 62.

Tony Cheng's (p. 52) CHINATOWN *CHINESE* Upstairs, despite the name, Tony Cheng's Seafood Restaurant serves from a wide-ranging Chinese menu. Downstairs, Tony Cheng's Mongolian Barbecue offers grill and hot-pot cooking. Entrees come with a wide range of prices, from less than $10 to about $30.... *Tel 202/371-8669. 619 H St. NW, between 6th and 7th sts. Gallery Place–Chinatown Metro. AE, MC, V. Sun–Thurs 11am–11pm; Fri–Sat 11am–midnight. $$*

See Map 4 on p. 62.

The Tombs (p. 50) GEORGETOWN *AMERICAN* Brick walls, wooden tables and sporting paraphernalia mark this as a classic college hangout but with above-par food. Try the superb crab cakes, tasty french fries, and thick, juicy veggie burger.... *Tel 202/337-6668. www.tombs.com. 1226 36th St. NW, between Prospect and N sts. Take Georgetown Connection Rte. 2 shuttle bus from Rosslyn or Dupont circle Metrorail station, or ride 30-series Metrobus. Reservations not accepted. AE, DC, DISC MC, V. Mon–Thurs 11:30am–11pm; Fri 11:30am–midnight; Sat 11am–midnight; Sun 9:30am–11pm. $*

See Map 6 on p. 65.

2Amys (p. 49) UPPER NORTHWEST *PIZZA/ITALIAN* Real Neapolitan pizza that kids will like because it's pizza and adults will like because it's sophisticated and the best in town. Folks gather in the evening to sip wine or beer and nibble on small plates of Italian hors d'oeuvres.... *Tel 202/885-5700. www.2amyspizza.com. 3715 Macomb St. NW, just west of Wisconsin Ave., near National Cathedral. Take 30-series Metrobus. Reservations not accepted. MC, V. Mon 5–10pm; Tues–Wed 11am–10pm; Thurs–Sat 11am–11pm; Sun noon–10pm. $*

See Map 3 on p. 60.

Vidalia (p. 51) DOWNTOWN *SOUTHERN/MODERN AMERICAN* Named for the sweet Southern onion, Vidalia uses the South as a starting point for culinary explorations that go all over the map. Shrimp and grits, for instance, or roasted loin of rabbit stuffed with sweetbreads and wrapped in apple-wood bacon.... *Tel 202/659-1990. www.vidaliadc.com. 1990 M St. NW, between 19th and 20th sts. Dupont Circle Metro. Reservations recommended. AE, DC, DISC, MC, V. Mon–Fri 11:30am–2:30pm; Mon–Thurs and Sun 5:30–10pm; Fri–Sat 5:30–10:30pm. $$$*

See Map 4 on p. 62.

DINING

THE INDEX

Zaytinya (p. 50) PENN QUARTER *MEDITERRANEAN* Settle in beside the tall windows, grab a Greek wine or beer, and watch night descend on the city. Some highlights from the large menu of small plates of goodies are: *kolokithokeftedes* (zucchini-cheese patties), *manty nejla* (beef-stuffed pasta), and *adana kebab "Tike"* (ground lamb with grilled tomatoes and sumac onions).... *Tel 202/638-0800. www.zaytinya.com. 701 9th St. NW, at G St. Gallery Place–Chinatown Metro. AE, DC, DISC, MC, V. Sun–Mon 11:30am–10pm; Tues–Thurs 11:30am–11:30pm; Fri–Sat 11:30am–midnight. $$*

See Map 4 on p. 62.

Zola (p. 57) PENN QUARTER *MODERN AMERICAN* The black-clad waiters in this spy-themed restaurant will offer you a thick wine book with a wide range of prices. The best food on the menu may be the crispy french fries. For a main course, try the broiled jumbo prawns.... *Tel 202/654-0999. www.zoladc.com. 800 F St. NW, at 8th St. Gallery Place–Chinatown Metro. Reservations recommended. AE, DC, DISC, MC, V. Mon–Fri 11:30am–midnight; Sat 5pm–midnight; Sun 5–10pm. $$$*

See Map 4 on p. 62.

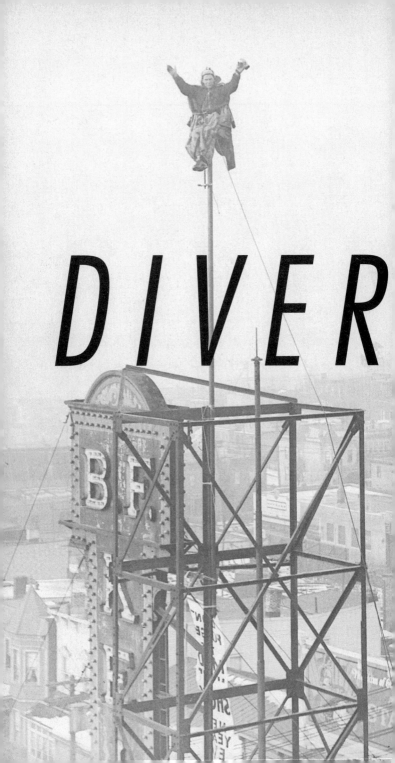

DIVER

SIONS

3

Basic Stuff

Washington certainly lives up to its nickname, "Capital of the Free World." Most of what makes Washington special—government buildings, monuments, museums, memorials—is free. All Americans pay for Washington's attractions through their taxes, of course. But since you have to pay whether you see them or not, come on out and get your money's worth.

Getting Your Bearings

Washington can be a daunting place to get around at first glance. But if you understand how the city is organized, you'll always have a good idea of where you are and a reasonably good idea of how to get where you want to go. To paraphrase Daniel Boone, you might get befuddled from time to time, but you'll never get lost.

Washington originally was a perfect diamond, carved out of Virginia and Maryland, with its corners pointing due north, south, east, and west. Later, Virginia's contribution was returned, so Washington's southwestern border is formed by the Potomac River, and the perfect diamond no longer exists. (Those lucky Virginia residents of the former D.C., therefore, are full-fledged U.S. citizens, while the former Marylanders are subject to the whims of a Congress in which they have no vote.) We still use the street scheme based on that diamond, and that's why most Washington addresses are easy to locate today.

Although it's not the physical center of D.C., the Capitol dome is the center of Washington's street grid. North Capitol, East Capitol, and South Capitol streets extend north, south, and east from the dome. There is no West Capitol Street, but if there were, it would run straight down the middle of the National Mall, and that line helps to define the grid. Those four "streets" carve the District into four quadrants: Northeast (NE), Southeast (SE), Southwest (SW), and Northwest (NW). The numbered streets run north and south, and their names get higher as they get farther from North and South Capitol streets. The first north–south street west of South Capitol Street, for instance, is (usually) 1st Street SW. The first street east, is 1st Street SE and so on. Streets that run east–west have names that run up the alphabet according to their distance from East Capitol Street and that center line of the Mall. The streets closest to East Capitol and the Mall have letters (A St., B St., etc.). Then they get two-syllable names (Adams St., Bryant St.). Then three-syllable names. Then they're named for plants (Aspen, Butternut). Most of the time, this is all you need to know to figure out where you're going. If you decide to have dinner at the Prime Rib, at 2020 K St. NW, you know it is in the Northwest quadrant, just west of 20th Street.

This is the seat of the federal government so, naturally, things get more complicated. But if you focus on the grid, you can fight your way through the complications, which include: There are no J, X, Y, or Z streets. There are no B Streets in the heart of D.C., because they've been named Constitution and Independence avenues. Half streets pop up from time to between Capitol and 1st streets. Most avenues cut diagonally across the grid and are named for states. Washington also has roads, drives, and places, which don't necessarily follow the grid rules. Some streets break the alphabet and syllable rules willy-nilly. Squares and circles pop up all over the place, causing street names to disappear and drivers to go apoplectic. Roadways run into physical barriers and disappear, only to reappear again several blocks away.

Pennsylvania Avenue is the grand boulevard of the nation, connecting the White House and the Capitol. Wisconsin Avenue and M Street are the raucous main drags of Georgetown. Massachusetts Avenue between Dupont Circle and 34th Street (where the vice president's mansion sits on the grounds of the U.S. Naval Observatory) has many embassies and is called Embassy Row. K Street downtown is known for lobbyists and lawyers. Connecticut Avenue is a major shopping artery. At Dupont Circle, Connecticut collides with (and dips under) New Hampshire and Massachusetts avenues and 19th and P streets, creating the ultimate in circular confusion for the Washington newbie. A huge proportion of Washington's stellar attractions are on or near the Mall, the large expanse of green between the Lincoln Memorial and the Capitol. (Originally, the western section was under the Potomac.)

The Lowdown

Since you've been gone... If you haven't been to Washington lately, some new or improved sights await you, especially in the world of art. The Smithsonian Institution's **American Art Museum** and the **National Portrait Gallery,** which share the Old Patent Office Building in Penn Quarter, closed for a several-hundred-million-dollar renovation in 2000 and reopened mid-2006. The **Phillips Collection** opened new space in April 2006 and added a 180-seat auditorium, a hands-on activity room, a courtyard, a new cafe, and a new shop, among other facilities. The **National Zoo**

has been drawing big crowds to see baby panda Tai Shan (and mother Mei Xiang and father Tian Tian) since its birth in July 2005. The **National Archives,** home to *billions* of documents—including the Constitution, the Declaration of Independence, and the Bill of Rights—has made efforts to make its documents more accessible, putting all four pages of the Constitution in its main public exhibition area, for instance. On the negative side, the **National Museum of American History** closed for renovations in 2006 and won't reopen until summer 2008 (larger projects won't open until 2014).

If you haven't been to D.C. in a few years, don't miss two major additions: The **World War II Memorial** and the **National Museum of the American Indian** both opened in 2004.

Covering all points of view... Post-9/11 security concerns (some would say hysteria) curtailed access to one of Washington's most wonderful views: from the terrace at the **Capitol**'s West Front. It used to be that anyone could climb the West Steps or wander around from the East Front. Now, if you're lucky, you can get there during or after a formal Capitol tour. Otherwise, you can walk to the bottom of the steps and content yourself with a ground-level view of the Mall and its environs—except when the Capitol cops have the entire West Lawn fenced off, which they do from time to time.

From the Capitol Reflecting Pool, between the Mall and the Capitol, you can get a great look at the Capitol itself. Somewhat ironically, the best long-range view of Mall monuments and the august buildings of the federal government is from the porch of **Arlington National Cemetery**'s Arlington House, once the home of Robert E. Lee, who tried and failed to destroy the nation that the capital still governs. From the nearby **U.S. Marine Corps War Memorial** (commonly known as the Iwo Jima Memorial), you can see an imposing alignment of the **Capitol, Washington Monument,** and **Lincoln Memorial.** The steps of the **Thomas Jefferson Memorial** offer a gorgeous view of the Tidal Basin (especially at cherry-blossom time), the Washington Monument, and the White House beyond.

Other great viewing spots: the **Washington Monument, Lincoln Memorial, Old Post Office Pavilion, John F. Kennedy Center for the Performing Arts** roof terrace,

Washington National Cathedral tower, and Washington Harbour. After dark Washington truly is an alabaster city gleaming.

Monumental achievements... The **Washington Monument** is the tallest structure in the city and the most distinctive element of the Washington skyline—but it's never had it easy. Construction of the 555-foot obelisk began in 1848 and wasn't completed until 1884, the 36-year gap caused first by a depletion of funds and then by the Civil War. By the time there was enough money to finish the project, the marble used in the early construction couldn't be matched perfectly, hence the two-tone effect you see today. From 1998 to 2000, the monument endured a face-lift during which the exterior was cleaned, the commemorative stones inside were repaired or replaced, and the observation deck was remodeled. Since 9/11 the monument has been subjected to a series of security upgrades. Among the best recent improvements was the new elevator cab, which whisks visitors to the top in 70 seconds, then lets them down slowly over 2 minutes and 18 seconds so they can view 45 of the commemorative stones.

The **Lincoln Memorial,** a limestone-and-marble temple housing a pensive statue of President Abraham Lincoln, has always spoken of the present and future as well as the past. On Easter Sunday 1939, the famed black singer Marian Anderson performed on the memorial's steps after the Daughters of the American Revolution barred her from their Constitution Hall because of her race. Martin Luther King Jr. delivered his immortal "I Have a Dream" speech from these steps (with an encore performance by Marian Anderson) at the great civil rights march of 1963. The Vietnam War was protested here, and other major political demonstrations have used the monument as a backdrop.

Enormous controversy accompanied the construction of the **Jefferson Memorial,** which has become one of the most beloved structures in the country. Strong opposition was voiced to the selection of the architect, the design for the memorial, and its location. Environmentalists feared construction would damage the Tidal Basin. Early tree-huggers chained themselves to cherry trees slated for removal from the memorial's site. In a protest that presaged objections to the World War II Memorial, some opponents alleged that Jefferson's memorial would detract from Lincoln's and that too many structures were being placed on and near the Mall. Miraculously, it got built, in a style that suggests Jefferson's home at Monticello. Ever since, Jefferson's 19-foot statue has gazed across the water to the White House where, for 8 years, he applied his enormous talents to leading the country.

FDR is the latest president to be memorialized here, at an off-by-itself spot at the southwest edge of the Tidal Basin. The **Franklin Delano Roosevelt Memorial** opened in 1997 in typical Washington fashion—with controversy, debates, and delays. For one thing, Roosevelt said he wanted a memorial the size of his desk, and this puppy is huge—four open-air "rooms" on 7.5 acres of land. It also opened without a depiction of Roosevelt in his now-famous wheelchair, an image he worked hard to hide during his life. Advocates for the handicapped howled, and a statue of the president in a wheelchair was added. The "rooms" tell the story of Roosevelt's four terms—twice as many as any other president ever will serve unless we repeal the 22nd Amendment, which was adopted in reaction to FDR's unprecedented electoral longevity. You'll also find depictions of first lady Eleanor and first dog Fala, whose statue shines where visitors pet it.

War memorials... Perhaps the most controversial memorial of all was the **Vietnam Veterans Memorial,** which also has since become one of the most-visited and most-loved spots in the capital. The private Vietnam Veterans Memorial Fund, led by returned vets, wanted a memorial that bypassed the political polarization of the war years and simply remembered the American soldiers who fought. The fund set up a competition, to be judged by a panel of architects, and Maya Lin, a young Chinese-American, produced the winning design—a V-shaped wall of black granite, carved into the ground near the Lincoln Memorial, and etched with the names of the U.S. war dead. Criticism was intense, but Lin's plan survived. Later, to placate the critics, a more traditional statue of three soldiers was erected near the wall. Still later, in a nod to military women, a statue of female military nurses at work was added. But it's the wall that brings the enormous crowds of reverent visitors, who search for familiar names or are simply overcome by the enormous loss the names represent.

Across the Reflecting Pool, the **Korean War Veterans Memorial** honors (finally) the "silent generation" of soldiers who fought the "forgotten war" in the early '50s. Here 15 soldiers, two Marines, one Navy medic, and one Air Force observer—ghostly and larger than life—are frozen in perpetual patrol in a field of juniper.

Controversy also accompanied the **World War II Memorial,** though not because the war was controversial. Like the Vietnam wall's, this memorial's design spawned contention, and so did its location. Critics complained the memorial's placement—between the **Lincoln Memorial** and the **Washington Monument**—would disrupt the breathtaking view from Lincoln's seat to the **Capitol** dome, which had been interrupted only by Washington's thin spire. They also complained that it would be too big and bulky and that it got the symbolism all wrong; individual columns for each state and territory made no sense, they said, in commemorating a war the nation fought in unity. It also represented a dramatic break in the trend, started by the Vietnam wall, toward simplicity in memorial design. You can decide for yourself by climbing Lincoln's steps to study the view to the Capitol and by wandering around the World War II Memorial and studying its components.

Just north of Arlington Cemetery stands the **U.S. Marine Corps War Memorial,** much better known as the Iwo Jima Memorial. Six-times-life-size, the statue depicts five Marines and a Navy hospital corpsman raising the American flag on Mount Suribachi on February 23, 1945, during the bloody battle for the Pacific island of Iwo Jima. Modeled on a Pulitzer Prize–winning photograph by Joe Rosenthal, the statue by Felix W. de Weldon looks impressive enough as you drive by on George Washington Parkway. But it's worth a closer look to see the lifelike faces modeled after the actual flag raisers. The Marine Corps Band—once led by John Philip Sousa—performs here in summer according to a schedule that can change. At this writing the key time is 7pm Tuesday, when the Marine Drum and Bugle Corps and Silent Drill Platoon conduct a parade, and the band performs a concert. Parking at the memorial is limited, but free shuttle buses take visitors back and forth from Arlington Cemetery, or you can take the 10-minute stroll. Bring a lawn chair or blanket and pack a picnic for this concert under the stars...and stripes.

DIVERSIONS

At the **U.S. Navy Memorial,** across Pennsylvania Avenue from the National Archives at the edge of Penn Quarter, you can walk across a 100-foot-diameter granite map of the world and peruse 26 bronze reliefs that depict important moments in U.S. naval history. Inside the Naval Heritage Center here, you can look at exhibits and watch a film about, well, naval heritage.

Prepare to have your emotions assaulted at the **U.S. Holocaust Memorial Museum,** which tells the story of this obscene chapter in European history. Prepare your children, too, if you plan to take them. The museum recommends that no one younger than 11 visit the permanent collection, for which you must obtain tickets. But exhibits on the first floor and concourse can be entered without tickets, and one of them—"Daniel's Story"—is designed for elementary- and middle-school children. The museum is about hope and heroism as well as suffering, telling about non-Jews who hid Jews at great risk to themselves, for instance. In some respects, the most disturbing programs at the museum are those that remind us that genocide is not just a historic artifact but a recurring event.

More memorials... The blue-gray marble walls of the **National Law Enforcement Officers Memorial** in Judiciary Square display the names of 18,000 federal, state, and local officers killed in the line of duty since the first known death in 1792. Less solemn—in fact downright whimsical—is the **Albert Einstein Memorial** on the grounds of the National Academies near the Mall. Sculptor Robert Berks' lumpy style imbues the bronze statue with more warmth than you'd expect from 4 tons of metal. The great physicist is depicted sitting on steps, and children love to climb up and sit in his lap. A map of the universe spreads out at his feet. Einstein quotes are engraved on the steps, including one about his "joy and amazement at the beauty and grandeur of this world."

Where to get booked... You can't check books out of the **Library of Congress.** (It's for *Congress,* you see.) But you can tour the library's magnificent Thomas Jefferson Building, and you can do research here if you're so inclined. This is the world's largest library, with 530 miles of shelves holding nearly 30 million books and other printed materials, 2.7 million films and recordings, 12 million photographs,

4.8 million maps, and 58 million manuscripts. It opened in 1801 with 740 books and three maps, was destroyed by the British in 1814, and was replenished with Jefferson's private collection of 6,487 volumes in 1815. Now the library is heavily into electronic media and boasts one of the government's best websites, www.loc.gov.

Anglophiles (You don't care the bloody Brits burned our library?) might skip across the street to the **Folger Shakespeare Library,** a private institution founded by Henry Clay Folger, who made his millions at Standard Oil of New York, which later become Mobil Oil and now ExxonMobil. The Folger boasts the world's largest collection of Shakespeare's printed works, as well as other rare Renaissance publications and manuscripts. Scholars do research here. Tourists can visit changing exhibitions and tour the building. The 250-seat Folger Theater—a replica of an Elizabethan performance venue—is a great place to take in a Shakespeare play. It also stages works by other playwrights and hosts poetry readings and early-music concerts.

Where to see your tax $$$ at work... The **U.S. Capitol**—where Congress meets—is the heart of American government. You can tour the building and sit in the House and Senate visitor galleries to watch your legislature in action. Unfortunately, you usually won't see much happening in the legislative chambers. Most congressional business really is done in committee meetings and private negotiations. "Debates" on the House and Senate floors usually consist of one lawmaker speaking to a nearly empty chamber. Just about everyone shows up for the roll calls, but they're pretty boring affairs unless some monumental issue is being decided in a toss-up vote.

The Capitol almost never closes. Since 9/11, however, the building is open only to people who have business appointments or are on Monday-through-Saturday guided tours. Your representative or senator can get you tour tickets. They're also the people to ask for passes to the visitor galleries. Or you can get first-come, first-served tour tickets at the Capitol Guide Service kiosk, along the curving sidewalk southwest of the Capitol near the intersection of 1st Street SW and Independence Avenue.

Most committee meetings are held in nearby congressional office buildings, are open to the public, and don't require tickets. You may have to stand in line to get into an especially important committee meeting, and those kinds of meetings often fill the meeting room to capacity with lobbyists and journalists. For committee schedules, check out the "Today in Congress" feature at the *Washington Post* website (www.washingtonpost.com/congress) or the *Washington Times*'s "Daybook" (www.washingtontimes.com/national/daybook.htm). Many committees publish their schedules on their websites. Start looking at www.house.gov or www.senate.gov.

Another hit attraction is the **Bureau of Engraving and Printing,** where U.S. currency, postage stamps, bonds, and White House invitations have been engraved and printed since 1914. It's a cheerful place overlooking the Tidal Basin where tour guides wear bright red ties festooned with vivid greenbacks. They show a lighthearted introductory video entitled *The Buck Starts Here,* and signs on the printing presses playfully taunt: "Have you ever been so close and yet so far away?" This good humor is evident in the bureau's website as well, titled www.moneyfactory.com.

Until 1935 the **Supreme Court** conducted its business in various locations, including the Capitol. William Howard Taft—who had been president before becoming chief justice—convinced Congress to give the court its own home. It's designed to scream "The Majesty of the Law" and to fit with the architectural style of the Capitol. Your lawmakers can get you tour tickets. Or you can wander around on your own, checking out the displays on the ground floor and the imposing architecture inside and out. You can watch a film about the court and attend a lecture in the courtroom when it's not in use. The court's oral arguments—held from the first Monday in October into late spring—are open to the public. Two lines form outside the court for admission to the arguments, one for attending an entire hour-long argument, the other for taking a 3-minute peek. Competition for seats is fierce when a highly controversial topic is being addressed.

The **State Department** occupies a plain gray box in the appropriately named Foggy Bottom neighborhood. The drab corridors inside are even duller. But tourists can't really see them anyway (state secrets, you know). What you can see—on a guided tour for which you must make reservations—are the Diplomatic Reception Rooms, where the secretary of state and other high-ranking officials entertain visiting dignitaries. The rooms are interesting for what occurs in them, for their collection of Revolutionary-era arts and furniture (Thomas Jefferson's desk, for instance), and for the view from the eighth-floor terrace outside. See p. 179 for tips on getting tickets.

Where you can't see your tax $$$ at work... White House tours have been severely curtailed since 9/11, although things are better now than they were the first couple years after the terrorist attacks and presumably will continue to get better as time passes. To find out how much of the president's mansion is open during your visit, check the White House website at www.whitehouse.gov/history/tours or phone Tel 202/456-7041. At this writing, you have to form a group of 10 and ask your senator or representative for tickets if you want to visit the mansion. Otherwise, you can stroll the perimeter of the White House grounds (outside the fence!) and visit the White House Visitor Center, which is located—pay attention, now!—not at the White House but in the Great Hall of the Commerce Department building. Even when tours flowed in their most expansive state, visitors got to see just a tiny portion of the president's digs, which serve as both home and office for the chief executive and a prestigious workplace for his highest ranking aides and the White House press corps. The best time to visit is when the mansion is done up big-time for Christmas.

The tour of **FBI Headquarters**—especially popular with little boys who like things that go *bang*—was suspended for building renovations in 2004. To find out if it's been resumed by the time of your D.C. visit, check the FBI website (www.fbi.gov/aboutus/tour/tour.htm) or phone Tel 202/324-3447. The attraction isn't the building's architecture, which has been described as Penitentiary Moderne. It's what the guide shows you inside: information on the Ten Most Wanted list, famous FBI cases, and other aspects of FBI operations, as well as a walk through a functioning crime lab and usually a demonstration at the firing range (frightening to some young children). Pistol-packin' G-Poppas—or Mommas—shoot first and ask the audience for questions later.

Tours of the **Pentagon**—once highly popular—have become even more exclusive than White House visits. The tours are open now only to religious groups, educational institutions, government agencies, and military organizations. Reservations must be made at least 2 weeks in advance

DIVERSIONS

by calling Tel 703/697-1776. Damage suffered when American Airlines Flight 77 slammed into the Pentagon on September 11 was repaired with remarkable speed. To memorialize the 184 victims—passengers and crew on the aircraft and workers in the building—a discolored stone block from the damaged west wall was inscribed with the date of the attacks and installed in the repaired wall. Behind it is a memorial capsule containing such items as letters of condolence from schoolchildren and a plaque containing the victims' names. Inside the building another memorial displays the victims' names, photos, and biographies. A memorial park was scheduled to be dedicated at the southwest corner of the building in the fall of 2006.

Having a ball on the Mall... Over the years the National Mall has been the site of open sewers, railway stations, wartime barracks, and postwar office buildings. Today it serves as a combination city park, playing field, concert arena, and public meeting grounds. The crypt in the first Smithsonian Institution building—known as the **Smithsonian Castle**—contains institution founder James Smithson's remains. It also contains a state-of-the-art information center that should be your first stop on a Smithsonian visit. It opens at 8:30am, 90 minutes before the Smithsonian museums that occupy most of the Mall between the Capitol and 14th Street. Here you will find brochures, electronic maps, touch-screen information monitors in multiple languages, a 24-minute film overview of all the Smithsonian museums...even helpful human beings. Behind the Castle, the Enid A. Haupt Garden (6:30am–dusk) is one of the largest rooftop gardens in the world. Though it looks like it's at ground level, it's actually above the underground Ripley Center International Gallery, **Sackler Gallery,** and **National Museum of African Art.**

Artful Mall museums... In its Italian Renaissance–style building surrounding a courtyard, the **Freer Gallery of Art,** on the south side of the Mall, has the cool austerity of a monastery. The Freer has a split personality. Part of it goes for modern American art—or at least what was modern from the late 19th through early 20th centuries, when Charles Lang Freer collected it. The lion's share of the gallery, though, is devoted to Asian art acquired by and after Freer. Your eyes will pop at the Peacock Room, a London dining room that James McNeill Whistler painted—the whole room, not a picture—in an elaborate blue and gold peacock design in 1876–77. There's more Asian art next door, down in the subterranean **Arthur M. Sackler Gallery,** whose first thousand pieces of Asian art were donated by physician/publisher Arthur M. Sackler. Sackler's underground neighbor, the **National Museum of African Art,** spotlights traditional and contemporary art from throughout that continent. Completing this art museum row, the **Hirshhorn Museum and Sculpture Garden** looks the way a modern-art museum ought to look: like an impenetrable piece of modern art. A donut-shaped, stilted bunker with one horizontal slit of windows, it resembles headgear for one of Homer Simpson's colleagues at the nuclear power plant. Curving galleries display modern and contemporary heavies. The outdoor sculpture garden is fun, especially when snowfall decorates the statues. The **National Gallery of Art,** an independent affiliate of the Smithsonian, consists of two separate buildings that are known, rather artlessly, as the West Building and the East Building, and are connected by a subterranean passageway with an airport-style moving walkway. The three-block-wide West Building opened in 1941, the building and initial artworks donated by former treasury secretary Andrew Mellon. It is filled with European works from the 13th into the early 20th centuries and American art from the 18th into the 20th. Here you will find, among many others, Raphael, Rembrandt, El Greco, and the only da Vinci painting in the Western Hemisphere. The East Wing is modern—in both architecture and collection. Financed by Mellon's children, Paul Mellon and Ailsa Mellon Bruce, the sharply angled structure was designed by famed architect I.M. Pei. You can see how one especially sharp corner near the entrance has been polished by the marveling touches of countless visitors. The collection focuses on 20th—and now 21st—century works, the most prominent being a giant Calder mobile in the central court. Outside is a sculpture garden with a cafe, where you can listen to live jazz Friday evenings in summer, and a rink where you can ice-skate in the winter. The gallery offers an extensive menu of lectures, concerts, films, and other events.

Artless Mall museums... The **National Air and Space Museum** already was one of the most popular museums in the world when the late-2003 opening of its annex at

Dulles International Airport caused the visitor count to soar even higher. You can trace the entire history of human flight at the original Mall museum, from the first manned flight in the Wright Brothers' 1903 Flyer to the latest space technology. Beat the inevitable crowds by arriving when the doors open in the morning. Immediately buy tickets for an IMAX movie or the Einstein Planetarium later in the day, and then tour the exhibits before the place fills up. At the annex—the **National Air and Space Museum Steven F. Udvar-Hazy Center,** which can house much larger vehicles—you can walk among the Space Shuttle *Enterprise,* the first shuttle, which was used in tests; the Lockheed SR-71 Blackbird reconnaissance plane, the fastest and highest-flying jet aircraft ever built with a top speed over 2,200 mph at altitudes exceeding 85,000 feet; the Boeing Dash 80, the prototype for the 707; and the Boeing B-29 Superfortress Enola Gay, which dropped the first atomic bomb on Japan during World War II. Altogether more than 120 aircraft, more than 140 large space artifacts, and more than 1,500 smaller items are housed in nearly 350,000 square feet of display space. Knowledgeable docents explain the displays and answer visitors' questions.

With more than three million artifacts of American political, social, and technological history, the **National Museum of American History** is really too much to swallow in one gulp. Among the most-gaped-at exhibits: Archie Bunker's chair from the *All in the Family* TV series; Judy Garland's ruby slippers from the film *The Wizard of Oz;* first ladies' inaugural gowns; and the 15-star flag that inspired Francis Scott Key to write "The Star Spangled Banner." The hands-on history and science rooms are great for kids 5 and older. Unfortunately, if you arrive before mid-2008, you'll probably find the museum closed for renovations. It was scheduled to reopen that summer.

You may not be overly thrilled about petting a tarantula, picking up a giant hissing cockroach, or crawling through a mock termite mound, but your kids will put those among the highlights of visiting the **National Museum of Natural History,** which has, among many other things, a hands-on insect zoo. Other highlights for the whole family: the African elephant in the main-floor Rotunda; the 45.52-carat Hope Diamond in the Hall of Geology, Gems and Minerals; and exhibits about humans, under the theory that we're part of natural history, too.

The 250,000-square-foot **National Museum of the American Indian** displays 10,000 years worth of artifacts related to Indians of the Americas. Leaders of Indian communities participated in planning the institution, which some critics charge loaded the place up with too much myth and not enough hard history. The limestone exterior was designed to evoke a stone mass carved over time by wind and water. The museum's Mitsitam Cafe, serving traditional Indian foods, is the best place to eat on the Mall. This museum also has some of the most interesting shopping in town.

While you're on the Mall, you might as well stroll down to the **U.S. Botanic Garden,** where the Mall bumps into the base of Capitol Hill. In addition to the 4,000 plants on display inside the nation's greenhouse, there are outdoor gardens adjacent to the building and across Independence Avenue where you can see a fountain created by Frederic August Bartholdi, the French designer of the Statue of Liberty. Poinsettias bring lots of color to the greenhouse during Christmas season, and it's a nice warm place to duck out of the cold throughout the winter.

Places to dawdle... You could have a pretty good time in Washington without ever leaving **Union Station,** an architecturally distinguished, historically significant structure with more than 100 shops, restaurants and fast-food stands, and a nine-screen cinema complex. Oh, and a train station, a Metrorail station, a tour bus staging area, and a parking garage. Located on the edge of what had been a rough Capitol Hill shantytown known as Swampoodle, Union Station opened in 1908, designed by Chicago architect Daniel H. Burnham to ape the dimensions and grandiosity of ancient Rome. The main entrance copies the Arch of Constantine; the Main Hall re-creates the central hall of the Baths of Diocletian; fountains splash inside and outside. Note the 96-foot-high barrel-vaulted ceiling, and statues by Augustus Saint-Gaudens of 36 Roman legionnaires at attention on a surrounding balcony.

When it opened downtown in 1899, the **Old Post Office Pavilion,** with its tower, was the largest and tallest government building in Washington. Not everyone thought highly of its busy, Romanesque architecture, which one senator described as "a cross between a cathedral and a cotton mill." Outdated within 15 years, it somehow dodged the wrecking ball long enough to evolve into a national treasure.

You can ride the elevator 270 feet to the clock tower's observation deck for a great view without the long lines of the Washington Monument. Attempts to create a dining and shopping magnet here have not met early expectations. Only a handful of food stands and shops do business here.

Artful converted mansions... Built between 1799 and 1801, the **Octagon Museum** downtown actually has six sides, plus a rounded entrance hall that may have spawned the name. Round rooms in the 18th century often were formed from eight angled walls that were plastered smooth in a circle and were referred to as "octagon salons." This is among the facts you can learn touring the house, which the American Architectural Foundation employs as a museum. Serious history has happened within these—whatever number—walls. After the British burned the White House in 1814, the Octagon was temporary residence for President James Madison and his wife, Dolley. The next year, the Treaty of Ghent, which ended that war with Great Britain, was signed here. During World War II the CIA predecessor OSS was headquartered here, as was the National Trust for Historic Preservation after that war. Closed to the general public throughout 2006, the Octagon was scheduled to reopen in 2007.

Across Pennsylvania Avenue from the White House, the **Renwick Gallery** displays American crafts in an 1859 Second Empire mansion designed by noted architect James Renwick Jr. to house the art collection of William Wilson Corcoran. What was Washington's first art museum later moved down the street and became the **Corcoran Gallery of Art,** which features American and European art and has the distinction today of being Washington's largest private art museum. Renwick also designed the Smithsonian's Castle. The Renwick Gallery is part of the Smithsonian's **American Art Museum.**

Opened in 1921, the **Phillips Collection** sprang from the private collection of Jones & Laughlin Steel Company scion Duncan Phillips, whose 1890s Georgian Revival mansion near Dupont Circle feels less like a museum than a gallery in an elegant private home. Expansions gave the gallery modern exhibition space as well. The Phillips calls itself America's first museum of modern art, but Duncan Phillips also collected the works of earlier artists who influenced the moderns. He acquired an El Greco from around

1600, for example, because Phillips considered the painter to be the "first impassioned expressionist." The gallery hosts lectures most Thursday evenings and concerts at 5pm Sunday from October through May.

Marjorie Merriweather Post, heir to the Post Toasties fortune, purchased a Georgian mansion in Upper Northwest in 1955, renamed it Hillwood, and had it enlarged to display her art collection. Now known as **Hillwood Museum and Gardens,** this mansion and grounds overlooking Rock Creek Park is open for tours. Of Post's four husbands, number three was Joseph E. Davies, U.S. ambassador to the Soviet Union, and that marriage turned her on to the Russian art that would become her passion (instead of, apparently, Davies). A bracing Royalist antidote to all that democracy on the Mall, Hillwood displays an extensive collection of Russian decorative art, including Faberge eggs, as well treasures from France and elsewhere.

The stunning **Kreeger Museum**—in another affluent Upper Northwest neighborhood, this one just north of Georgetown—was built in 1967 for Geico Insurance Co. founder David Lloyd Kreeger and his wife Carmen. The building—modern with influences from Byzantium, Egypt, and Rome—was designed to be a residence, museum, and concert space. It was opened the public in 1994, displaying primarily works acquired by the Kreegers. The collection ranges from the mid–19th century to the 1970s and includes works by Monet, Renoir, Pissarro, Picasso, Munch, Miró, Calder, and Washington Color School artists, as well as some traditional art from Africa and the Americas.

Where bureaucrats roamed... Can your stamps pass the "lickometer test"? Find out at the delightful **National Postal Museum,** in the former main city Post Office on Capitol Hill. This compact museum mingles serious postal history and rare stamps with oddities and amazing facts. Kids like the interactive exhibits. Enter the 1887 block-wide, red-brick **National Building Museum,** originally the Pension Building, and you get a big surprise: This structure by Judiciary Square is hollow. The Great Hall—316 feet long, 116 feet wide, and up to 159 feet high—has a central fountain and eight Corinthian columns, 75 feet tall, painted to look like marble, that come straight from a C. B. DeMille epic. Numerous shorter columns line the walls. It looks just like an Italian Renaissance palace, which was what architect and engineer Montgomery C. Meigs intended. Perhaps setting precedent for his successors at the Army Corps of Engineers—who never met a multibillion-dollar project they didn't like—General Meigs clearly committed overkill in his design. But he also demonstrated practical genius, deploying windows, vents, and open archways to flood the Great Hall with air and light. The hall has hosted inaugural balls since 1885. Museum exhibits focus on the building process, architectural styles, and construction techniques. It also hosts forums on such timely topics as managing suburban growth, saving landmarks, preserving communities, and revitalizing urban centers. Kids enjoy the hands-on exhibits.

The **American Art Museum** and the **National Portrait Gallery** share the old Patent Office Building, a pillared Greek Revival structure in Penn Quarter that no less an artist than Walt Whitman called "the noblest of Washington buildings." President Andrew Jackson laid the cornerstone for this "temple to the industrial arts" in 1836. Construction wasn't completed until 1867, establishing an unfortunate tradition. The building's current renovation project closed the two museums from 2000 into 2006 and wasn't scheduled for completion until mid-2007. When open, the museums deliver what they promise: portraits and American art.

Where history was made... The most amazing things about **Ford's Theatre,** where Lincoln was assassinated on April 14, 1865, by John Wilkes Booth, are that it's still around at all and that it's still used as a theater. The War Department blocked John T. Ford's plan to reopen the summer following the assassination by seizing the theater and converting it to a department office building that for a while also housed the Library of Medicine and the Army Medical Museum. In 1893 the building's interior collapsed, killing 22 government clerks. The building housed a warehouse and publications depot from then until 1932, when the Lincoln Museum opened on the first floor. Finally on February 5, 1969, after an extensive restoration, Ford's staged its first performance in more than a century. Now you can take in a play in a theater that looks just as it did when Lincoln attended. And you can explore museum displays that include Booth's Derringer, Lincoln's coat, and a bloodstained pillow that cushioned the president's head as he lay dying in **Peterson House,** directly across the street, which also is open to visitors.

War of 1812 hero Commodore Stephen Decatur is far less known than Lincoln, of course, but Federal-style **Decatur House** is worth a visit even if you don't care who lived there. When it was built in 1818, it was the first private home on Lafayette Square, opposite the White House. The house is furnished as it would have been in the early 19th century. The **Frederick Douglass National Historic Site** preserves the home of the great African-American abolitionist who also became a D.C. Council member, D.C.'s U.S. marshal, and U.S. minister to Haiti. Tours include a film on Douglass's life and exhibits that demonstrate his diverse and impressive accomplishments. The **Woodrow Wilson House** was, surprisingly, until recently, the only post-presidential home in town. Until first lady Hillary Clinton was elected to the Senate from New York and bought a D.C. house with hubby Bill, Wilson was the only president who stayed here after leaving office. He's still the only president buried in Washington— at National Cathedral. Wilson's home, north of Dupont Circle, isn't far from Hill and Bill's digs near the Veep's house on the Naval Observatory grounds.

Really not for women only... The great irony of the **National Museum of Women in the Arts** is that its downtown home is an ornate palace originally built for one of the most famous all-men's organizations in the world: the Masons. Since 1987, though, it's housed the only museum in the world devoted exclusively to female artists. The **Daughters of the American Revolution** complex, an entire block of prime real estate just a matron's throw from the White House, offers a rare close-up view of patrician America. The best-known part of the site is DAR Constitution Hall, a performance venue infamous for barring a concert by famed black singer Marian Anderson, who made civil rights history by performing instead at the Lincoln Memorial on Easter Sunday 1939. But there's also a library and a museum that focuses on furnishings and decorative arts. "Period Rooms," furnished and decorated as they would have been at a particular time in U.S. history, include, among others, a Pilgrim dwelling, an upper-middle-class Victorian parlor, a Beaux Arts board room (which the DAR board uses), an 18th-century tavern, and an attic filled with toys and dolls.

DIVERSIONS

Where to find real party animals... The **National Zoological Park** in Upper Northwest—better known as the National Zoo—has been through some rough times. First it was the fruitless marriage of Ling-Ling and Hsing-Hsing, the adorable but somnolent giant pandas who emigrated from the People's Republic of China in 1972 and died (Ling-Ling, the female, in 1992, Hsing-Hsing, the male, in 1999) without giving us surviving American-born offspring. They've been replaced by Tian Tian and Mei Xiang, who finally gave us a D.C.-native panda in 2005 and are expected to produce more. In 1995, a mentally disturbed woman wandered into the lion's den and didn't wander back out. In 2000, a 16-year-old punk shot up a traditional family day at the zoo. And, more recently, zoo employees made several boneheaded mistakes that killed the animals they're supposed to care for. It's still a great place to visit (if not live)—especially for kids. Check out the Think Tank, which probes animals' abilities to communicate and reason; the O Ring, which lets orangutans move between buildings by swinging freely on overhead cables; and Amazonia, which replicates a South American rainforest. Children like to visit Kids Farm, where they can pet animals, help to groom them, and play with a giant pizza that teaches that if you want to eat something, you have to grow it first. For parents, the Kids Farm also has benches for sitting. The best time to see animals in action is early or around dusk. During the middle of the day, many nap or find nooks and crannies where they can hide from human zoo visitors.

The **National Aquarium,** founded in 1873, has been tucked away in the basement of the Commerce Department downtown since the building opened in 1931. The cool, dark aquarium has 80 exhibits that display some 1,000 specimens of marine life including sharks, piranhas, and alligators. Come at 2pm for the feedings: piranhas on Tuesday, Thursday, and Sunday; sharks on Monday, Wednesday, and Saturday; alligators on Friday. Compared to the free National Zoo, with 2,400 animals on 163 acres of land, the aquarium's $5 admission charge for most visitors makes it about the worst financial deal in town.

Sea adventures... The U.S. Navy's first onshore facility, Washington Navy Yard, was established in 1799 on the north bank of the Anacostia River. Here the **Navy Museum** contains exhibits on every war the United States has ever fought, including obscurities like the Quasi War with France in the West Indies (1798–1800). Highlights include a portion of the USS *Constitution*'s fighting top, examples of Navy guns, and a collection of Navy ship models, and the USS *Berry,* a destroyer launched in 1955 that saw action in Vietnam.

Attractions that won't bore the kids... The privately owned **International Spy Museum** is sure to perk up the kids after a day of historical sights. It's got a coat-button camera, lipstick pistol, Enigma cipher machine, and artifacts from such pop-culture fiction as *Mission Impossible, Get Smart, The Avengers,* and James Bond. The Smithsonian gives children lots to do on the Mall. At the **National Museum of American History**'s Hands-On History Room, for example, they can tap out Morse code telegrams, pick cotton, ride high-wheeler bikes, and don 18th-century waistcoats or corsets. Dinosaurs who would eat Barney for lunch (and nibble Baby Bop and B.J. for dessert) roam the **National Museum of Natural History.** Just about all of the **National Air and Space Museum** is mandatory for kid tourists. Make a beeline for IMAX movie tickets as soon as you enter the building. Lines also form to touch the moon rock and to walk through Skylab. Interactive exhibits at the **National Postal Museum** on Capitol Hill are fun enough to keep kids' attention, especially the machines that custom-design souvenir postcards. And the **National Zoo,** off Connecticut Avenue in Upper Northwest, never fails to please the young ones.

The **National Geographic Museum at Explorers Hall** downtown often mounts visits that are fascinating to kids. Because exhibits change, it pays to call ahead to find out if there's anything that interests your family. Little boys especially like the big bangs of agents' guns during the firing-range demonstration at **FBI Headquarters.** The tour was suspended during building renovations. Check if it's back on during your visit. Even if your kids can't learn how the FBI catches bank robbers during your D.C. trip, they can see how currency is engraved and printed at the **Bureau of Engraving and Printing** near the Tidal Basin. (Let them come up with the "free samples" line on their own.) The **U.S. Holocaust Memorial Museum** next door presents "Daniel's Story," an exhibit designed for children 8 and older that follows one Jewish boy into and out of the Holocaust. Children also appreciate the pomp and precision of the changing of the guard at the Tomb of the

Unknowns in **Arlington National Cemetery,** as long as they're old enough to understand what it's about and to treat it with the required respect.

A museum meant for older kids... The National Academy of Sciences has long advised public officials through reports prepared by those infamous "distinguished panels of experts." In 2004, the academy opened the **Marian Koshland Science Museum** in Penn Quarter to educate rank-and-file citizens about that important intersection where science meets public policy. Built around studies regularly published by the academies, the museum's first exhibits explored the hotly debated issue of global warming and the many mind-boggling applications of the science of DNA. As this book was being written, the museum was preparing a new interactive exhibit about infectious diseases. The exhibits are aimed at adults and children older than 12.

Where soldiers, statesmen, celebrities, and politicians rest... Arlington National Cemetery contains the graves of more than 300,000 war dead, veterans, and their dependents on more than 600 rolling acres beside the Potomac River, across Memorial Bridge from the Lincoln Memorial. Two presidents are buried here (Kennedy and Taft), many famous warriors (Gen. Philip Sheridan, Adm. Richard E. Byrd, Gen. Omar Bradley, Gen. George Marshall), plus many ex-soldiers more celebrated for achievements in other arenas: heavyweight champion Joe Louis, civil rights leader Medgar Evers, and mystery writers Mary Roberts Rinehart and Dashiell Hammett. The most gratifying way to experience Arlington may be to wander among the memorials and graves. But it's a long wander. So, for most folks, it makes the most sense to ride the Tourmobile. It stops at the cemetery highlights, where you can get off and wander at your heart's content, then reboard to continue your tour. Plain black marble stones and an eternal flame mark President John F. Kennedy's gravesite. Also buried there are Jacqueline Kennedy Onassis and two Kennedy infants who died before the president. Brother Robert Kennedy, assassinated while running for president in 1968, rests beneath a plain white cross nearby. Self-guided tours are offered at Arlington House, Robert E. Lee's mansion. Pierre L'Enfant is buried nearby with a panoramic view of the city he designed. The Tomb of the Unknowns marks graves of unidentified soldiers from World War I, World War II, and Korea. Due to the triumphs of modern science, no Vietnam War unknown is buried here because all Vietnam remains have been identified so far, as have the dead from our subsequent conflicts. Changing of the guard takes place every half-hour from April through September, on the hour the rest of the year. Nearby, marked by a standard-issue stone, lies Audie Murphy, America's most decorated World War II soldier—and less decorated postwar movie star.

The difference between spit-and-polish Arlington and the gently dilapidated **Congressional Cemetery** bespeaks the difference between the chaotically operated legislative branch and the meticulously regimented military. Judging by the number of visitors, Congressional Cemetery today is about as popular as Congress itself, although the Association for the Preservation of Historic Congressional Cemetery was in the midst of a restoration and preservation project aimed for completion by the cemetery's bicentennial in 2007. Founded in 1807 on a 30-acre slope near where Pennsylvania Avenue SE crosses the Anacostia River (now a not-so-nice part of town), Congressional contains graves of 19 U.S. senators and 71 representatives, along with monuments to 120 others who died in office. Many more nonlegislators are buried here. Notable occupants include Elbridge Gerry, a Declaration of Independence signer, vice president, and Massachusetts governor who signed a legislative districting bill that inspired the term "gerrymander"; Civil War photographer Matthew Brady; "March King" John Philip Sousa, with a bar of "Stars and Stripes Forever" engraved on his tomb; and FBI Director J. Edgar Hoover.

Only two celebrities are in **St. Mary's Catholic Church Cemetery** in the suburb of Rockville, Maryland: author F. Scott Fitzgerald and his wife Zelda. Why Rockville? Because Francis Scott Key Fitzgerald was descended from the same old Maryland family that produced the composer of "The Star Spangled Banner," and he wished to be buried among his Maryland ancestors. When he died in 1940, though, he was barred from Catholic St. Mary's Cemetery because he wrote dirty books. So he was buried in the Rockville Union Cemetery, where Zelda joined him in 1948. In 1975, the church relented and let the Fitzgeralds' daughter, Scottie, transfer her parents' remains to St. Mary's; Scottie joined them here in 1986. Scott and Zelda's grave marker is inscribed with the final words of *The Great Gatsby:* "So we beat on, boats against the current, borne back ceaselessly into the past."

Where to pray for our government... Washington may be the only city in the world that doesn't bill itself the "City of Churches," but it does have important and unusual religious edifices. **Washington National Cathedral** has the highest profile in a city of high profiles. Its towers aren't as tall as the Washington Monument, but its setting atop a tall hill causes it to rise above the monument and everything else in town and to be visible from almost everywhere. Officially named the Cathedral Church of Saint Peter and Saint Paul, it is the world's sixth-largest cathedral and the seat of the Episcopal bishop of Washington. Teddy Roosevelt and the Bishop of London helped to lay the foundation stone in 1907, but work wasn't completed until 1990. Martin Luther King Jr. delivered his last Sunday sermon here on March 31, 1968, a few days before his assassination. The tomb of the only president buried in D.C., Woodrow Wilson, is near the Space Window, which is embedded with a shard of moon rock from the Apollo XI moon landing in 1969. Every Tuesday and Wednesday at 1:30pm, the cathedral offers "Tour and Tea" with a view from a tower gallery for $22. Don your white gloves and dial as much as 6 months in advance for the required reservations (Tel 202/537-8993). Ask about the occasional Teddy Bear Tea for kids. Children 6 to 12 enjoy the crafts program presented from 10am to 2pm Saturday in the crypt ($5 for a group of up to four, a dollar for each additional child).

Across Lafayette Square from the White House, **St. John's Church** bills itself as the "Church of Presidents," because every presidential fanny since James Madison's in 1815 has occupied Pew 54 at least once. Some of its stained-glass windows honor presidents and members of Congress. The **New York Avenue Presbyterian Church** has been called "Lincoln's Church" because Old Abe regularly worshipped with this congregation during the Civil War. The church, about three blocks from the White House, displays Lincoln's pew and a Lincoln stained-glass window. Now the building houses an activist congregation and often is the site for liberal activist gatherings. The Clintons worshiped regularly at the **Foundry United Methodist Church,** a 185-year-old activist congregation near Dupont Circle that welcomes all races, classes, and sexual orientations. President Clinton didn't abandon his Baptist roots but followed lifelong Methodist Hillary's lead to Foundry. The Clintons liked the congregation's diversity, and Pastor Phil Wogaman became one of the president's most important counselors during Monicagate. Like other churches in the vicinity of the White House, Foundry can boast that most presidents since its founding have sat in the sanctuary from time to time.

The **Metropolitan African Methodist Episcopal (A.M.E.) Church** downtown is known as the Cathedral of African Methodism, a denomination founded in 1787 when a group of blacks walked away from segregation at a Philadelphia Methodist church. The Washington church has served as an Underground Railroad stop for runaway slaves, offered a forum for such civil rights leaders as Frederick Douglass and Martin Luther King Jr., and opened its doors to presidents. President Clinton and Vice President Albert Gore attended inaugural worship services here in 1993 and 1997.

Northeast Washington has created a virtual Roman Catholic Bible Belt with Catholic University, Trinity College, and the **Basilica of the National Shrine of the Immaculate Conception,** the largest Catholic church in the Western Hemisphere. The basilica's tower and dome are prominent features of Washington's away-from-the-Mall skyline. Its Crypt Church displays a gold-embroidered stole and tiara of Pope John XXIII. Also in the area is the century-old **Franciscan Monastery,** officially known as the Memorial Church of the Holy Sepulcher. The Franciscans are charged with preserving Roman Catholicism's holiest shrines, and here they've built replicas to be visited by Americans who can't get to the Holy Land.

Map 7: Washington, D.C., Diversions

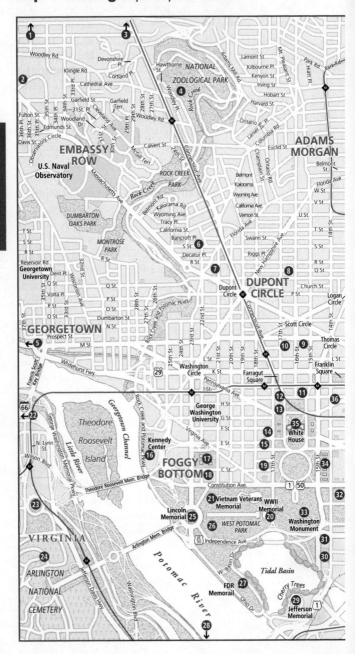

See map key on next page

Key for Map 7: Washington, D.C., Diversions

American Art Museum **39**
Arlington National Cemetery **24**
Arthur M. Sackler Gallery **49**
Basilica of the National Shrine of
   the Immaculate Conception **68**
Bureau of Engraving and Printing **30**
Capitol **61**
Congressional Cemetery **57**
Corcoran Gallery of Art **15**
Daughters of the American Revolution **19**
Decatur House **12**
Frederick Douglass National
   Historic Site **56**
Einstein Memorial **18**
FBI **42**
Folger Shakespeare Library **59**
Ford's Theatre/Peterson House **41**
Foundry United Methodist Church **8**
Franciscan Monastery **69**
Franklin Delano Roosevelt Memorial **27**
Freer Gallery of Art **48**
Hillwood Museum and Gardens **3**
Hirshhorn Museum and
   Sculpture Garden **51**
International Spy Museum **38**
Thomas Jefferson Memorial **29**
John F. Kennedy Center for the
   Performing Arts **16**
Korean War Veterans Memorial **26**
Kreeger Museum **5**
Marian Koshland Science Museum **63**
Library of Congress **58**
Lincoln Memorial **25**
Metropolitan African Methodist Episcopal
   (A.M.E.) Church **9**
National Air and Space Museum **52**
National Air and Space Museum Steven F.
   Udvar-Hazy Center **22**
National Aquarium **34**
National Archives **45**

National Building Museum **65**
National Gallery of Art **62**
National Geographic Museum at
   Explorers Hall **10**
National Law Enforcement Officers
   Memorial **64**
National Museum of African Art **50**
National Museum of American History **32**
National Museum of the
   American Indian **53**
National Museum of Natural History **46**
National Museum of Women in
   the Arts **37**
National Portrait Gallery **40**
National Postal Museum **66**
National Zoological Park **4**
Navy Museum **55**
New York Avenue Presbyterian Church **36**
Octagon Museum **14**
Old Post Office Pavilion **43**
Pentagon **28**
Phillips Collection **7**
Renwick Gallery **13**
St. John's Church **11**
St. Mary's Catholic Church Cemetery **1**
Smithsonian Institution Building
   (The Castle) **47**
State Department **17**
Supreme Court **60**
Union Station **67**
U.S. Botanic Garden **54**
U.S. Holocaust Memorial Museum **31**
U.S. Marine Corps War Memorial **23**
U.S. Navy Memorial **44**
Vietnam Veterans Memorial **21**
Washington Monument **33**
Washington National Cathedral **2**
White House **35**
Woodrow Wilson House **6**
World War II Memorial **20**

The Index

See Map 7 on the previous page for all Diversions listings.

American Art Museum (p. 87) PENN QUARTER The oldest Smithsonian art collection chronicles the gamut of American art. Gift shop.... *Tel 202/275-1500. www.americanart.si.edu. 8th St. NW, between F and G sts. Gallery Place–Chinatown Metro. Daily 11:30am–7:30pm. Closed Dec 25. Free admission.*

Arlington National Cemetery (p. 88) VIRGINIA America's most famous military cemetery. No cars allowed beyond on-site parking lot. Tourmobile stops at Kennedy gravesite, Arlington House (Robert E. Lee's home), Tomb of the Unknowns.... *Tel 703/607-8000. www.arlingtoncemetery.org. VA side of Memorial Bridge, opposite Lincoln Memorial. Arlington Cemetery Metro. April–Sept daily 8am–7pm; Oct–March daily 8am–5pm. Free admission; charge for Tourmobile and parking.*

Arthur M. Sackler Gallery (p. 97) NATIONAL MALL Underground gallery of Asian art. Museum shop.... *Tel 202/633-4880. www.asia.si.edu. Between Smithsonian Castle, Independence Ave. SW, and 12th St. Smithsonian Metro. Daily 10am–5:30pm. Closed Dec 25. Free admission.*

Basilica of the National Shrine of the Immaculate Conception (p. 109) NORTHEAST Largest Roman Catholic church in Western Hemisphere. Gift shop, bookstore, restaurants for breakfast and lunch.... *Tel 202/526-8300. www.nationalshrine.com. 400 Michigan Ave. NE, at 4th St. Brookland/Catholic University Metro or take a cab. April–Oct daily 7am–7pm; Nov–March daily 7am–6pm. Guided tours Mon–Sat 9–11am and 1–3pm; Sun 1:30–4pm. Masses Mon–Sat 7, 7:30, 8, 8:30am, 12:10, and 5:15pm; Sun 7:30, 9, 10:30am, noon (solemn), 1:30 (Spanish), and 4:30pm.*

Bureau of Engraving and Printing (p. 94) TIDAL BASIN March through August, get up to four free timed tickets after 8am on day of tour at ticket kiosk (Raoul Wallenberg Place on 15th St. side of building). Tickets usually gone by 9am. Tickets not required September through February.... *Tel 202/874-2330 (866/874-2330). www.moneyfactory.com. Entrance on 14th St. SW, near C St.; ticket kiosk on Raoul Wallenberg Place SW. Smithsonian Metro. Tours May–Aug Mon–Fri 9–10:45am, 12:30–2pm, and 5–7pm; Sept–April 9–10:45am and 12:30–2pm; visitor center Sept–April 8:30am–3pm, May–Aug till 7:30pm. Closed weekends, federal holidays, and Dec 25–Jan 1. Free admission.*

Capitol (p. 88) CAPITOL HILL Get tickets from your senator or representative to watch the legislative bodies in action (or inaction) and for a VIP tour. Or get in the tour line with the commoners. Shop, restaurants.... *Tel 202/225-6827 (recorded info). (Call senators at Tel 202/224-3121, representatives at Tel 202/225-3121.) www.aoc.gov. First-come, first-served tour tickets distributed at kiosk along curving sidewalk near 1st St. SW and Independence Ave. beginning at 9am daily. Capitol S. Metro. Tours Mon–Sat 9am–4:30pm except Thanksgiving and Dec 25. Free admission.*

Congressional Cemetery (p. 107) SOUTHEAST Semiofficial burial ground for Congress members and others. Not a neighborhood to get lost in.... *Tel 202/543-0539. www.congressionalcemetery. org. 1801 E St. SE, at 18th St. Drive or take a cab and reserve one for return trip. Daily dawn–dusk. Free admission.*

Corcoran Gallery of Art (p. 100) DOWNTOWN Washington's first art museum features a coherent display of American art plus many European works. Many lectures, seminars, courses, performances. Shop, cafe.... *Tel 202/639-1700. www.corcoran.org. 500 17th St. NW, between New York Ave. and E St. Farragut W. Metro. Wed–Sun 10am–5pm; Thurs till 9pm. Open some Mondays. Closed Jan 1, Thanksgiving, and Dec 25. Admission charged.*

Daughters of the American Revolution (p. 103) DOWNTOWN Complex of DAR's Constitution Hall auditorium, museum, library, offices, gift shop.... *Tel 202/628-1776. www.dar.org. 1776 D St. NW, between 17th and 18th sts. Farragut W. Metro. Museum Mon–Fri 9:30am–4pm; Sat 9am–5pm. Period Rooms tours Mon–Fri 10am–2:30pm; Sat 9am–4:30pm. Library Mon–Fri 8:30am–4pm; Sat 9am–4:30pm. Headquarters offices Mon–Fri 8am–4pm; closed Sat. All closed Sun, federal holidays, and varied dates in late June/early July. Admission charged to use library, others free.*

Decatur House (p. 103) DOWNTOWN Home of early naval hero Commodore Stephen Decatur. Museum shop.... *Tel 202/842-0920. www.decaturhouse.org. 1610 H St. NW, at Jackson Place. Farragut W. Metro. Tues–Sat 10am–5pm; Sun noon–4pm. Donations requested.*

Einstein Memorial (p. 92) FOGGY BOTTOM Robert Berks's sculpture is behind the National Academies headquarters.... *Constitution Ave. NW, between 21st and 22nd sts. Foggy Bottom/GWU Metro. Daily 24 hours. Free admission.*

FBI Headquarters (p. 95) PENN QUARTER Call or check website to find out if tours have resumed. Tip from informant: Ask senator or representative for VIP tour tickets.... *Tel 202/324-3447. www.fbi.gov/aboutus/tour/tour.htm. E St. NW, at 9th St. Archives–Navy Memorial Metro. Free admission.*

Folger Shakespeare Library (p. 93) CAPITOL HILL Impressive collection of Shakespearean and Renaissance stuff, an Elizabethan theater, concerts, plays, readings.... *Tel 202/544-4600 (box office 202/544-7077). www.folger.edu. 201 E. Capitol St. SE, at 2nd St. Capitol S. Metro. Mon–Sat 10am–4pm; tours Mon–Sat 11am and Sat 1pm; building and exhibition tours Mon–Fri 11am and Sat 11am and 1pm; garden tours April–Oct 3rd Sat of month 10 and 11am. Closed Sun, federal holidays, and Dec 26. Free admission.*

Ford's Theatre/Peterson House (p. 102) PENN QUARTER Ford's, the scene of the Lincoln assassination, is still functioning, with a Lincoln museum in the basement. Peterson House, where Lincoln died, is across the street.... *Tel 202/426-6924. Box office 202/347-4833. www.nps.gov/foth and www.fordstheatre.org. 511 10th St. NW, between E and F sts. Metro Center Metro. Daily 9am–5pm. Closed Dec 25. Theater closed to visitors during performances, rehearsals, and set work. Free admission. Fee for performances.*

Foundry United Methodist Church (p. 109) DUPONT CIRCLE Activist urban-melting-pot congregation was first family's first choice for worship during Clinton administration.... *Tel 202/332-4010. www.foundryumc.org. 1500 16th St. NW, at P St. Dupont Circle Metro. Services Sun 9:30 and 11am; Wed 6:45pm. Offerings accepted.*

Franciscan Monastery (p. 109) NORTHEAST Serene edge-of-D.C. setting for replicas of important Christian shrines. Well-stocked religious gift shop; snack bar.... *Tel 202/526-6800. http:// www.myfranciscan.org. 1400 Quincy St. NE, at 14th St. Take a cab. Daily 10am–5pm. Tours Mon–Sat 10am, 11am, 1pm, 2pm, and 3pm; Sun 1, 2, and 3pm. Services Mon and Wed–Fri 6 and 7am; Tues 6, 7, 9am, and 5:30pm; Sat 6 and 7am; Sun 6, 7, 8, 10am, and noon. Spanish mass daily 5pm. Offerings accepted.*

DIVERSIONS

THE INDEX

Franklin Delano Roosevelt Memorial (p. 90) TIDAL BASIN Huge, buildinglike memorial for president who said he preferred a monument the size of his desk.... *Tel 202/426-6841. www. nps.gov/fdrm. W. Basin Dr. SW, at Ohio Dr. Half-hour walk from Smithsonian Metro, or take cab or Tourmobile. Daily 8am–midnight. Closed Dec 25. Free admission.*

Frederick Douglass National Historic Site (p. 103) ANACOSTIA Residence of the celebrated African-American abolitionist. Limited space, so reserve.... *Tel 202/426-5961 (800/967-2283). www.nps.gov/frdo. 1411 W St. SE, at 14th St. Take a taxi. Oct 16–April 14 daily 9am–4pm; April 15–Oct 15 till 5pm. Last house tour starts 30 minutes before closing. Closed Jan 1, Thanksgiving, and Dec 25. Fee for reservation.*

Freer Gallery of Art (p. 96) NATIONAL MALL Turn-of-the-20th-century American art and treasures from Asia. Gallery shop.... *Tel 202/633-4880. www.asia.si.edu. Between Smithsonian Castle, Independence Ave. SW, and 12th St. Smithsonian Metro. Daily 10am–5:30pm; Thurs in July till 8pm. Closed Dec 25. Free admission.*

Hillwood Museum and Gardens (p. 101) UPPER NORTHWEST Imperial Russian decorative art dominates Marjorie Merriweather Post's collection in the mansion she bought to display it. Museum shop, cafe for lunch or tea.... *Tel 202/686-5807 (877/445-5966). www.hillwoodmuseum.org. 4155 Linnean Ave. NW, east of Connecticut Ave. near Upton St. About 8-block stroll from Van Ness/UDC Metro through affluent residential neighborhood, or take a taxi. Tues–Sat 10am–5pm. Closed Jan and most federal holidays. Children younger than 6 allowed in gardens but not in mansion. Reservations suggested. Admission charged.*

Hirshhorn Museum and Sculpture Garden (p. 97) NATIONAL MALL Modern and contemporary works inside and outside on the Mall. Museum shop.... *Tel 202/633-1000. www.hirshhorn.si.edu. Independence Ave. SW, at 7th St. Smithsonian Metro. Museum daily 10am–5:30pm; plaza 7:30am–dusk; sculpture garden daily 7:30am–dusk. Closed Dec 25. Donations accepted.*

International Spy Museum (p. 105) PENN QUARTER Date- and time-specific tickets can be purchased in advance at the museum or from Ticketmaster (Tel 800/551-7328; www.ticketmaster.com). Limited supply same-day tickets are sold at the museum.... *Tel 202/393-7798 (866/779-6873). www.spymuseum.org. 800 F St. NW, between 8th and 9th sts. Gallery Place–Chinatown Metro. Nov–Feb daily 10am–6pm; March daily 9am–6pm; April through mid-Aug daily 9am–8pm; mid-Aug through Oct Sun–Fri 10am–6pm, Sat 10am–8pm. Closed Jan 1, Thanksgiving, Dec 25. Admission charged.*

John F. Kennedy Center for the Performing Arts (p. 88) FOGGY BOTTOM A living memorial to the slain president. Free performances daily at 6pm on the Millennium Stage in the Grand Foyer.... *Tel 202/467-4600 (800/444-1324). www.kennedy-center. org. 2700 F St. NW, between New Hampshire Ave. and Rock Creek Pkwy. Foggy Bottom/GWU Metro. Free shuttle from Metro every 15 minutes Mon–Fri 9:45am–midnight, Sat 10am–midnight, Sun noon–midnight, federal holidays 4pm–midnight. Tours Mon–Fri 10am–5pm; Sat–Sun 10am–1pm. Free admission; charge for performances.*

Korean War Veterans Memorial (p. 91) NATIONAL MALL Remembers those who fought in this "forgotten war."... *Tel 202/ 426-6841. www.nps.gov/kwvm. French Dr. SW, at Independence Ave., southeast of the Lincoln Memorial. Foggy Bottom/GWU Metro. Daily 8am–midnight. Closed Dec 25. Free admission.*

Kreeger Museum (p. 101) UPPER NORTHWEST Stunning modern mansion/museum shows off art from the mid–19th century to the 1970s. Children younger than 12 welcomed only on Saturday.... *Tel 202/338-3552 (877/337-3050). www.kreegermuseum. com. 2401 Foxhall Rd. NW, north of W St. Take a cab. Tours Tues–Fri 10:30am and 1:30pm. Open Sat 10am–4pm for tours and unguided exploration. Closed Aug. Reservations required except Sat. Admission charged.*

Library of Congress (p. 92) CAPITOL HILL Anybody can join a guided tour of Jefferson Building. Get limited-supply tickets at the visitor center. Better: Ask your representative or senator for tickets for the congressional tour. Exhibits, shop.... *Tel 202/ 707-8000. www.loc.gov. 1st St. SE, between E. Capitol St. and Independence Ave. Capitol S. Metro. Jefferson Building Mon–Sat 10am–5:30pm. Tours Mon–Sat 10:30, 11:30am, 1:30, and 2:30pm, also Mon–Fri 3:30pm. Free admission.*

Lincoln Memorial (p. 88) NATIONAL MALL See some of Washington's best views—looking at the memorial and from its east and west terraces. With museum and bookstore.... *Tel 202/ 426-6841. www.nps.gov/linc. West end of Mall at 23rd St. Foggy Bottom/GWU Metro. Daily 24 hours. Free admission.*

Marian Koshland Science Museum (p. 106) PENN QUARTER Who better to create a science museum than the National Academy of Sciences?... *Tel 202/334-1201 (888/567-4526). www.koshland-science-museum.org. 6th and E sts. NW. Gallery Place–Chinatown Metro. Wed–Mon 10am–6pm; last admission at 5pm. Closed Tues, Thanksgiving, Dec 25, and Jan 1–13. Admission charged.*

Metropolitan African Methodist Episcopal (A.M.E.) Church (p. 109) DOWNTOWN Historic, socially active cathedral for African Methodism.... *Tel 202/331-1426. www.metropolitan amec.org. 1518 M St. NW, between 15th and 16th sts. McPherson Sq. or Farragut N. Metro. Services Sun 7:30 and 11am; Wed noon. Offerings accepted.*

National Air and Space Museum (p. 97) NATIONAL MALL Aviation's sacred relics, interactive exhibits, and compelling prognostications of what's going to happen next. Several restaurants and shops.... *Tel 202/633-1000. Tours and reservations Tel 202/633-2563. IMAX Theater and planetarium Tel 202/633-4629 (877/932-4629). Lectures and programs Tel 202/633-2398. www.nasm.si.edu. Independence Ave. SW, between 4th and 7th sts. L'Enfant Plaza Metro. Daily 10am–5:30pm. Summer 9am–5:30pm. Closed Dec 25. Free admission; fees for IMAX Theater and planetarium.*

National Air and Space Museum Steven F. Udvar-Hazy Center (p. 98) VIRGINIA The popular museum's annex at Dulles International Airport displays large vehicles for which there's no room on the Mall. Also an IMAX theater and aircraft control tower. Buy shuttle-bus tickets in advance to make sure you can get on.... *Phone, Internet, and hours info same for both facilities. 14390 Air and Space Museum Pkwy., Chantilly, VA, off U.S. 28 south of Dulles International Airport. Parking on-site. Shuttle bus between the two Air and Space Museum facilities leaves Mall at 9 and 11am and 1 and 3pm, leaves annex at 11am and 1, 3, and 5pm. Free admission; fee for shuttle bus and annex parking.*

National Aquarium (p. 104) DOWNTOWN The oldest aquarium in the country, founded in 1873, at current site since 1931.... *Tel 202/482-2825. www.nationalaquarium.com. Commerce Department Building, 14th St. NW, between Pennsylvania and Constitution aves. Federal Triangle Metro. Daily 9am–5pm. Closed Thanksgiving and Dec 25. Admission charged.*

National Archives (p. 88) DOWNTOWN *Billions* of American historical documents. Avoid lines and reserve tickets 6 weeks in advance by sending e-mail to visitorservices@nara.gov or volunteer@nara.gov for guided tour.... *Tel 202/357-5000. www.archives.gov. Constitution Ave. NW, between 7th and 9th sts. Archives/Navy Memorial Metro. Exhibition Hall Memorial Day weekend–Labor Day daily 10am–9pm; day after Labor Day–March to 5:30pm; April–Memorial Day weekend to 7pm. Closed Dec 25. Free admission.*

National Building Museum (p. 101) DOWNTOWN Exhibits on architecture and construction seem puny compared with the building itself and its great Great Hall. Gift shop features architecture books and cunning gadgets.... *Tel 202/272-2448. www.nbm.org. 401 F St. NW, between 4th and 5th sts. Judiciary Sq. Metro. Mon–Sat 10am–5pm; Sun 11am–5pm. Guided tours Mon–Wed 12:30pm; Thurs–Sun 11:30am, 12:30, and 1:30pm. Tours of exhibitions Fri–Sun 2:30pm. Closed Jan 1, Thanksgiving, Dec 25, and during special events. Donation suggested.*

National Gallery of Art (p. 97) NATIONAL MALL The West Building is old, the East Building new—in age of structure and of art contained therein. Several restaurants, great shops, sculpture garden.... *Tel 202/737-4215. www.nga.gov. Constitution Ave. NW, between 3rd and 7th sts. Archives/Navy Memorial Metro. Mon–Sat 10am–5pm; Sun 11am–6pm. In summer, sculpture garden open to 7pm Sat–Thurs and 9:30pm Fri. Closed Jan 1 and Dec 25. Free admission.*

National Geographic Museum at Explorers Hall (p. 105) DOWN-TOWN Interactive exhibits on science, society, and discovery at National Geographic Society headquarters. Frequent lectures, films, and other programs. Gift shop.... *Tel 202/857-7588. www.nationalgeographic.com/museum. 17th St. NW, at M St. Farragut N. Metro. Mon–Sat 9am–5pm; Sun 10am–5pm. Closed Dec 25. Free admission.*

National Law Enforcement Officers Memorial (p. 92) DOWN-TOWN Engraved with names of officers killed in the line of duty.... *Tel 202/737-3213 (866/569-4928). www.nleomf.com. E St. NW, between 4th and 5th sts.; visitor center with exhibits 605 E St. NW, at 6th St. Judiciary Sq. Metro. Memorial daily 24 hours; visitor center Mon–Fri 9am–5pm, Sat 10am–5pm, Sun noon–5pm. Free admission.*

National Museum of African Art (p. 96) NATIONAL MALL Underground museum with African art and research center.... *Tel 202/633-4600. www.si.edu/nmafa. 950 Independence Ave. SW, midway between 7th and 12th sts. Smithsonian Metro. Daily 10am–5:30pm. Closed Dec 25. Free admission.*

National Museum of American History (p. 88) NATIONAL MALL Vast collection mingles serious history and technology with light cultural stuff. Huge museum store. Several eateries.... *Tel 202/633-1000. www.americanhistory.si.edu. Between Constitution Ave. NW, Madison Dr., and 12th and 14th sts. Smithsonian Metro. Daily 10am–5:30pm. Closed until summer 2008. Closed Dec 25. Free admission.*

National Museum of Natural History (p. 98) NATIONAL MALL Big museum has big diamonds, even bigger dinosaurs. Shops, eateries.... *Tel 202/633-1000. www.mnh.si.edu. Between Constitution Ave. NW, Madison Dr., and 9th and 12th sts. Smithsonian Metro. Daily 10am–5:30pm; Memorial Day weekend through Labor Day weekend till 7:30pm. Closed Dec 25. Free admission.*

National Museum of the American Indian (p. 88) NATIONAL MALL Smithsonian's newest museum, opened in fall of 2004, displays 10,000 years worth of Indian artifacts. Excellent cafe, stores.... *Tel 202/633-1000. www.nmai.si.edu. Independence Ave. SW, at 4th St. L'Enfant Plaza Metro. Daily 10am–5:30pm. Closed Dec 25. Free admission.*

National Museum of Women in the Arts (p. 103) DOWNTOWN World's only art museum for women only—artists that is. Anyone can visit. Shop.... *Tel 202/783-5000 (800/222-7270). www. nmwa.org. 1250 New York Ave. NW, at 13th St. Metro Center Metro. Mon–Sat 10am–5pm; Sun noon–5pm. Closed Jan 1, Thanksgiving, and Dec 25. Admission charged.*

National Portrait Gallery (p. 87) PENN QUARTER Just what its name promises. Lots of portraits of Americans, from formal oils of founding fathers to contemporary cartoons.... *Tel 202/ 633-1000. www.npg.si.edu. 8th St. NW, between F and G sts. Gallery Place–Chinatown Metro. Hours daily 11:30am–7pm. Closed Dec 25. Free admission.*

National Postal Museum (p. 101) CAPITOL HILL Fun exhibits on postal history, in basement of Washington's one-time main post office. Museum store, functioning post office on-site.... *Tel 202/ 633-5555. www.postalmuseum.si.edu. 2 Massachusetts Ave. NE, across 1st St. from Union Station. Union Station Metro. Daily 10am–5:30pm. Closed Dec 25. Free admission.*

National Zoological Park (p. 104) UPPER NORTHWEST Rock Creek Park home for more than 2,400 animals on 163 acres of land. Several gift shops, snack bars, outdoor picnic tables, grassy places to lounge while snacking or resting.... *Tel 202/ 673-4821. www.natzoo.si.edu. 3001 Connecticut Ave. NW, north of Cathedral Ave. For easier walking, use Cleveland Park Metro to zoo, Woodley Park–Zoo Metro when leaving. Grounds April–Oct daily 6am–8pm; Nov–March till 6pm. Buildings April–Oct daily 10am–6pm; Nov–March till 4:30pm. Closed Dec 25. Free admission; fee for parking.*

Navy Museum (p. 104) SOUTHEAST The oldest U.S. Navy facility, the Washington Navy Yard, houses this military museum. You must call ahead for a reservation before visiting. Monday through Friday enter at 11th and O streets SE; Saturday and

Sunday at 6th and M streets SE.... *Tel 202/433-6897. www. history.navy.mil/branches/nhcorg8.htm. Take a cab. Mon–Fri 9am– 5pm; Sat–Sun and federal holidays 10am–5pm. Free admission.*

New York Avenue Presbyterian Church (p. 108) DOWNTOWN Lincoln's church during the Civil War, about three blocks from the White House.... *Tel 202/393-3700. www.nyapc.org. 1313 New York Ave. NW, between 13th and 14th sts. Metro Center or McPherson Sq. Metro. Services in summer Sun 10am; rest of year 8:45 and 11am.*

Octagon Museum (p. 100) DOWNTOWN Architecture exhibits and period rooms in Federal-style house built 1799–1801.... *Tel 202/638-3221. www.archfoundation.org/octagon. 1799 New York Ave. NW at 18th St. Farragut W. Metro. Tues–Sun 10am–4pm. Closed throughout 2006. Closed Jan 1, Thanksgiving, and Dec 25. Admission charged.*

Old Post Office Pavilion (p. 88) DOWNTOWN Great view from tower, which is run by National Park Service. Some shops, fast-food stands, free entertainment in atrium.... *1100 Pennsylvania Ave. NW, at 11th St. Federal Triangle Metro. Pavilion: Tel 202/289- 4224. www.oldpostofficedc.com. March–Aug Mon–Sat 10am–8pm, Sun noon–7pm; Sept–Feb Mon–Sat 10am–7pm, Sun noon–6pm. Tower: Tel 202/606-8691. www.nps.gov/opot/index.htm. June– Labor Day Mon–Fri 9am–7:45pm, Sat–Sun and holidays 10am– 5:45pm; rest of year Mon–Fri 9am–4:45pm, Sat–Sun and holidays 10am–5:45pm. Free admission.*

Pentagon (p. 95) VIRGINIA Since 9/11 attacks, tours limited to religious, educational, and government groups. Call at least 2 weeks in advance to find out if you qualify.... *Tel 703/697-1776. www.defenselink.mil/pubs/pentagon. Arlington, VA. Pentagon Metro. Group tours by appointment. Free admission.*

Peterson House (p. 103) See Ford's Theatre.

Phillips Collection (p. 87) DUPONT CIRCLE Modern art and earlier works that influenced it. Museum shop, cafe.... *Tel 202/ 387-2151. www.phillipscollection.org. 1600 21st St. NW, at Q St. Dupont Circle Metro. Tues–Sat 10am–5pm; Thurs till 8:30pm. Sun June–Sept noon–5pm; Oct–May till 7pm. Closed federal holidays. Admission charged weekends and special exhibitions; children under 18 free. Donations accepted Mon–Fri.*

Renwick Gallery (p. 100) DOWNTOWN Smithsonian collection of American crafts across street from White House. Museum shop.... *Tel 202/633-2850. www.americanart.si.edu/renwick. 1661 Penn- sylvania Ave. NW, at 17th St. Farragut W. Metro. Daily 10am–5:30pm. Closed Dec 25. Free admission.*

St. John's Church (p. 108) DOWNTOWN Episcopal church across Lafayette Square from White House, known as "Church of Presidents" because it's been worshipped in by every president who's held office since it opened in 1815.... *Tel 202/347-8766. www.stjohns-dc.org. 1525 H St. NW, at 16th St. McPherson Sq. Metro. Services summer Sun 7:45 and 10:30am, 1pm (Spanish); rest of year 8, 9, and 11am, 1pm (Spanish). Offerings accepted.*

St. Mary's Catholic Church Cemetery (p. 107) MARYLAND Reburial site of F. Scott and Zelda Fitzgerald.... *Tel 301/424-5550. www.stmarysrockville.org. 520 Veirs Mill Rd., at Rockville Pike (MD Rte. 355), Rockville, MD. Rockville Metro. Free admission.*

Smithsonian Institution Building (The Castle) (p. 96) NATIONAL MALL Information center for all things Smithsonian.... *Tel 202/633-1000. www.si.edu/visit/infocenter/sicastle.htm. 1000 Jefferson Dr. SW, east of 12th St. Smithsonian Metro. Daily 8:30am–5:30pm; guided tours at varying times. Free admission.*

State Department (p. 94) FOGGY BOTTOM Visitors can tour only the Diplomatic Reception Rooms. Reservations required, usually a month in advance. Not recommended for children younger than 12. Strollers not permitted.... *Tel 202/647-3241. www.state.gov/www/about_state/diprooms/index.html. 23rd St. between C and D sts. Foggy Bottom Metro. Guided tours only Mon–Fri 9:30 and 10:30am, 2:45pm. Arrive 30 minutes early for security check. Free admission.*

Supreme Court (p. 94) CAPITOL HILL Witness justice in action when court's hearing arguments, attend lectures on judicial system in courtroom when it's not, learn about American justice in basement visitor center. Shop, cafeteria, snack bar.... *Tel 202/479-3211. www.supremecourtus.gov. 1 1st St. NE, at Maryland Ave. Capitol S. or Union Station Metro. Mon–Fri 9am–4:30pm. Lectures, when courtroom not in use, every hour on the half-hour 9:30am–3:30pm. Court hears arguments first Mon of Oct through late spring—usually 2 weeks on, 2 weeks off—Mon, Tues, Wed mornings beginning at 10am, sometimes also in afternoon. Closed federal holidays. Free admission.*

Thomas Jefferson Memorial (p. 88) TIDAL BASIN Bronze statue of third president, in Monticello-like columned rotunda, has gorgeous view of Tidal Basin, Washington Monument, and White House.... *Tel 202/426-6841. www.nps.gov/thje. East Basin Dr. SW, on southeast side of Tidal Basin. 15- to 25-minute walk from Smithsonian Metro, or take taxi or Tourmobile. Daily 8am–midnight. Closed Dec 25. Free admission.*

Union Station (p. 99) CAPITOL HILL Magnificent Beaux Arts transportation hub, with more than 100 places to eat, drink, and shop, plus nine movie screens.... *Tel 202/289-1908. www.union stationdc.com. 50 Massachusetts Ave. NE, at 1st St. Union Station Metro. Station daily 24 hours; stores Mon–Sat 10am–9pm, Sun noon–6pm; holiday hours vary. Some restaurants open earlier and later. Free admission to station.*

U.S. Botanic Garden (p. 99) CAPITOL HILL Where Capitol Hill and the Mall collide, greenhouse, gardens, and warm respite in winter.... *Tel 202/225-8333. www.usbg.gov. 100 Maryland Ave. SW, at 1st St. and Independence Ave. Federal Center SW Metro. Conservatory daily 10am–5pm; outdoor gardens dawn–dusk. Free admission.*

U.S. Holocaust Memorial Museum (p. 92) TIDAL BASIN Grim subject matter presented effectively in a stark, stunning building. Date- and time-specific tickets, required only for permanent exhibition, available free beginning at 8am on day of visit or in advance for $1.75. Shop, cafeteria.... *Tel 202/488-0400 (800/ 400-9373 for advance tickets). www.ushmm.org (www.tickets. com for advance tickets). 100 Raoul Wallenberg Place SW, south of Independence Ave. Smithsonian Metro. Daily 10am–5:30pm. April to mid-June Tues and Thurs till 7:50pm. Closed Yom Kippur and Dec 25. Free admission; charge for advance tickets to permanent exhibition.*

U.S. Marine Corps War Memorial (p. 88) VIRGINIA Impressive, larger-than-life sculpture of World War II Iwo Jima flag-raising by five Marines and one Navy hospital corpsman.... *Tel 703/ 289-2500. www.nps.gov/gwmp/usmc.htm. Limited parking at site, north of Arlington Cemetery. Free shuttle bus or 10-minute walk from cemetery parking garage. Arlington Cemetery Metro. Daily 24 hours. Free admission; fee for cemetery parking.*

U.S. Navy Memorial (p. 92) PENN QUARTER Outdoor plaza with navy friezes, masts, fountains. Indoor Naval Heritage Center with film, interactive exhibits.... *Tel 202/737-2300 (800/821-8892). www.lonesailor.org. 701 Pennsylvania Ave. NW, at 7th St. Archives/ Navy Memorial Metro. Memorial daily 24 hours; Heritage center March–Oct Mon–Sat 9am–5:30pm; Nov–Feb Tues–Sat 9am– 5:30pm. Free admission.*

Vietnam Veterans Memorial (p. 90) NATIONAL MALL Black granite wall bearing names of more than 58,000 Vietnam War dead.... *Tel 202/426-6841. www.nps.gov/vive. Bacon Dr. NW between Constitution Ave. and the Lincoln Memorial. 10-block walk from Foggy Bottom/GWU Metro. Take taxi or Tourmobile. Daily 8am–midnight. Closed Dec 25. Free admission.*

DIVERSIONS

THE INDEX

Washington Monument (p. 88) NATIONAL MALL Free time-specific tickets for the elevator to the top are distributed on day of visit at kiosk at 15th St. from 8am until they run out, which is usually early. Get advanced tickets for a fee.... *Tel 202/426-6841 (800/967-2283 for advance tickets). www.nps.gov/wamo (www. reservations.nps.gov for advance tickets). Between Constitution Ave. NW, Independence Ave. SW, and 15th and 17th sts. Smithsonian Metro. Daily 9am–4:45pm. Closed Dec 25. Free admission; charge for advance reservations.*

Washington National Cathedral (p. 89) UPPER NORTHWEST Officially the Cathedral Church of Saint Peter and Saint Paul, this is the seat of the Episcopal bishop of Washington. Site of Reagan's state funeral.... *Tel 202/537-6200 (recorded info 202/ 364-6616). www.cathedral.org/cathedral. Wisconsin Ave. NW, at Massachusetts Ave. Take 30-series Metrobus or, from Dupont Circle, an N2, N3, N4, or N6 Metrobus. Mon–Fri 10am–5:30pm, June–Labor Day till 7:45pm; Sat 10am–4:30pm; Sun 8am–6:30pm. Cathedral tours Mon–Sat 10–11:30am and 12:45–3:15pm; Sun 12:45–2:30pm. Other tours (gardens, gargoyles, etc.) at various times. Services Sun 8, 9, 10, 11am, 4, and 6:30pm; Mon–Sat 7:30am, noon, 2:30 and 5:30pm. Offerings accepted.*

White House (p. 95) DOWNTOWN You must form a group of at least 10 and make a reservation (up to 6 months ahead) through a senator or representative.... *Tel 202/456-7041. www. whitehouse.gov/history/tours. 1600 Pennsylvania Ave. NW, between 15th and 17th sts. McPherson Sq. Metro. Tours Tues–Sat 7:30am–12:30pm, except federal holidays. Visitors Center: Tel 202/208-1631. www.nps.gov/whho/WHVC/index.htm. 1450 Pennsylvania Ave. NW, between 14th and 15th sts. Federal Triangle Metro. Daily 7:30am–4pm. Closed Jan 1, Thanksgiving, and Dec 25. Free admission.*

Woodrow Wilson House (p. 103) DUPONT CIRCLE Authentically furnished 1915 town house where ex-president lived from when he left the White House in 1921 until he died here in 1924.... *Tel 202/387-4062. www.woodrowwilsonhouse.org. 2340 S St. NW, between 23rd and 24th sts. Walk about 8 blocks uphill from Dupont Circle Metro, or take an N-series Metrobus up Massachusetts Ave. or catch a cab. Tues–Sun 10am–4pm. Closed major holidays. Admission charged.*

World War II Memorial (p. 88) NATIONAL MALL A long-overdue memorial, opened in mid-2004.... *Tel 202/619-7222. www.nps. gov/nwwm. In the middle of the Mall between Lincoln Memorial and Washington Monument. Smithsonian Metro. Daily 24 hours. Free admission.*

GETTING

OUTSIDE

Basic Stuff

There's plenty to do outside when you're inside the Capital Beltway. Washington has lots of parkland. And D.C.'s weather makes outdoor recreation comfortable—or at least plausible—most of the year. The first really cold and snowy winter weather usually doesn't arrive till January, and usually, it's gone before March. The oppressive heat, humidity, and frequent thunderstorms of July and August may make you want to stay inside. But, if you take it easy, you can still mosey around the green spaces and lounge under the trees—except during those thunderstorms, of course.

As you'd expect for the national government's company town, Washington makes a federal case out of outdoor recreation. Most of the city's parklands—even little vest-pocket parks—belong to the federal government. Rock Creek Park, one of the largest urban parks in the country, is run by the National Park Service. The Department of Agriculture takes care of the vast National Arboretum. The pathways traversing the National Mall are popular running trails—in the morning, evening, and around lunchtime. The Mall—"America's lawn"—also is the best place in town to pick up a game of something a bit more physical than hardball politics—softball and volleyball being especially big vote-getters.

GETTING OUTSIDE

The Lowdown

Leaving the city behind in Rock Creek Park...
Extending from the mouth of Rock Creek at the Potomac River beside Georgetown all the way to Washington's northwestern border with Maryland, **Rock Creek Park** (Tel 202/895-6070; www.nps.gov/rocr) takes up 1,755 acres of D.C. real estate, 4% of the entire city. (You can download a terrific interactive map at www.nps.gov/rocr/ROCRmap1.pdf.) It's more than twice the size of New York's Central Park. On a map the park looks something like an IV bag—the narrow southern tip limited to a strip of land on either side of the creek, bulging to more than a mile wide in the north. Rock Creek Park also serves as something of a socioeconomic boundary: West of the park, running to the Potomac and the Maryland border, are the affluent, mostly white neighborhoods of Northwest Washington. Affluence defines many of the neighborhoods immediately east of the park as well. But fewer of the residents are white. And as you continue to

travel further east, the neighborhoods become less white and less affluent.

Congress established the park in 1890, and President Teddy Roosevelt, the great outdoorsman, used the place for vigorous hikes. Even today, some of the park's less-traveled roads can make you feel like you're winding through the rural mountains of West Virginia. High-traffic jogging and bike paths run the length of the park. On holidays and weekends, portions of **Beach Drive** are closed to cars and become the exclusive property of bicyclists, in-line skaters, walkers, runners, and parents pushing strollers and carriages. The drive is closed from Broad Branch Road to Military Road, from Picnic Grove 10 to Wise Road, and from West Beach Drive to the D.C.–Maryland border from 7am to 7pm holidays and from 7am Saturday to 7pm Sunday on weekends. If you drive on Beach Drive on weekdays, you, too, can participate in one of D.C.'s favorite outdoor sports: playing chicken with spandex-suited cyclists who are ferociously determined not to use the bike path that runs parallel to the roadway. *Be warned:* There's a disturbingly high chance that the bike rider you're about to slam into is a lawyer.

All that's free, of course, but Rock Creek Park also has recreational facilities you can pay for. The 18-hole **Rock Creek Golf Course** (Tel 202/882-7332; www.golfdc.com/gc/rc/news.cfm; 16th and Rittenhouse sts. NW; dawn–dusk) is short but requires some attention to accuracy. **Rock Creek Park Horse Center** (Tel 202/362-0117; www.rockcreekhorsecenter.com; 5100 Glover Rd. NW, just south of Military Rd.) runs escorted trail rides through the park (Tues–Thurs 1:30pm; Sat–Sun noon, 1:30, and 3pm). Reservations are required, at least a week ahead for weekend rides. You can reserve 1 of 5 indoor and 25 outdoor tennis courts for a fee at the **Rock Creek Tennis Center** (Tel 202/722-5949; www.rockcreektennis.com; 16th and Kennedy sts. NW; daily 7am–11pm). Three outdoor courts are available near **Pierce Mill** (Tel 202/722-5949; Park Rd. NW just east of Beach Dr.). The courts are free, first-come-first-served, and unattended at **Montrose Park** (near R St. NW between 30th and 31st sts. in upper Georgetown). The Park Service asks players to limit their play to an hour when others are waiting.

Among the best deals in Washington are the free summer performances by the Washington Shakespeare Theater and the National Symphony Orchestra at the

Barron Amphitheater (Tel 202/426-0486; www. rocr/cbarron; 16th St. and Colorado Ave. NW). Amphitheater hosts paid performances as well. If got kids along, head for **Rock Creek Nature Center** 2/895-6070; www.nps.gov/rocr/naturecenter; 5200 Rd. NW, south of Military Rd.; Wed–Sun 9am–5pm; closed Jan 1, July 4, Thanksgiving, Dec 25), where they can investigate a working beehive, watch true-life adventure films, take nature hikes, visit a small planetarium, and play in the hands-on Discovery Room. You may be mystified by the little **Joaquin Miller Cabin** (Beach Dr. just north of the Military Rd. overpass). Miller, the 19th- and early-20th-century "Poet of the Sierras," was a colorful adventurer who lived in this cabin on Meridian Hill near Adams Morgan in the 1880s during one of his many stints away from California. The Park Service moved the cabin here, where it now serves as the site of outdoor poetry readings at 7:30pm Tuesdays in June and July (www.wordworks dc.com/miller_cabin.html). The readings are followed by a reception at a nearby church, a benefit of putting your wilderness cabin in the heart of a big city.

Tranquil spots just away from the fray... One of the strangest places on Capitol Hill is a roofless red brick structure called the **Summer House** (www.aoc.gov/cc/grounds/art_arch/summer_house.cfm; Union Station Metro). Created by famed landscape architect Frederick Law Olmsted, who was hired by Congress in 1874 to spruce up the Capitol grounds, it's essentially a grotto with fountains and waterfalls, sort of burrowed into the hillside northwest of the Senate wing of the Capitol. Olmstead intended it to provide rest and refreshment to Capital Hill pedestrians. He wanted to build a second version on the House side of the Hill, but quite a few congressmen didn't like the first one, so that plan was never realized. **Bartholdi Park** (www.usbg.gov/gardens/barthodli-park.cfm; in the triangle created by 1st St. SW and Independence and Washington aves.; Federal Center Southwest Metro) focuses on the Bartholdi Fountain, a massive relic of the Gilded Age that was designed in 1878 by Statue of Liberty sculptor Frederic Bartholdi. In nice weather you can stroll and sit in the park's gardens, which are part of the **U.S. Botanic Garden** across the avenue. A favorite spot for brown-bagging bureaucrats, **Pershing Park** (14th St. and Pennsylvania Ave. NW; Metro Center Metro) offers picnic tables, fountains, and a protected setting to deaden the traffic noise. In the winter, for a fee, you can ice-skate (Tel 202/737-6938; www.pershingparkicerink.com). One of the best places to sit and contemplate Washington is on a bench in **Lafayette Square** (across Pennsylvania Ave. NW from the White House; McPherson Sq. Metro). Ugly makeshift security barriers mar the view nowadays, but you can pretend they're not there and take in the White House with the Washington Monument popping up over the roof in the distance. Historic 19th-century houses line the west side of the square. According to the National Park Service, the square boasts "the highest density of squirrels per square acre ever recorded." Office workers on lunch hour and demonstrators seeking the president's attention claim equal rights to share the square. Say hello to William Thomas and Concepcion Picciotto, who have spent a substantial portion of the last quarter century protesting for peace here.

The garden behind the **Organization of American States' Art Museum of the Americas** (201 18th St. NW, at Constitution Ave. NW; Farragut West Metro) is serene. Its centerpiece is a pool guarded by the Aztec god of flowers, Xochipili. To get away from the Georgetown bustle, duck into the garden at **The Old Stone House** (Tel 202/426-6851; www.nps.gov/rocr/oldstonehouse; 3051 M St. NW, between 30th and 31st sts.; Georgetown Connection shuttle bus or 30-series Metrobus), one of the very oldest buildings in Washington, erected in 1765. In Georgetown's northern reaches the **Dumbarton Oaks Gardens** (Tel 202/339-6401; www.doaks.org; R St. NW at 31st St.; Georgetown Connection shuttle bus or 30-series Metrobus; Tues–Sun mid–Mar through Oct 2–6pm, admission charged; Nov to mid-Mar 2–5 pm, admission free) bloom from mid-March into October. The garden closes in bad weather, on federal holidays, and December 24. A garden off Massachusetts Avenue NW, north of 30th Street, marks the **Khalil Gibran Memorial,** which honors the Lebanese-American writer.

A park with a past... Neighborhood residents cast out the drug dealers and brought good people back to **Meridian Hill Park** (Tel 202/895-6070; www.nps.gov/rocr/cultural/merid.htm; between 15th, 16th, W, and Euclid sts. NW; U St./Cardozo Metro), which is also sometimes referred to as Malcolm X Park in honor of the civil rights activist. People come to this hill to take in the panoramic view of Washington, to play soccer, or to gaze in wonder at the eclectic collection of statuary. It's still wisest to visit during the daytime. The park's most striking feature is a waterfall that cascades through 13 basins and that looks longer from the bottom than it actually is. That's because of some optical gerrymandering: Each basin is larger than the one above it. Joan of Arc riding her horse here is Washington's only equestrienne statue. It's a copy of a statue at the Cathedral of Rheims in France and was a 1922 gift from the "Ladies of France in Exile in New York." Also among the park's eclectic collection of sculpture are Dante Alighieri, author of *The Divine Comedy*, and James Buchanan, who is remembered—if he's remembered at all—as our only bachelor president.

GETTING OUTSIDE

Exploring the urban wilderness... Theodore Roosevelt Island Park (Tel 703/289-2500; www.nps.gov/this; off the northbound lanes of the George Washington Memorial Pkwy. just north of Theodore Roosevelt Memorial Bridge) is a swatch of wilderness (well, not really wilderness) within Washington's city limits. The island sits in the middle of the Potomac, an easy George-Washington-dollar's-throw from the Kennedy Center, Georgetown, and Virginia's Rosslyn business district. One reason it's so unspoiled is that it's so hard to get to. From D.C., take Constitution Avenue west. Follow signs to I-66, the Theodore Roosevelt Bridge, and then the George Washington Parkway. *Immediately* after you enter the parkway, watch for the park's parking lot on your right. Once you get parked, you walk across another bridge to the island. The most direct way to get here, actually, is by canoe from the Thompson Boat Center (see "Boats and bikes by the hour," below). Fishing, bird-watching, and strolling the 2.5 miles of flat trails are the principal activities on the island. The primary unnatural thing here is the monument to TR—an outsized statue at a vast plaza surrounded by forest that suggests the worship site of some strange woodland cult.

Sort of a mini–Rock Creek Park, the 183-acre **Glover Archbold Park** is a narrow swath of forest and trails that stretches from the C&O Canal in Georgetown to Van Ness Street in Upper Northwest. The **Glover Archbold Trail** runs 3.1 miles from one end of the park to the other. The southern trail head is at the Potomac near Canal Road's intersection with MacArthur Boulevard. The northern trail head is east of 41st Street on Van Ness. There's also access from several cross streets.

The nation's garden... The **National Arboret**
(Tel 202/245-2726; www.usna.usda.gov; 3501 New York
Ave. NE, west of Bladensburg Rd.; daily 8am–5pm; closed
Dec 25; free admission) is well worth the drive, especially
from late April into late May, when the blooming azaleas
will rock your eyeballs and blow your mind. Most visitors
drive to the arboretum and use their cars to explore the 9
miles of road through the 446-acre Agriculture Department research facility and living museum. It's also a great
place to ride a bike. You can get here by the X6 Metrobus
(www.usna.usda.gov/Information/metrosched.html),
which makes a 17-minute express run to and from Union
Station every 40 minutes on weekends and holidays. The
first bus leaves Union Station at 7:55am; the last leaves
arboretum at 4:56pm. For a fee, you can take a tram tour
on weekends and holidays from mid-April through mid-
October at 11:30am, 1, 2, 3, and 4pm, and sometimes
10:30am. The National Bonsai and Penjing Museum (daily
10am–3:30pm) shows off these arts of training miniature
trees (Bonsai is the Japanese technique; Penjing is Chinese)
in three pavilions. The National Herb Garden throws in
grapevines and roses for good measure. You'll also notice
(how could you not?) a grove of 22 Corinthian columns
standing at attention with nothing to support. They were
transplanted here after being removed from the Capitol
during a renovation. You'll think you've stumbled onto the
ruins of a lost civilization—and sometimes Washington
does feel that way. Check this Web page to find out what's
blooming while you're in town: www.usna.usda.gov/
Education/blooming.html.

Cruising D.C. (no, not that kind)... You become
another tourist's wackiest Washington memory when you
waddle down the street in **DC Ducks'** amphibious tour
vehicles (Tel 202/832-9800; www.historictours.com/
washington). These converted World War II troop-and-
supply carriers drive past major Washington sights, and
then dip into the Potomac for a cruise. The tour guide's
patter includes urging passengers to quack at passersby.
The 90-minute tours leave from Union Station on Capitol
Hill. Duck season is mid-April through October (daily
10am–4pm; closed Sun of Memorial Day weekend, July
4th, and the day of the Marine Corps Marathon). No
advance reservations. Seating is first-come, first-served.

Once you step aboard the **Dandy** (Tel 703/683-6076; www.dandydinnerboat.com; 0 Prince St., at the river in Alexandria), you'll be on the water till you disembark at the end of your lunch, brunch, or dinner-with-dancing cruise. The boat sails from Alexandria to Georgetown and back, offering river's-eye views of the monuments, memorials, and waterfronts. Men must wear jackets for dinner and Sunday brunch. "Dressy casual" attire is required for lunch.

From mid-April to mid-September you can cruise the **C&O Canal** on a mule-drawn canal boat (www.nps.gov/choh/boatrides/publicboatrides.html). Boats ply the canal from Georgetown (Tel 202/653-5190; 1057 Thomas Jefferson St. NW, south of M St.; Foggy Bottom/GWU Metro, Georgetown Connection shuttle bus, or 30-series Metrobus) and Great Falls (Tel 301/767-3714; 11710 MacArthur Blvd., Potomac, MD, 15 miles west of Georgetown). Boatmen (and women) clad in 19th-century garb provide running commentary about the sights and about life on the canal when it was an important mode of transporting people and products.

Happy historic trails for you... Washington has loads of scenic running/jogging/hiking/walking/cycling trails in historically significant locales. You can run in a circle—or at least in an ellipse—on **The Ellipse** (.6 mile, just south of the White House). For a long, sort-of-circular route, go round and round the **Tidal Basin** (1.8 miles). Walkers, runners, and cyclists share the often-crowded path/sidewalk that parallels **Rock Creek Parkway** and **Beach Drive** from the Potomac north into Maryland. Enjoy breathing the fumes from passing cars as you get your aerobic exercise; **Rock Creek Park**'s less-beaten paths are more pleasant. The **C&O Canal Towpath** begins near the **C&O Canal National Historical Park**'s Georgetown visitor center at 1057 Thomas Jefferson St. NW, south of M Street. It travels northwest for 184.5 miles to Cumberland, Maryland. Most of the route is wide and composed of hard-packed dirt, making it ideal for bicycle and foot traffic. The **Mount Vernon Trail** runs 18.5 miles along the Virginia bank of the Potomac from Theodore Roosevelt Island to George Washington's estate at Mount Vernon. Like the Rock Creek Parkway trail, this one parallels a busy road, the George Washington Memorial Parkway. But it doesn't always run right along the road, the views across the river to the

Washington skyline are terrific, and the riverside becomes ever-more idyllic as you move further south of Alexandria.

Boats and bikes by the hour... Strategically situated where Rock Creek flows into the Potomac, the **Thompson Boat Center** (Tel 202/333-9543; www.thompsonboatcenter. com; Virginia Ave. NW, west of Rock Creek Pkwy.; roughly mid-April into Oct, daily 8am–6pm, till 7pm in summer) rents canoes, kayaks, rowing shells, sailboats, and bikes. **The Boathouse at Fletcher's Cove** (Tel 202/244-0461; www.fletcherscove.com; off Canal Rd. northwest of Reservoir Rd.; early Mar through fall daily 7am–7pm) rents bikes, rowboats, kayaks, and canoes and sells fishing supplies and refreshments. You'll find **Jack's** under the Key Bridge in Georgetown (Tel 202/337-9642; www.jacksboat house.com; 3500 K St. NW; Mon–Fri 10am–8pm, Sat–Sun 8am–8pm; closed Dec–Mar). Jack rents kayaks and canoes. For a slow, energy-draining cruise around the Tidal Basin, rent one of those wacky, flat-bottomed, pedal-powered boats from **Tidal Basin Paddle Boats** (Tel 202/479-2426; 1501 Maine Ave. SW, at 15th St.; daily 10am–6pm; closed Columbus Day–Mar 14). You get a great water view of the Jefferson Memorial. And, if you can get the kids to pedal, they'll fall asleep *really fast* that night.

For land transit alone, **Better Bikes** (Tel 202/293-2080; www.betterbikesinc.com) will deliver a rental bike to you, along with trail map, lock, and helmet. Not only that, these guys never close. If you want somebody to tell you where to go, **Bike the Sites** (Tel 202/842-2453; www.bikethesites. com; 12th St. NW between Pennsylvania and Constitution aves.; Federal Triangle Metro) offers guided bike tours (Mar–May and Sept–Nov Thurs–Tues 10am–1pm and 2:30–5:30pm; late Mar–May and Sept–early Nov also 6:30–9:30pm; June–Aug Thurs–Tues 10am–1pm, 2:30–5:30pm, and 7–10pm, Fri also at 6–8:30pm; Sat also 9:30am–noon and 6–8:30pm; no tours Dec–Feb). You can rent from a variety of bikes to take on your own, as well (Mon–Sat 9am–6pm, till 9pm in summer; Sun 9:30am–6pm). In conjunction with Scootaround Mobility Solutions (Tel 888/441-7575; www.scootaround.com), Bike the Sites also rents "mobility scooters"—sit-upon powered vehicles for persons with disabilities or those who just don't want to pedal.

GETTING OUTSIDE

Par for the course... Our great golfing presidents—Ike, Gerry Ford, and Bill Clinton—have all been more likely to play at exclusive country clubs, but D.C. does offer a few public golf courses for the masses. Most scenic (and crowded) is the **East Potomac Golf Course** (Tel 202/554-7660; www.capitalcitygolf.net/gc/ep/gc.htm; 972 Ohio Dr. SW, in East Potomac Park; Memorial Day–Labor Day daily 6am–8:30pm, rest of year 6:30am–6pm). It has one 18-hole course, one 9-hole course, and one 9-hole par-3 course, plus a driving range (summer Wed–Mon 6am–10pm, Tues 10am–10:30pm; rest of year 7am–8pm, Tues 10am–9pm) and a miniature golf course that managed to get itself on the National Register of Historic Places (summer Tues–Sun 11am–7pm, Mon 2:30–7pm; closed rest of year). Great views of the Washington skyline. Line up a shot with the Washington Monument. To play links that tell a significant story about American history, head for **Langston Golf Course** (Tel 202/397-8638; www.golfdc.com/gc/lng/golf course.htm; Benning Rd. NE at 26th St.; daily dawn–dusk), just south of the National Arboretum. Langston was opened in 1939, the fruit of a campaign by black golfers for a place to play 18 holes in the then-segregated, thoroughly Southern Washington area. Blacks could play only on a 9-hole course, located, at that time, on the National Mall. Otherwise, they had to travel to Northern cities—as far as Philadelphia, New York, Boston, or Pittsburgh—to find integrated courses. Langston offers 18 holes, golf lessons, golf shop, driving range, putting green, and snack bar. There's also the 18-hole **Rock Creek Golf Course;** see the Rock Creek Park section at the beginning of this chapter.

Good skates... Because acrobatic in-line skating can destroy property as well as break bones, many plazas, parks, and memorials post signs specifically banning it. But you can still merrily roll along the bike paths in Rock Creek Park and along the Potomac River.

In winter, ice skaters can glide (or fall) at two picturesque outdoor rinks in central D.C. Near the White House is the **Pershing Park** rink (Tel 202/737-6938; www.pershingparkicerink.com; 14th St. and Pennsylvania Ave. NW; Metro Center Metro). Across 7th Street from the National Gallery of Art's West Building on the Mall, you'll find the **Sculpture Garden Ice Rink** (Tel 202/289-3360;

www.nga.gov/ginfo/skating.htm; between Constitution Ave. NW, Madison Dr., and 7th and 9th sts.; Archives–Navy Memorial Metro).

Sportin' life on the Mall... To fall into casual pickup games, there's no place better than the **National Mall,** particularly west of 17th Street. You'll find volleyball courts, softball fields, and even a polo ground. Anywhere on the giant lawn that grows between the Capitol and the Potomac south of the White House, you'll find impromptu games of Frisbee, touch football, soccer, and rugby. Sometimes lawmakers' staffs play here for pride and bragging rights.

Go fly a kite... The open space around the **Washington Monument** is prime kite-flying territory. At the beginning of the Cherry Blossom festival in late March each year, the Smithsonian throws its annual Kite Festival here. See www.kitefestival.org.

Spy the friendly skies... Watch airplanes take off and land at National Airport from two inauspiciously named spots along the Potomac: **Gravelly Point** and **Daingerfield Island,** both on the east side of the George Washington Memorial Parkway. At Gravelly, barely north of the airport's main runway, you'll feel you can reach up and touch the planes. Daingerfield, a bit further away to the south of the runways, gives you a wider view of the airport and the D.C. skyline beyond. There's a boat slip at Gravelly from which you can begin an on-the-water exploration of the area—if you've BYOB (brought your own boat). On Daingerfield you'll find the **Washington Sailing Marina** (Tel 703/548-9027; www.washingtonsailingmarina.com), the **Indigo Landing** Southern and seafood restaurant (Tel 703/548-0001; www.indigolanding.com), picnic tables, and parking for hikers and cyclists exploring the Mount Vernon Trail. Rent bikes daily from 9am to 5pm all year and sailboats from 11am to 5pm from spring to mid-October. You must have on-the-water certification or pass a written test at the Marina.

Basic Stuff

Although shopoholics wouldn't put Washington high on their list of destinations, there's plenty to capture the fancy of visitors who overdose on the National Mall and crave a close encounter with a mall of another type.

What to Buy

Books, magazines, treatises, manuals. Washingtonians are readers, with plenty of busy newsstands and world-renowned bookstores to support their habit. Washington is, of course, a major stop on the author's tour circuit, and "signed by the author" volumes abound. For book signings and readings, check the listings in the "Book World" supplement to Sunday's *Washington Post* or in the weekly *Washington City Paper*, which lists them in the "Books" area of its "Events" section.

The business of Washington is politics, and the most locally relevant gift items are politically oriented souvenirs and memorabilia sold in the city's huge array of museum gift shops and specialty stores. "Property of White House"–type souvenirs are in large supply. History is everywhere, too, and you can buy all manner reproductions and commemoratives. The Smithsonian's varied shops are noteworthy for their wide selections catering to every age and budget (astronaut ice cream at the Air and Space Museum is a perennial bestseller for children). During December, droves of Washingtonians and visitors head to Decatur House for the latest annual-issue White House Christmas ornament.

Target Zones

Downtown D.C. is no longer the shopping hub it was in the 1950s when seven fine department stores anchored major blocks. Although some chic shopping can be found in the neighborhood around Connecticut and L streets as well as eclectic shopping farther north on Connecticut Avenue around trendy Dupont Circle, serious shoppers head for other parts of town. The oldest section of the District, Georgetown, boasts the densest concentration of antiques shops and art galleries, which radiate out from the main intersection of Wisconsin Avenue and M Street. Shoppers craving luxury goods will find many new choices, from designer-clothing boutiques to the high-end home-furnishings shops in Cady's Alley. Georgetown also appeals to the young and the restless with stores selling biker boots, organic beauty products, vintage comic books, movie posters, and exotic clothing. Georgetown University students rub elbows with out-of-town celebrities and tons of tourists in this enclave of shops and restaurants. Georgetown Park, a four-story mall encrusted with Victorian glitz and adjacent to the C&O Canal, is the spot for concentrated recreational shopping. Drop by its ground-level concierge office to pick up free directories to neighborhood antiques shops, galleries, and other points of interest.

Designers and discounters cohabit in the Friendship Heights/Chevy Chase neighborhood straddling the D.C.–Maryland border along Wisconsin Avenue. Two small malls—Mazza Gallerie and Chevy Chase Pavilion—anchor two corners of the Wisconsin–Western avenues intersection. In or nearby these malls are Filene's Basement, T.J. Maxx, and Loehmann's for bargain hunters, and stores of the Saks/Tiffany's/Neiman Marcus ilk when money is no object. The new Chevy Chase Center, which opened in 2005, added top fashion names such as Barneys New York Co-op, Gucci, Jimmy Choo, and Louis Vuitton.

Two spots on Capitol Hill are worth a look if you're in the neighborhood. Historic Union Station, where the city's passenger trains arrive and depart, houses multilevel shopping in an architectural masterpiece. Skip the chain stores and head for the East Hall and West Hall to buy American and international crafts, classier-than-average souvenirs, toys, and gifts. Eastern Market, a Victorian-era market building, still houses stands for vendors selling fresh produce, meats, cheeses, baked goods, and flowers. Some of the city's chefs shop here. For out-of-towners, however, it's the Sunday flea market adjacent to and across from the 130-year-old building that's the big draw.

Washington's most ethnically diverse neighborhood is Adams Morgan, where shoppers scour import shops, unusual clothing boutiques, and secondhand stores. The U Street Corridor is the new up-and-coming neighborhood with funky and fancy stores, notably some with unusual home furnishings.

In Old Town Alexandria, Virginia, buildings of about the same vintage as Georgetown house a similar assemblage of galleries, antiques shops, and one-of-a-kind boutiques. For something completely different, there's Takoma Park, Maryland. Born in 1884 as a "railroad suburb" of Washington, it has evolved into a multiracial, nuclear-free bastion of 1960s hippiedom, sometimes referred to as the "People's Republic of Takoma Park." A funky collection of stores ranges around the Carroll Avenue shopping district, a short walk from the Takoma station on Metro's Red Line, and the area's best farmers' market germinates on a closed street here on Sunday from March through Thanksgiving.

SHOPPING

● ●

SHOPPING ON THE MALL, NOT AT THE MALL

The Smithsonian claims that to see everything its museums on the National Mall have to offer, you'd have to view thousands of items every day of your life. Its numerous gift shops have almost that much available for purchase. The price range fits every budget. Kids can buy souvenirs for less than $3, and adults can score a diamond necklace for $2,500. All the merchandise is at least tangentially related to the collection—e.g., crystal growing kits in the Natural History Museum, kites and model airplanes in Air and Space.

Tip: Before you leave home, go to www.smithsonianstore.com for a sneak peek at the goods, and consider becoming a Smithsonian member for as little as $19. With your membership, you get 10% off all your purchases for a year—from the shops, catalog, or website—plus 12 issues of Smithsonian magazine, discounts on the IMAX movies and planetarium tickets, and other perks. And you'll have the satisfaction of supporting these museums, which are already a great bargain: Admission is free.

● ●

Bargain Hunting

For a bargain orgy, Washingtonians head south to Virginia and Potomac Mills (Tel 703/490-5948, 800/VA-MILLS; www. potomacmills.com; off I-95, exit 158B), near Dale City, 30 miles from downtown D.C. A "super-regional" outlet and off-price mall of more than 200 stores and eateries, offerings include Washington's famed G-Street Fabrics and outlets for Nordstrom's and Saks Fifth Avenue. IKEA, the massive Swedish furnishings store, which used to be in the mall, is now across the street, and many other discounters have clustered in the immediate area of the mall. Millions of shoppers flock to Potomac Mills each year, making it one of the biggest tourist magnets in metropolitan Washington. If you go on the week-end, it will seem they've all come on the same day. You can skip your morning workout because all the stores are on one floor, and it's more than a mile walk from one end to the other.

Hours of Business

Most stores in D.C. are open daily (except Sun in some cases) from midmorning to early evening. Shops open later in the neighborhoods with lively nightlife. Best bet: Call ahead.

Sales Tax

D.C. charges 5.75%; Maryland, 5%; and Virginia, 4.5%.

The Lowdown

Books for special-interest groups... Near Dupont Circle, **Lambda Rising** claims to stock virtually every gay/lesbian book in and out of print. **ADC Map Store** is cartography heaven, containing topographic, nautical, decorative, and road maps, plus travel guides and gadgets. **Kramerbooks & Afterwords Cafe** in Dupont Circle proclaims it has served latte to the literati since 1976. The food, full bar, and live music are all good enough to attract non-readers, and the all-night hours on weekends make it popular with insomniacs. **Reiter's Bookstore** near George Washington University is an earnest nerdatorium that stocks thousands of scientific and technical titles—computers, medicine, law, science—plus a science section for kids and humorous T-shirts. Looking for a copy of *Rural Realignment in South Saharan Africa?* You'll find it, along with hundreds of other reports and technical documents in many tongues, plus travel gear, at the **World Bank InfoShop.**

Political connections... If you want to look the part, head to **America's Spirit** at Union Station, where you'll find polo shirts and other apparel bearing the insignias of staffers for the White House, the crew of Air Force One, and shirts with National Security Council, FBI, and CIA logos. The **Human Rights Campaign Store and Action Center** in Dupont Circle caters to the political—and whimsical—interests of the gay and lesbian community. While you're there, you can send a message via e-mail to your member of Congress.

Historical interest... The **Old Print Gallery** in Georgetown sells pieces of history in the form of the area's largest selection of antique prints and maps. Views of Washington as a country town, images of historical events, and sweeping cosmopolitan vistas help to adjust your perspective on D.C.

Hippie-dippy-dom... Head to Takoma Park for out-of-the-mainstream items. **House of Musical Traditions,** a nationally known empire of unpluggedness (folk, ethnic, blues, jazz), sells musical instruments from around the world, new and used CDs and tapes, and sheet music. Go bead-crazy, baby, at Dupont Circle's **Beadazzled,** which carries a collection of Indonesian and Indian crafts and textiles, North African jewelry, handmade goods, and a collection of loose beads ranging from darling $1 numbers to $150 Indonesian manik-manik beads. If you like your goods to be organic, try **Habitat** in the U Street Corridor. Jewelry and home accents are made from organically grown wood and leather, as well as glass, metal, or shell.

Alternative art-gazing... If you'd like to stray from pre-dictable art-museum offerings, try hitting the **Torpedo Factory** in Alexandria (yes, this was an actual World War II torpedo factory), where the public can watch artists at work in more than 80 design studios. Chitchat with cre-ators while they work, or fall in love with a piece and make it yours.

Crafty design... Union Station's **Appalachian Spring** has earned a national reputation for selling crafts, not just from Appalachian artisans but from all over the United States. Downtown's **Pangea Artisan Market and Café,** a project of the World Bank, offers shopping, dining, and education. Sales of these high-quality crafts from all over the world help create sustainable livelihoods for the artisans in devel-oping nations. Scan the bar code of an object at Pangea's computer kiosk to learn about the people who made it. Since 1938, the **Indian Craft Shop,** housed in the Depart-ment of the Interior, has been purveying Native American crafts from over 40 tribal areas. The colors and lights in **go mama go!** in the U Street Corridor will lure you in for a look at the housewares and gifts from around the globe.

The other side of the Hill... Seven blocks east of the Capitol, in the heart of Capitol Hill, stands **Eastern Mar-ket,** more than 130 years old and the last remaining D.C. public market. It was part of Pierre L'Enfant's plans for the city. The market proper is old-fashioned, with butchers, bakers, greengrocers, and flower growers. On Sunday, an outdoor flea market offers arts and crafts, antiques, jewelry, and international handmade goods. **Pulp,** on Pennsylvania Avenue, will amuse you with hip stationary, political paper dolls, weird greeting cards, and other assorted oddities.

Incredible edibles... **Dean & Deluca Café,** an outpost of New York's fancy-schmancy gourmet foodery, sits next to Georgetown Park mall in the historic Markethouse building.

If you can't wait to eat the goodies you've bought, you can sit down in the open-air dining area.

Kid stuff... Kids will go ape for **Discovery Channel Store Destination D.C.,** a science store/attraction in Union Square, with fossils and minerals, planes, science kits, and lots of gooey playthings. Adults who are fond of Discovery's array of TV shows will find amusements here, too. **Flights of Fancy,** on the upper level of the station, offers a wide array of games and toys in a small space.

Home suite home... Tucked amidst the art galleries of the Penn Quarter neighborhood, **Apartment Zero** has adopted that art gallery feel for its exhibits of ultracontemporary furniture and housewares by noted designers, all of which are for sale. In the U Street Corridor, **Muléh**'s Southeast Asian imports include furniture made by traditional craft methods to produce strikingly contemporary pieces; it has women's fashions as well. Muléh's neighbor, **Vastu,** or "the art of placement" in Sanskrit, combines modern furniture with original artwork; there are art receptions every couple of months. For more Victorian tastes, **The Brass Knob** in Adams Morgan carries a huge selection of architectural antiques salvaged from area homes.

Nifty gifties... Local favorite **Chocolate Moose** sells all manner of oddities, from purses resembling watering cans to shower curtains with political themes—and Belgian chocolates, too. Down in Alexandria, Washington's steamy summers often drive visitors indoors to Alexandria's **Christmas Attic,** in a historic building where you can fantasize about winter while choosing from a huge array of nutcrackers, Radko glass ornaments, and decorations from around the world. For Asian goods, **Ginza** in Dupont Circle sells all things Japanese, including a wide range of authentic kimonos.

The price is right... **Loehmann's,** an off-price mecca for men and women since the first store opened in Brooklyn in 1921, has one location in Upper Northwest D.C. The famous Back Room sells designer clothes at 30% to 65% off regular retail. The Swedish international chain **H&M** sells inexpensive, trendy clothes, both downtown and in Georgetown Park.

Map 8: Washington, D.C., Shopping

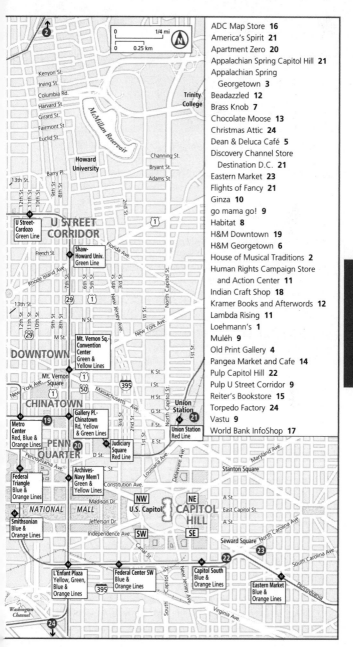

SHOPPING

The Index

See Map 8 on the previous page for all Shopping listings.

ADC Map Store (p. 143) DOWNTOWN Maps and atlases.... *Tel 202/628-2608. www.adcmap.com. 1636 I St. NW. Farragut W. or Farragut N. Metro. Mon–Thurs 8am–6:30pm; Fri 8am–5:30pm; Sat 11am–5pm.*

America's Spirit (p. 143) CAPITOL HILL No home should be without White House guest towels or an Air Force One polo shirt (even if they're actually made in Honduras).... *Tel 202/842-0540. www.americastore.com. 50 Massachusetts Ave. NE, in Union Station. Union Station Metro. (Also at Reagan National and Dulles airports.) Mon–Sat 10am–9pm; Sun noon–6pm.*

Apartment Zero (p. 145) PENN QUARTER Ultramodern home furnishings by international designers.... *Tel 202/628-4067. www. apartmentzero.com. 406 7th St. NW. Archives/Navy Memorial Metro. Wed–Sat 11am–6pm; Sun noon–5pm.*

Appalachian Spring (p. 144) CAPITOL HILL/GEORGETOWN Wide selection of fine American crafts.... Capitol Hill: *Tel 202/ 682-0505; 50 Massachusetts Ave. NE, in Union Station; Union Station Metro; Mon–Sat 10am–9pm, Sun noon–6pm.* Georgetown: *Tel 202/337-5780; 1415 Wisconsin Ave. NW; take Georgetown Connection shuttle bus Rte. 1 from Foggy Bottom/ GWU Metrorail station or take 30-series Metrobus; Mon–Fri 10am–8pm, Sat–Sun 10am–6pm.*

Beadazzled (p. 143) DUPONT CIRCLE Beads for all occasions plus one-of-a-kind crafts abound here.... *Tel 202/265-2323. www. beadazzled.net. 1507 Connecticut Ave. NW. Dupont Circle Metro. Mon–Sat 10am–8pm; Sun 11am–6pm.*

The Brass Knob (p. 145) ADAMS MORGAN Architectural antiques, from garden ornaments to chandeliers.... *Tel 202/332-3370. www.thebrassknob.com. 2311 18th St. NW. Take 98 Metrobus from Woodley Park–Zoo Metrorail Station. Mon–Sat 10:30am–6pm; Sun noon–5pm.*

Chocolate Moose (p. 145) DOWNTOWN Gifts and cards galore for the easily amused, and chocolate, too.... *Tel 202/463-0992. www.chocolatemoosedc.com. 1743 L St. NW. Farragut N. Metro. Mon–Sat 10am–6pm.*

Christmas Attic (p. 145) VIRGINIA Nutcrackers, Radko ornaments, and decorations from around the world, housed in a historic warehouse.... *Tel 703/548-2829 (800/881-0084). www.christmas attic.com. 125 S. Union St., Alexandria, VA. Mon–Sat 10am–9pm; Sun noon–6pm.*

Dean & Deluca Café (p. 144) GEORGETOWN Fabulous food and kitchenware, across from the Georgetown Park mall.... *Tel 202/ 342-2500. www.deandeluca.com. 3276 M St. NW. Take Georgetown Connection shuttle bus Rte. 2 from Dupont Circle or Rosslyn Metrorail Station. Mon–Sun 10am–8pm.*

Discovery Channel Store Destination D.C. (p. 145) CAPITOL HILL This attraction/retail store begs for you to explore your world.... *Tel 202/842-3700. www.discovery.com. 50 Massachusetts Ave. NE, in Union Station. Union Station Metro. Mon–Sat 10am–9pm; Sun noon–6pm.*

Eastern Market (p. 144) CAPITOL HILL Washington's Victorian-era market still offers fresh meats, seafood, produce, breads, flowers, and cheese, plus an outdoor flea market on Sunday.... *Tel 202/544-0083. www.easternmarket.net. 225 7th St. SE. Eastern Market Metro. South Hall Food Merchants: Tues–Sat 7am– 6pm; Sun 9am–4pm. Open Air Farmers' Line: Sat–Sun 8am–6pm. Market 5 Gallery: Tues–Fri 11am–5pm; Sat–Sun 8am–5pm. Market Festival Arts & Crafts Fair: Sat 10am–5pm. Flea Market: Sun 10am–5pm.*

Flights of Fancy (p. 145) CAPITOL HILL Toys galore, from kites to Playmobile.... *Tel 202/371-9800. 50 Massachusetts Ave. NE, in Union Station. Union Station Metro. Mon–Sat 10am–9pm; Sun noon–6pm.*

Ginza (p. 145) DUPONT CIRCLE Everything Japanese from fountains to kimonos.... *Tel 202/331-7991. www.ginzaonline.com. 1721 Connecticut Ave. NW. Dupont Circle Metro. Mon–Fri 11am– 7pm; Sat 11am–7:30pm; Sun noon–6pm.*

go mama go! (p. 144) U STREET CORRIDOR A huge array of international gifts and housewares.... *Tel 202/299-0850. www.go mamago.com. 1809 14th St. NW. U St./Cardozo Metro. Mon noon–7pm; Tues–Sat 11am–7pm; Sun noon–5pm.*

Habitat (p. 144) U STREET CORRIDOR Home accessories and jewelry that's organically correct.... *Tel 202/518-7222. www.habitat style.com. 1510 U St. NW. U St./Cardozo Metro. Mon–Sun noon–6pm and by appointment.*

H&M (p. 145) DOWNTOWN/GEORGETOWN From Sweden, a hip international chain store offering trendy, inexpensive clothing for the whole family.... *Downtown: Tel 202/347-3306; www.hm.com; 1025 F. St. NW, between 10th and 11th sts. Metro Center Metro; Mon–Sat 10am–8pm, Sun noon–6pm. Georgetown: Tel 202/298-6792; 3222 M St. NW; take Georgetown Connection shuttle bus from Foggy Bottom/GWU, Dupont Circle, or Rosslyn Metrorail station, or take 30-series Metrobus; Mon–Sat 10am–9pm, Sun 11am–6pm.*

House of Musical Traditions (p. 143) MARYLAND Folk and Irish/Celtic music store for albums, instruments, sheet music, lessons.... *Tel 301/270-9090. www.musicaltraditions.com. 7040 Carroll Ave., Takoma Park, MD. Takoma Metro. Tues–Sat 11am–7pm; Sun–Mon 11am–5pm.*

Human Rights Campaign Store and Action Center (p. 143) DUPONT CIRCLE Buy equality wear and contact your legislator, all in the same place.... *Tel 202/232-8621. www.hrc.org. 1629 Connecticut Ave. NW. Dupont Circle Metro. Mon–Sat 10am–9pm; Sun 11am–7pm.*

Indian Craft Shop (p. 144) FOGGY BOTTOM Some of the city's best examples of Native American crafts. Bring ID; it's inside the Interior Department.... *Tel 202/208-4056. www.indiancraftshop. com. 1849 C St. NW. Farragut W. Metro. Mon–Fri 8:30am–4:30pm; third Sat each month 10am–4pm.*

Kramerbooks & Afterwords Cafe (p. 143) DUPONT CIRCLE A bookstore and restaurant combined with live music and late hours.... *Tel 202/387-1400. www.kramers.com. 1517 Connecticut Ave. NW. Dupont Circle Metro. Daily 7:30am–1am; all night Fri and Sat.*

Lambda Rising (p. 143) DUPONT CIRCLE Gay and lesbian bookstore and cultural center.... *Tel 202/462-6969. www.lambda rising.com. 1625 Connecticut Ave. NW. Dupont Circle Metro. Sun–Thurs 10am–10pm; Fri–Sat 10am–midnight.*

Loehmann's (p. 145) UPPER NORTHWEST Designer clothes at big discounts in the famed Back Room.... *Tel 202/362-4733. www.loehmanns.com. 5333 Wisconsin Ave. NW. Friendship Heights Metro. Mon–Sat 10am–9:30pm; Sun 11am–6pm.*

Muléh (p. 145) U STREET CORRIDOR Two floors of dramatic home furnishings with an Asian flair plus a line of designer women's clothing.... *Tel 202/667-3440. www.muleh.com. 1831 14th St. NW. U St./Cardozo Metro. Tues–Sat 11am–7pm; Sun noon–5pm.*

Old Print Gallery (p. 143) GEORGETOWN The area's largest selection of antique prints and maps.... *Tel 202/965-1818. www.old printgallery.com. 1220 31st St. NW. Take Georgetown Connection shuttle bus from Foggy Bottom/GWU, Dupont Circle, or Rosslyn Metrorail station, or take 30-series Metrobus. Mon–Sat 10am–5:30pm.*

Pangea Artisan Market and Café (p. 144) DOWNTOWN A World Bank project to support artisans in developing countries; offers handbags, jewelry, table settings, and more.... *Tel 202/872-6432. www.pangeamarket.com. 2121 Pennsylvania Ave. NW. Farragut N. or Farragut W. Metro, or take 30-series Metrobus. Mon–Fri 7am–7pm; Sat 9am–5pm.*

Pulp (p. 144) CAPITOL HILL/U STREET CORRIDOR Stationary, gifts, and political statements to wear or hang on the wall.... *Capitol Hill: Tel 202/543-1924; www.pulpdc.com; 303 Pennsylvania Ave. SE; Capitol S. Metro; Mon–Fri 9:30am–7:30pm; Sat 10am–7pm; Sun noon–5pm. U St. Corridor: Tel 202/462-7857; 1803 14th St. NW; U St./Cardozo Metro; daily 11am–7pm.*

Reiter's Bookstore (p. 143) DOWNTOWN Well-stocked store for technical, medical, and scientific books.... *Tel 202/223-3327 (800/537-4314). www.reiters.com. 2021 K St. NW. Farragut W. Metro. Mon–Fri 8am–8pm; Sat 9:30am–6pm; Sun noon–5pm.*

Torpedo Factory (p. 144) VIRGINIA Explore 84 working artists' studios and six art galleries.... *Tel 703/838/4565. www.torpedo factory.org. 105 N. Union St., Alexandria, VA. King St. Metro, then DASH Bus east to waterfront. Daily 10am–5pm; open till 9pm on the second Thurs of every month for Art Night in Alexandria.*

Vastu (p. 145) U STREET CORRIDOR Modern furniture paired with original art works.... *Tel 202/234-8344. www.vastudc.com. 1829 14th St. NW. U St./Cardozo Metro. Tues–Sat 11am–7pm; Sun noon–5pm.*

World Bank InfoShop (p. 143) DOWNTOWN All the books you need to plan your own international development project.... *Tel 202/458-4500. www.worldbank.org/infoshop. 701 18th St. NW, at Pennsylvania Ave. Farragut W. Metro. Mon–Fri 9am–5pm.*

THE INDEX

SHOPPING

Basic Stuff

Despite conservative daytime appearances, D.C. really does know how to cut loose come sundown. And, because Washingtonians come from all over the country and all over the world, there's a scene for everyone: Capitol Hill bars for people who've left work to talk about work before turning in early; mammoth dance clubs where glow-stick-adorned ravers bounce happily till the sun comes up; hot gay clubs where shirtless men flaunt their gym-perfect physiques; live-music clubs, featuring everything from country to jazz; quiet, romantic cocktail lounges; hip hotels with hip hotel lounges. And there's no shortage of happy hours and special-feature nights. Hey, running the world's a tough job. No wonder Washington power brokers (and wannabes) need to party.

The Lay of the Land

The D.C. nightlife scene is scattered all over town. **Georgetown** is, in a sense, the most interesting area because it's such a study in contrasts. The quiet residential side streets are the most exclusive in Washington and house people whose names and faces are recognized around the world. Democratic presidential candidate John Kerry and Veep-wannabe John Edwards were Georgetown neighbors when they ran together in the 2004 election, for instance. Former secretary of state Madeleine Albright lives in the neighborhood, as do many other people who ran—or run—the government or influence the people who do. As the home of Georgetown University, Georgetown also is awash in student rooming houses and nightspots and other establishments that cater to people in their late teens and early 20s. M Street and Wisconsin Avenue, the main Georgetown thoroughfares, are lined with shops (tacky, exclusive, and hip), restaurants, and nightspots. They attract buttoned-down lobbyists, scruffy college kids, and common folk of all kinds out for a good time. Weekend nights, these streets and their sidewalks can be gridlocked.

Dupont Circle—probably as famous as Georgetown—is best known as the hub of D.C.'s large and active gay community. But its many shops, restaurants, and nightspots serve folks of all sexual persuasions, ages, and incomes. There are bars and restaurants worth talking about on Capitol Hill (and we will). But they tend to be more sedate, catering to Hill workers and residents.

NIGHTLIFE

Adams Morgan is the hottest real nightclubbing part of town, a compact, multicultural, multiethnic place where bar-hoppers cruise the streets looking for a good time. The up-and-coming nightlife areas are **U Street Corridor** and **Penn Quarter,** two very different neighborhoods. The area spreading out from U and 14th streets NW is spawning a growing number of clubs and eateries in a neighborhood that still requires caution after dark. Penn Quarter—bounded roughly now by Pennsylvania and Massachusetts avenues and 6th and 10th streets but quite likely to expand—has become a lively arts and entertainment center. Here you'll find galleries, restaurants, theaters, the big-crowd-magnet Verizon sports/concerts venue (nicknamed the Phone Booth under its previous appellation as the MCI Center), even a shamefully overpriced bowling alley nightspot. While much of the U Street Corridor area remains a shabby striver working its way up, Penn Quarter is sparkling and affluent. It, Georgetown, and Dupont Circle are essentially safe spots for nighttime play, as are the main streets of Adams Morgan and the most popular section of U Street itself. In all parts of the city, however, it pays to avoid alleys and dark streets at night.

Where to Get the Inside Scoop

Weekend, the *Washington Post*'s Friday entertainment tabloid, is the best source for up-to-the-minute news, reviews, and listings about concerts, clubs, films, theater, museums, galleries, and special events. Online, click on **City Guide** at the *Post*'s website, www.washingtonpost.com. The free weekly *Washington Blade* (www.washblade.com), the city's leading newspaper for homosexuals, reports serious news of importance to gays and lesbians and publishes comprehensive reporting and listing of gay/lesbian-oriented entertainment. *Washington City Paper* (www.washingtoncitypaper.com)—the free weekly alternative to the *Post*—offers its alternative take on the entertainment scene. Both freebies are found throughout the Washington area in bars, restaurants, hotels, bookstores, libraries, and other public venues.

Find out where to hear the blues in the night by checking the **D.C. Blues Society** website, www.dcblues.org. If your tastes run more to folk music and dance, the **Folklore Society of Greater Washington** will be happy to tell you what's happening (Tel 202/546-2228; www.fsgw.org).

NIGHTLIFE

Liquor Laws & Drinking Hours

The drinking age is 21, and most clubs that serve alcohol will ask to see ID before allowing young folks through the door. Some clubs admit those over 18 on a nonalcohol-drinking basis, distinguishing them from drinkers with hand stamps or wristbands. Others admit 18- to 20-year-olds only on certain nights or before certain hours. Call to find out before you go, because the burley guy at the door probably won't be interested in debating the matter.

The Lowdown

Special places after dark... The unique part of Washington's nightlife is the view. The Capitol, White House, monuments, and memorials gleam pure white in the glow of bright floodlights after dark. That's why flying into National Airport is such a thrill when your plane is landing at night from the northwest, floating over the Potomac, the Lincoln Memorial and Washington Monument gleaming below, the White House a little further in the distance, the Capitol dome shining across the river as the plane taxis on the runway after touching down. Even better is to climb Lincoln's steps and gaze down the entire length of Mall or to sit on Jefferson's steps and look across the Tidal Basin to the Washington Monument and the White House. In most cities, when you talk about nightlife, you're referring to restaurants, bars, lounges, clubs, and other commercial entertainment venues. Washington has all that, of course, in addition to its special views. And in some places, you can get everything at once. The **Sky Terrace,** for instance, is an open-air restaurant and bar on the top floor of the Hotel Washington, the closest hotel to the White House. From April through October, you can stop by for food or drink until 12:30am and gaze on the president's mansion nearby and other Washington landmarks in the not-too-far distance.

Carouse with the insiders... House staffers frequent **Bullfeathers** for several reasons, not least being its location in the shadows of the House office buildings. It's a noisy, friendly pub with reasonably good food at reasonably good prices and happy hour from 4 to 8pm every night but Sunday (when it's closed). A little further from the Capitol on

Pennsylvania Avenue, peaceniks and warmongers gather at the **Hawk 'n' Dove.** For one thing, it's got six rooms, so you don't have to look at people you despise. For another, it's a traditional post-softball-game retreat, where the losing representative's aides buy the beer for the winners. The **Capitol Lounge** draws House staffers to three rooms on Pennsylvania Avenue SE with sports-tuned televisions, a pool table, and political memorabilia—especially stuff associated with the only president to resign from office, Richard Nixon. Another true House hangout is the **Tune Inn,** also on Pennsylvania. It's a dive, but staff and representatives love it.

Over on the Senate side of the Hill, where lawmakers and their aides think of their digs as the "Upper Chamber," the upscale bar at **Bistro Bis** is a favorite hangout. The bar and its patrons are bright and brassy. (Well, actually, the bar is zinc, but you get the idea.)

The **Old Ebbitt Grill,** the **Round Robin Bar,** and downstairs at **The Occidental** will fulfill your fantasies about what insider drinking spots should look like, and you can easily bump into White House aides and other movers and shakers unwinding after a hard day of governing and influencing. All three sport lots of polished mahogany. The Occidental's walls are covered with pictures of famous and powerful folks who have wandered through over the last hundred years or so. Old Ebbitt, which dates to 1856 (in another address), displays artifacts collected over the decades, such as an antique clock, antique beer steins, and a walrus head that may have been bagged by Teddy Roosevelt (who is said to have been among several presidents who dined and/or drank at the saloon in an earlier location). The Round Robin, in the Willard Inter–Continental Washington hotel, also predates the Civil War and asserts that Sen. Henry Clay of Kentucky introduced Washington to the mint julep on its premises. That also would have been in an earlier building on the same site. But the current Willard is no spring chicken, dating as it does to 1901. The bar honors Clay with an annual Kentucky Derby party.

Where the international crowd lets down its hair...

It figures that Washington's nightlife would be as international as the rest of the town. Diplomats from around the world take temporary residence here. Hyphenated-American citizens of all ethnicities come here to ply the political trade. So, naturally, they spawn a market for international entertainment.

We'll start with the Irish, because they've been running much of the U.S. government for a long time now, especially on Capitol Hill. So it's no surprise that two of the Hill's most popular drinking spots are **Kelly's Irish Times** and **The Dubliner,** next door to each other near Union Station and thus particularly popular with those who work in the Senate and the journalists who cover them. Both serve up Irish food, Irish music, and Irish booze, and both have sidewalk tables in good weather. The Times attracts lots of college kids. The Dubliner enjoys a better rep for the eats, though people seem to go more for the burgers than the corned beef. Actually, in both places, they go more for the beer and the music—live every night at The Dubliner, Friday and Saturday at the Times.

At **Chi Cha Lounge,** which parties to the wee hours on U Street, folks sit on sofas, nibble Spanish tapas, sip Latin-American drinks, and puff on Middle Eastern water pipes. At **Habana Village,** founded by a Cuban ex-pat in Adams Morgan, you can eat Cuban food while listening to Latin music. Then you can dance—or take lessons if you need them. Salsa and merengue are taught Wednesday through Saturday nights.

99 bottles of beer... Well, actually, that's a pretty paltry sum if you frequent **The Brickskeller.** Your bus ride would have to be a lot, lot longer if you were to work your way through this Dupont Circle bar's beer list—more than 1,000 varieties and counting. This is a classic American tavern—exposed brick walls, red-and-white checkered tablecloths, classic rock on the jukebox, beer bottles and cans decorating the walls, and a surprisingly diverse menu. **Capitol City Brewing Company** doesn't have nearly as many beers as The Brickskeller, but then The Brickskeller doesn't make its own beers on-site. Cap City (go for beer, not spelling lessons) does, in historic buildings downtown and on Capitol Hill. These are modern, sparkling brewpubs of the type that welcome families with kids as well as dating couples and singles stopping by for a snort after work. Typical modern pub food.

Top spots for live music... The **9:30 Club**—a converted warehouse on a dingy-looking corner in the U Street Corridor area—has top-of-the-line musical acts, state-of-the-art sound, and...hardly any seats! Most patrons don't mind standing, because this is considered one of the best live-music venues in the city. Fans under 35 flock to catch the likes of Pink, Cat Power, Sheryl Crow, Smashing Pumpkins, Shawn Colvin, R.E.M., Red Hot Chili Peppers, Ice-T, Alanis Morissette...even, strange as it may seem, Tony Bennett. The 9:30 welcomes visitors of all ages, including teens who are served the music but not the alcohol. *Note:* 9:30 is open only when there's a performance. A top spot for indie rock, the **Black Cat** draws lots of folk who like to wear lots of black to another U Street Corridor–area warehouse. While the bill here periodically spotlights cult bands that have "death" or "black" or "war" in their names, all kinds of music can be found here on occasion, including jazz, swing, hip-hop, techno, and folk. Bright Eyes, the Roots, Cherry Poppin' Daddies, Foo Fighters, Korn, We Are Scientists, Yeah Yeah Yeahs, and—conceding nothing to nearby 9:30—Pete Seeger have been on the bill. Black Cat's eclecticism extends beyond the music. In addition to the large concert/dance hall, the Black Cat offers the Red Room, a lounge with pool tables, pinball machines, a jukebox, and a laid-back atmosphere. The Backstage hosts poetry readings and films. Food for Thought Cafe has edibles for vegans, vegetarians, and carnivores alike.

There is dancing, sometimes, in a portion of the **Birchmere,** but the primary activities in this Alexandria establishment are sitting and eating and drinking and listening to top-notch musicians. Birchmere's Band Stand has a dance floor that is used from time to time. The heart of the Birchmere, however, is the Music Hall, with 500 seats at tables where you order food and drink, keep quiet, and listen. Originally, the **Birchmere** was known for country and bluegrass music, personified by the locally grown and nationally influential Seldom Scene. But the roster now is broad and often big-time or formerly big-time: Garth Brooks, Jerry Jeff Walker, Tom Paxton, David Crosby, the Nitty Gritty Dirt Band, Crash Test Dummies, David Grisman, Nils Lofgren, Manhattan Transfer, Sweet Honey in the Rock, Roseanne Barr, Paula Poundstone, and—really and truly—Herman's Hermits.

NIGHTLIFE

Places to shake off that dance fever... Heaven is upstairs, and Hell is below at the Adams Morgan **Club Heaven & Hell,** just as you probably would anticipate. Also matching expectations, Hell is dark, creepy, and sports a pool table. This version of heaven, however, is not a place of blissful peace. It's a loud dance hall with different types of music playing on different nights. Thursday features an '80s dance party, Friday top-40 videos. Another Adams Morgan hot spot is **Chief Ike's Mambo Room,** where you'll find dancers of varied ages hopping to a variety of musical styles on the small dance floor. If things get too hot, you can retire to the terrace.

Built into an imposing old Penn Quarter bank building with plenty of marble in the floor, **Platinum** is a visually impressive dance club that attracts visually impressive dancers. The music usually revolves around R&B, hip-hop, and/or reggae. **Zanzibar,** on the Southwest waterfront, is a dance club with a view. Picture windows look out onto the boats tied up in the Washington Channel. Outdoor decks are opened in nice weather. This is a big place, with several rooms, bars, and dance floors on several levels. Tables and comfortable seating are scattered about. You'll find live and recorded music of various genres here, especially African, Latin, and jazz. Take salsa or cha-cha lessons from 7 to 8pm Wednesday. Enjoy champagne brunch from 11am to 4pm Sunday.

Painting the town rainbow... Long before Ennis and Jack rode up Brokeback Mountain, gay cowboys found compadres on Capitol Hill. That would be at **Remington's,** a country-western bar that offers Western dance lessons in case you don't know the Texas two-step. Mostly gay men mosey in here after a hard day on the Washington range. They're testament to Washington's large, active, and diverse gay community, which, though centered on Dupont Circle, lives throughout the city and its suburbs.

One of D.C.'s newest and most popular nightspots is **Halo,** which was named Washington's best gay and lesbian bar by voters in the *Washington Post*'s online readers' poll in 2005. It's a small, laid-back, comfortable place where people go to relax, talk, and sip cocktails. The bar features tropical drinks, and it went smoke-free by choice before the city's antismoking law was adopted in 2006. The spot is most popular with gay men but welcomes everyone.

Located near Logan Circle, it serves as a kind of neighborhood bar and attracts straight neighbors as well. Another comfortable neighborhood bar—this one back on Capitol Hill—attracts lesbians of all ages to its tables, pool table, and small dance floor. That would be **Phase One,** which differs greatly from Halo in its age—35 years old and still going strong.

A longtime magnet for attractive, upscale gay men is **JR's Bar and Grill,** near Dupont Circle. Popular television shows and movies are shown on the big screen at the bar. A balcony with pool tables offers an escape from the packed-like-sardines scene you'll often encounter on the main floor. Also big in Dupont Circle is **Omega DC,** another spot for men, with the action spread over two floors and several rooms, including a piano bar and a cigar/martini bar with a pool table. Known as a hangout for gays and lesbians, **Mr. Henry's** on Capitol Hill draws plenty of straight men and women, too. On Friday nights the attraction is live jazz on the second floor. The rest of the time, it's the comfortable, cozy atmosphere and the reasonably priced food.

Noting that Washington could claim just one bar dedicated to lesbians, Bridget Hieronymus created what she dubbed **A Different Kind of Ladies Night.** Actually "nights." These essentially are happy hours for women that Hieronymus organizes frequently in various bars around town. Hieronymus describes her goal as replicating a "hip, funky, martini-type bar where women could sit around and actually talk and mingle and have a drink." Drink specials and no cover charge are part of the deal. Info is at her website, www.adifferentkindofladiesnight.com.

All that jazz... **Blues Alley** really is in an alley, off Wisconsin Avenue in Georgetown, but the emphasis is more jazz than blues. In fact, it's been Washington's premier jazz club for 4 decades, presenting the biggest stars in a classic jazz club/supper club setting. Dizzy Gillespie, Charlie Byrd, Stanley Turrentine, Ahmad Jamal, and Ramsey Lewis cut live albums here. You're advised to make reservations and arrive early for dinner to get a decent spot in this first-come, first-served room. The **Bohemian Caverns** presents jazz and blues where Duke Ellington, Pearl Bailey, and other jazz greats performed when the U Street Corridor was one of America's black entertainment capitals. The old

Crystal Caverns, which jumped and wailed from the '20s into the '60s, was renovated and expanded into this jazz club and restaurant. Phone or check the website to find out what's playing when.

When all you need is love... A quiet, romantic spot for sipping a drink while listening to the tinkling of piano ivories is the **Blue Bar** in Penn Quarter Thursday, Friday, and Saturday nights. The bar is a warren of nooks that lets you feel a sense of privacy while the music plays.

It starts with "P."... Washington's gotten caught up in the trend to yuppify nasty pool halls into charming "billiard cafes" with microbrewery beers and more female customers. **Georgetown Bar and Billiards** serves microbrews and adds a hot CD jukebox, Ping-Pong, foosball, air hockey, and dart boards to its pool tables. The joint likes students from the local colleges so much, it gives them discounts on Tuesday nights. Pool is half-price for everyone from 6 to 8pm nightly. A slightly more well-heeled crowd (translation: college graduates) can be seen at **Buffalo Billiards,** along with the occasional bicycle messenger tired of hanging out in nearby Dupont Circle's park. Buffalo shows sporting events on high-definition TVs and serves food on a patio. **Bedrock Billiards** in Adams Morgan attracts a really eclectic crowd, male and female, who can slake their thirst with a wide variety of beers and other libations. It's small, so you may have to wait a while to play at popular times.

It starts with "B."... Nightclub bowling has come to Washington in the form of **Lucky Strike Lanes,** next door to Verizon Center in Penn Quarter. The only thing resembling the traditional blue-collar bowling of old are the lanes and the pins, which are bathed in a nightclub-blue light and sport giant TV screens above the pin spotters. Here you've got a bar with $10 cocktails and $5 beer, a disk jockey, a menu with such items as "ancho citrus chicken skewers," and brightly colored balls whose speed is reported on the automatic scoreboards. This bowling alley also has a dress code that bans, among other things, sweats, athletic wear, sports jerseys, construction shoes, "excessively baggy clothing," and chains. Any idea whom they're shutting out? For real bowling, head for Marvin Center on the

George Washington University campus in Foggy Bottom, where the **Hippodrome** is open to the public during the school year.

Politics is not the only game in town.... It makes sense that ESPN, the all-sports cable TV network, would run a pretty spectacular sports bar. Washington's **ESPN Zone** in Penn Quarter offers 200 television screens tuned to sports, as well as electronic games, a restaurant, and booze. **Grand Slam,** in Penn Quarter's Grand Hyatt, attracts a transient and therefore somewhat more ecumenical clientele. There are 3 widescreen TVs and 24 smaller ones that provide many options for watching the action. If you want to *be* part of the action, pick from pool, video games, and a dance floor. **Senators Grill,** in the Capitol Hill Holiday Inn, spent an all-star's ransom to cover every visible surface with caps, yearbooks, photos, uniforms, documents, and trinkets recalling the late, lamented Washington Senators, who decamped for Minnesota after the 1960 baseball season, and were replaced immediately by an expansion team carrying the same name, and then turned into the Texas Rangers in 1972. Now the TVs here can show the games of the Washington Nationals, who moved here from Montreal in 2005 and adopted a name that had been used interchangeably with the Senators when Washington had its earlier Big League teams, which usually weren't all that good. No longer can local fans lament that Washington is "first in war, first in peace, and last in the American League." The new Nats are National Leaguers.

The laughs aren't all on Capitol Hill.... But the best comedy in D.C. is homegrown. **The Capitol Steps** really did blossom on the Capitol steps. They were congressional aides who saw the humor around them and had the talent to turn it into an enduring musical act. Their scores of parody songs include "It's a Whole Newt World," "Send in the Clones," "Enron-Ron-Ron," "The Wreck of the Walter Fritz Mondale," "Dutch, the Magic Reagan," "Here's to You, Reverend Robertson," and, more recently, "Papa's Got a Brand New Baghdad" and "What a Difference Delay Makes." You can experience their topical humor every Friday and Saturday at 7:30pm in the amphitheater of the Ronald Reagan Building and International Trade Center downtown. At **The DC Improv,** also downtown, you can catch touring comics such as Dave Attell, Adam Ferrara, and Anthony Clark.

Good old-fashioned taverns... Clyde's no longer is the worn old tavern that attracted so much affection from regulars in its early years. Since its 1996 renovation, it has more of the theme-bar feel (large models of antique airplanes hanging under a skylight in one room, for instance). But in other rooms it's kept its saloon roots through the renovation. And it's still a good place to grab a beer—or a full meal—in the heart of Georgetown's M Street action. Except for its surprising sky-lit second-floor dining room, **Garrett's** remains a worn old tavern that gets more worn as the years wear on. The first-floor bar lets its music drift out to M Street. And what music it is! The jukebox is hooked up to the Internet and offers a near-limitless selection of song titles. Two more bars share space upstairs with the dining room and let you play a golf game. The main Georgetown University hangout is **The Tombs** (once frequented by college student Bill Clinton), in the basement below the upscale 1789 Restaurant. This is a comfortable, attractive place that draws faculty and neighbors as well as students. It serves really good food, too.

Getting hip to what's hip... So, you want to prove your coolness by getting into the velvet-rope-type places? See if you can convince the doormen at **MCCXXIII** or the **Eighteenth Street Lounge,** both near Dupont Circle, to grant you admission. MCCXXIII appeals to the trendy, the wealthy, and the wannabes with at least enough bread to pay for the drinks here without taking out a loan. The nightspot features velvet couches and a soapstone bar. In one section of the top floor, you can reserve a bedlike banquette that can be enclosed in its own partition. The Eighteenth Street Lounge is so exclusive—and self-confident—that it purposely makes itself hard to find. ESL (as insiders call it) doesn't advertise and is identified only by a small plaque at the door. If you get inside, you'll discover the club sprawls over two floors of a restored mansion, sports multiple bars and fireplaces, and offers outdoor partying on a deck in nice weather.

Indebleu is a hip, attractive spot to grab a drink before or after attending events at Verizon Center or a Penn Quarter theater or browsing the neighborhood's galleries. The decor is colorful, creative, attractive, comfortable, playful—and noisy. A DJ spins tunes after 10:30pm Thursday, Friday, and Saturday nights. This is a place for folks who like cocktails with many ingredients and a tilt to sweetness—and who don't mind paying double-digit prices. (In some cases, triple digits!) This bar's fare includes a foie gras sandwich. The restaurant upstairs serves Indian-influenced contemporary French cuisine (hence the name). The bar at spy-themed **Zola,** also in Penn Quarter, is a popular after-work spot for drinking and gazing out the floor-to-ceiling windows at the street action in the growing arts and entertainment district. Select from an innovative wine-and-cocktail list.

Beyond classification... It's hard to know where to begin when describing **Madam's Organ** in Adams Morgan. Perhaps with a nod to the ancient and honorable art of punning. Or with the fact that *Playboy* named Madam's one of the 25 best bars in America in 2000. Or by Madam's self-description as a "blues bar and soul food restaurant where the beautiful people go to get ugly." But that is where the bar ventures into the realm beyond classification. While it's true Madam's offers more blues than anything else among its nightly live music offerings, it's also got a "funky jazz" night (Mon) and a bluegrass night (Wed), and none of the schedule is carved in stone. You also can catch, from time to time, R&B, smooth jazz, reggae, salsa, merengue, and who knows what else. Redheads get Rolling Rock for half price. The second-floor bar is called "Big Daddy's Love Lounge & Pick-Up Joint." Madam's is loud. It is sweaty. You can dance. Or you can go out on the roof deck to cool off and order something from the tiki bar! Madam's has been around long enough to earn venerable status on the D.C. bar scene.

Map 9: Washington, D.C., Nightlife

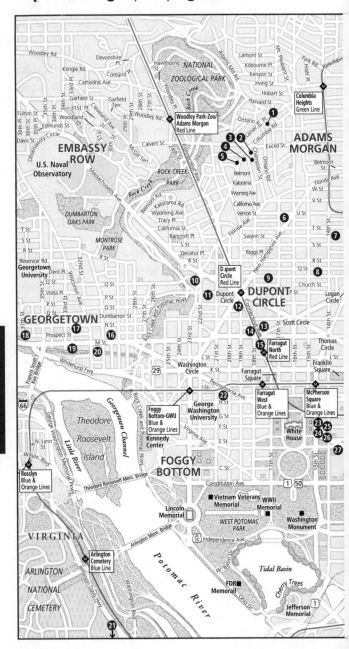

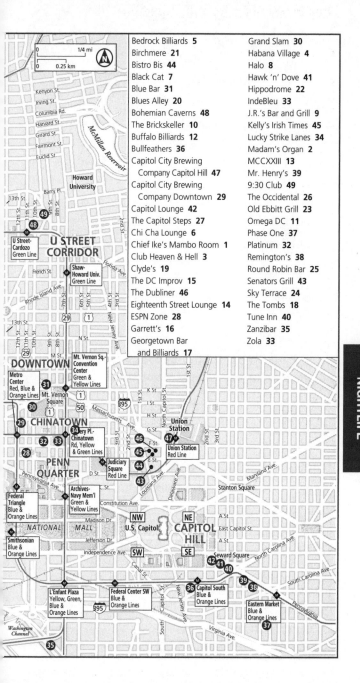

Bedrock Billiards **5**
Birchmere **21**
Bistro Bis **44**
Black Cat **7**
Blue Bar **31**
Blues Alley **20**
Bohemian Caverns **48**
The Brickskeller **10**
Buffalo Billiards **12**
Bullfeathers **36**
Capitol City Brewing
 Company Capitol Hill **47**
Capitol City Brewing
 Company Downtown **29**
Capitol Lounge **42**
The Capitol Steps **27**
Chi Cha Lounge **6**
Chief Ike's Mambo Room **1**
Club Heaven & Hell **3**
Clyde's **19**
The DC Improv **15**
The Dubliner **46**
Eighteenth Street Lounge **14**
ESPN Zone **28**
Garrett's **16**
Georgetown Bar
 and Billiards **17**

Grand Slam **30**
Habana Village **4**
Halo **8**
Hawk 'n' Dove **41**
Hippodrome **22**
IndeBleu **33**
J.R.'s Bar and Grill **9**
Kelly's Irish Times **45**
Lucky Strike Lanes **34**
Madam's Organ **2**
MCCXXIII **13**
Mr. Henry's **39**
9:30 Club **49**
The Occidental **26**
Old Ebbitt Grill **23**
Omega DC **11**
Phase One **37**
Platinum **32**
Remington's **38**
Round Robin Bar **25**
Senators Grill **43**
Sky Terrace **24**
The Tombs **18**
Tune Inn **40**
Zanzibar **35**
Zola **33**

NIGHTLIFE

The Index

See Map 9 on the previous page for all Nightlife listings.

Bedrock Billiards (p. 162) ADAMS MORGAN Want a microbrew with your pool game?... *Tel 202/667-7665. www.bedrockbilliards. com. 1841 Columbia Rd. NW, between Mintwood Place and Biltmore St. Take 98 Metrobus from Woodley Park–Zoo Metrorail Station. Mon–Thurs 4pm–2am; Fri 4pm–3am; Sat 1pm–3am; Sun 1pm–2am. Hourly pool rates $4–$10 per person depending on time. Cheaper for 3 or 4 players.*

Birchmere (p. 159) ALEXANDRIA Big music hall with food and drink in non–Old Town Alexandria. Come early for close-in free parking and close-in first-come, first-served seating. Tickets from Ticketmaster (Tel 800/551-7328; www.ticketmaster.com) or box office.... *Tel 703/549-7500. www.birchmere.com. 3701 Mount Vernon Ave., Alexandria, VA. Take cab. If driving, call or check website for directions. Doors open for box office and bar 5pm, food service starts 6pm; most concerts begin 7:30pm. Ticket prices vary with the act.*

Bistro Bis (p. 157) CAPITOL HILL Senate aides like to unwind in the sparkling upscale bar at this excellent restaurant.... *Tel 202/661-2700. www.bistrobis.com. 15 E St. NW., west of North Capitol St. Union Station Metro. Daily 11:30am–midnight, closes earlier on slow nights. No cover.*

Black Cat (p. 159) U STREET CORRIDOR Eclectic live music in dance hall. Jukebox, pool, pinball in Red Room Bar. Films, poetry readings in Backstage. Food at Food for Thought Cafe. All ages welcome, but those younger than 18 should have adult escort. Concert tickets available from Ticketmaster (Tel 800/551-7328; www.ticketmaster.com) and box office (cash only). Backstage tickets at door only.... *Tel 202/667-7960. www.blackcatdc.com. 1811 14th St. NW, between S and T sts. U St./Cardozo Metro. Red Room: Sun–Thurs 8pm–2am; Fri–Sat 7pm–3am. Cafe: Sun–Thurs 8pm–1am, Fri–Sat 7pm–2am. Mainstage opens Sun–Thurs 8:30pm, Fri–Sat 9:30pm. Opening act starts 30 minutes after opening. Backstage opens Sun–Thurs 8:30pm, Fri–Sat 9:30pm. No cover at Red Room Bar or Food for Thought Cafe; ticket price for live-music varies.*

Blue Bar (p. 162) PENN QUARTER Romantic bar with pianist from about 8pm Thursday, Friday, and Saturday.... *Tel 202/638-5200. www.henleypark.com. 926 Massachusetts Ave. NW, west of 9th St., in the Henley Park Hotel. Mount Vernon Sq. Metro. Sun–Thurs 11:30am–midnight; Fri–Sat till 1am. No cover.*

Blues Alley (p. 161) GEORGETOWN Big names in jazz in Georgetown supper club. Make reservations; arrive early for a good seat at dinner.... *Tel 202/337-4141. www.bluesalley.com. 1073 Wisconsin Ave. NW, in alley south of M St. Take Georgetown Connection shuttle bus from Dupont Circle, Foggy Bottom/GWU, or Rosslyn Metrorail Station, or ride 30-series Metrobus. Dinner at 6pm. Shows at 8 and 10pm most nights. Cover $2.50, minimum purchase $10 in addition to varying ticket price.*

Bohemian Caverns (p. 161) U STREET CORRIDOR Jazz and blues in renovated Crystal Caverns, which served up top-name performers from the '20s into the '60s.... *Tel 202/299-0801. www. bohemiancaverns.com. 2001 11th St. NW, at U St. U St./Cardozo Metro. Hours, cover vary.*

The Brickskeller (p. 158) DUPONT CIRCLE Descend to brick-lined catacombs to choose from among more than 1,000 varieties of beer; better food than you might expect.... *Tel 202/293-1885. www.thebrickskeller.com. 1523 22nd St. NW, between P and Q sts. Dupont Circle Metro. Mon–Thurs 11:30am–2am; Fri 11:30am–3am; Sat 6pm–3am; Sun 6pm–2am. No cover.*

Buffalo Billiards (p. 162) DUPONT CIRCLE Somewhat posh billiards cafe catering to young professionals and college grads.... *Tel 202/331-7665. www.buffalobilliards.com. 1330 19th St. NW, south of Dupont Circle. Dupont Circle Metro. Mon–Thurs 4pm–2am; Fri 4pm–3am; Sat 1pm–3am; Sun 4pm–1am. Hourly pool rates $6–$10 per person depending on time. Cheaper for 3 or 4 players. Must be 21 except before 6pm weekends.*

Bullfeathers (p. 156) CAPITOL HILL Popular hangout for House staffers and the occasional member of Congress. Attractive, bustling surroundings with decent food.... *Tel 202/543-5005. www.bullfeatherscapitolhill.com. 410 1st St. SE, south of D St. Capitol S. Metro. Mon–Sat 11:15am–midnight. No cover.*

Capitol City Brewing Company (p. 158) CAPITOL HILL/DOWNTOWN Beer brewed and consumed on renovated, historical premises. Standard modern pub fare.... *Capitol Hill: Tel 202/ 842-2337; www.capcitybrew.com; 2 Massachusetts Ave. NE, between N. Capitol St. and Union Station, in the old Post Office; Union Station Metro; Mon–Sat 11am–midnight, Sun 11am– 11pm. Downtown: Tel 202/628-2222; 1100 New York Ave. NW, at 11th and H sts.; Metro Center Metro; Sun–Thurs 11am–11pm, Fri–Sat 11am–midnight. No cover.*

THE INDEX

NIGHTLIFE

Capitol Lounge (p. 157) CAPITOL HILL Hangout for House staffers who like political memorabilia, sports on TV.... *Tel 202/547-2098. 231 Pennsylvania Ave. SE, between 2nd and 3rd sts. Capitol S. Metro. Sun–Thurs 11am–2am; Fri–Sat 11am–3am. No cover.*

The Capitol Steps (p. 163) DOWNTOWN This comedy troupe stimulates loud belly laughs with up-to-the-minute headline-based satirical songs and oldies-but-goodies from their quarter-century career. Tickets sold through Ticketmaster (Tel 800/551-7328; www.ticketmaster.com) or at the door beginning at 6pm.... *Tel 703/683-8330. www.capsteps.com. In the amphitheater of the Ronald Reagan Building and International Trade Center, 1300 Pennsylvania Ave. NW, between 13th and 14th sts. Federal Triangle Metro. Most Fri and Sat at 7:30pm. Tickets $39.*

Chi Cha Lounge (p. 158) U STREET CORRIDOR Comfortable oversize sofas and armchairs, tapas, Latin drinks, Latin music, and tobacco-only water pipes. Live music Sunday through Wednesday.... *Tel 202/234-8400. http://latinconcepts.com/chicha. 1624 U St. NW, between 16th and 17th sts. U St./Cardozo Metro. Sun–Thurs 5:30pm–1:30am; Fri–Sat 5:30pm–2:30am. Sometimes minimum $15.*

Chief Ike's Mambo Room (p. 160) ADAMS MORGAN Drinking and dancing to various danceable musical styles.... *Tel 202/332-2211. www.chiefikes.com. 1725 Columbia Rd. NW, west of 17th St. Take 98 Metrobus from Woodley Park–Zoo Metrorail Station. Sun–Thurs 4pm–2am; Fri–Sat till 3am. Cover $5 Sat–Sun and when band performs.*

Club Heaven & Hell (p. 160) ADAMS MORGAN Split-personality club offers danceable music upstairs and a dark bar with jukebox, pool table, and beer in the basement below.... *Tel 202/667-4355. 2327 18th St. NW, at Columbia Rd. Take 98 Metrobus from Woodley Park–Zoo Metrorail Station. Sun–Thurs 7:30pm–2am; Fri–Sat 7:30pm–3am. No cover.*

Clyde's (p. 164) GEORGETOWN This venerable, multiroom tavern—flagship of Clyde's local restaurant chain—has been modernized but still offers tastes of its roots. Oak bar, plank flooring among welcome aspects of preservation. Still a lively gathering place.... *Tel 202/333-9180. www.clydes.com. 3236 M St. NW, between Wisconsin Ave. and Potomac St. Take Georgetown Connection shuttle bus from Dupont Circle, Foggy/GWU, or Rosslyn Metrorail Station, or ride 30-series Metrobus. Mon–Thurs 11:30am–midnight; Fri 11:30am–1am; Sat 10am–1am; Sun 9am–midnight. No cover.*

The DC Improv (p. 164) DOWNTOWN Comedy club with inexpensive food and wine starting at $6 a glass. Big stars have played here but not all the time.... *Tel 202/296-7008. www.dcimprov.com.*

1140 Connecticut Ave. NW, between L and M sts. Farragut N.
Metro. Shows Tues–Thurs 8:30pm; Fri–Sun 8pm; Fri–Sat also
10:30pm; additional late shows for some acts. First-come, first-
served seating except for late shows. Ticket charge varies with act.
Also 2-item minimum.

A Different Kind of Ladies Night (p. 161) VARIOUS LOCATIONS
Parties for lesbians held frequently in various nightspots.
Upcoming events listed on website. www.adifferentkindofladies
night.com. No cover.

The Dubliner (p. 158) CAPITOL HILL Lively, friendly hangout for Hill
folk who like Irish beer, Irish music, and, perhaps, Irish food. Live
music every night starting at 9pm Monday through Saturday and
7pm Sunday.... Tel 202/737-3773. www.dublinerdc.com. 4 F St.
NW, at N. Capitol St. Union Station Metro. Sun–Thurs 11am–
1:30am; Fri–Sat till 2:30am. No cover.

Eighteenth Street Lounge (p. 164) DUPONT CIRCLE So exclusive
you can hardly find the sign.... Tel 202/466-3922. 1212 18th St.
NW, between M St. and Connecticut Ave. Dupont Circle Metro.
Tues–Wed 9:30pm–2am; Thurs 5:30pm–2am; Fri 5:30pm–3am;
Sat 9:30pm–3am. Cover $10–$20.

ESPN Zone (p. 163) DOWNTOWN It's a sports bar. A really big sports
bar.... Tel 202/783-3776. www.espnzone.com/washingtondc. 555
12th St. NW, between E and F sts. Metro Center Metro. Mon–Sat
11:30am–midnight; Sun 11:30am–11:30pm. Last seating 1 hr.
before closing; last entry 30 min. before closing. No cover.

Garrett's (p. 164) GEORGETOWN Well-worn tavern with great jukebox, electronic golf game.... Tel 202/333-1033. www.garretts
dc.com. 3003 M St. NW, at 30th St. Take Georgetown Connection
shuttle bus from Dupont Circle, Foggy Bottom/GWU, or Rosslyn
Metrorail Station, or ride 30-series Metrobus. Mon–Thurs
11:30am–1:30am; Fri–Sat noon–2:30am. No cover.

Georgetown Bar and Billiards (p. 162) GEORGETOWN Most players in this pool-hall-turned-billiards cafe are eds and coeds from
local colleges.... Tel 202/965-7665. www.georgetownbilliards.
com. 3251 Prospect St. NW, east of Potomac St., in the courtyard
behind Cafe Milano. Take Georgetown Connection shuttle bus
from Dupont Circle, Foggy Bottom/GWU, or Rosslyn Metrorail Station, or ride 30-series Metrobus. Sun–Thurs 6pm–2am; Fri–Sat till
3am. Hourly pool rates Sun–Thurs $7 per person, Fri–Sat $8.
Cheaper with more players.

Grand Slam (p. 163) PENN QUARTER Lots of TVs for watching sports, plus pool, video games, and a dance floor.... *Tel 202/ 582-1234. 1000 H St. NW, at 10th St., in the Grand Hyatt Washington hotel. Metro Center Metro. Sun–Thurs 11:30am–midnight; Fri–Sat till 1am. No cover.*

Habana Village (p. 158) ADAMS MORGAN Hot spot for live salsa and Latin jazz late on weekends, salsa and merengue lessons Wednesday through Saturday.... *Tel 202/462-6310. www. habanavillage.com. 1834 Columbia Rd. NW, between Biltmore St. and Belmont Rd. Take 98 Metrobus from Woodley Park–Zoo Metrorail Station. Wed–Thurs 6:30pm–1:30am; Fri–Sat till 2:30am. Cover $5 Fri–Sat.*

Halo (p. 160) DUPONT CIRCLE Comfortable gay/lesbian bar that pulls in straight neighbors as well. *Tel 202/797-9730. www. halodc.com. 1435 P St. NW, between 14th and 15th sts. Dupont Circle Metro. Mon–Thurs 5pm–2am; Fri–Sat 5pm–3am; Sun 2pm–2am. No cover.*

Hawk 'n' Dove (p. 157) CAPITOL HILL Lots of House staff members come here after work for cheap (for Washington) beer and food.... *Tel 202/543-3300. www.hawkanddoveonline.com. 329 Pennsylvania Ave. SE, between 3rd and 4th sts. Capitol S. Metro. Sun–Thurs 10am–2am; Fri–Sat 10am–3am. No cover.*

Hippodrome (p. 163) FOGGY BOTTOM Twelve-lane bowling alley on fifth floor of George Washington University's Marvin Center, open to residents of both (in GW-speak) GWorld and non-GWorld. Also table tennis, foosball, darts, billiards, air hockey, arcade games. No booze.... *Tel 202/994-3866. hippodrome.gwu.edu. 800 21st St. NW, 5th floor, at H St. Foggy Bottom/GWU Metro. Late Aug to mid-May Sun noon–midnight; Mon–Wed 6pm–midnight; Thurs–Fri 6pm–2am; Sat noon–2am. Closed in summer to walk-in customers. Bowling fees $4.50 per person per game ($3 for students, staff, alums). Other games $6–$8 per hour (non-GWorld), $5–$6 (GWorld).*

Indebleu (p. 165) PENN QUARTER For those who would like to sit on a swinging sofa and order a foie gras sandwich chased with a $120 glass of Remy Louis XIII cognac.... *Tel 202/333-2538. www.bleu.com/indebleu. 707 G St. NW, between 7th and 8th sts. Gallery Place/Chinatown Metro. Sun–Thurs 5pm–1:30am; Fri–Sat till 2:30am. No cover.*

JR's Bar and Grill (p. 161) DUPONT CIRCLE One of Washington's top gay bars, especially popular among good-looking male professionals.... *Tel 202/328-0090. www.jrswdc.com. 1519 17th St. NW, between P and Q sts. Dupont Circle Metro. Sun–Thurs 4pm–2am; Fri–Sat 2pm–3am. No cover.*

Kelly's Irish Times (p. 158) CAPITOL HILL The Dubliner's next-door rival in the competition for patrons who like all things Irish. Upstairs, Irish music, food, and booze. Downstairs, 20-somethings dancing to a pop jukebox.... *Tel 202/543-5433. 14 F St. NW, just west of N. Capitol St. Union Station Metro. Sun–Thurs 11am–1:30am; Fri–Sat 11am–2:30am. Live music starts Fri–Sat 10pm. No cover.*

Lucky Strike Lanes (p. 162) PENN QUARTER Not your father's bowling alley.... *Tel 202/347-1021. www.bowlluckystrike.com. 701 7th St. NW. Gallery Place/Chinatown Metro. Daily 11am–2am. Lane charge per person per game $4.95–$7.95 depending on time. Billiards $14–$21 per hour.*

Madam's Organ (p. 165) ADAMS MORGAN They do play the blues, but mostly they just play at this "neighborhood joint" that draws partiers from all over the D.C. area. Live music every night, lots of booze, lots of fun.... *Tel 202/667-5370. www.madamsorgan. com. 2461 18th St. NW, south of Columbia Rd. Take 98 Metrobus from Woodley Park–Zoo Metrorail Station. Sun–Thurs 5pm–2am; Fri–Sat 5pm–3am. Live music starts between 9 and 10pm. Cover $3–$7.*

MCCXXIII (p. 164) DUPONT CIRCLE This chic, high-priced club is the place to see and be seen by the swanky night crawlers of the capital. Enhance your chance of admission by following the club's dress suggestions: "designer chic or masquerade attire, jacket for men, sexy chic for ladies, casual wear discouraged, no blue jeans, no athletic wear." And wear a mask!... *Tel 202/ 822-1800. www.1223dc.com. 1223 Connecticut Ave. NW, between M and N sts. Dupont Circle Metro. Tues 9pm–2am; Wed–Thurs 6pm–2am; Fri 5pm–3am; Sat 8pm–3am; Sun 8pm–2am. Cover $10 after 10pm.*

Mr. Henry's (p. 161) CAPITOL HILL Comfortable restaurant/bar with live Friday-night jazz. Gay/lesbian hangout that attracts plenty of straights.... *Tel 202/546-8412. 601 Pennsylvania Ave. SE, at 6th St. Eastern Market Metro. Mon–Sat 11:15am–midnight; Sun 10am–midnight. Minimum $8 to hear jazz on second floor from 8:30pm Friday.*

9:30 Club (p. 159) U STREET CORRIDOR Arguably Washington's No. 1 live-music venue. Top stars perform. You can't sit down 'cause there are hardly any seats. Tickets sold at box office noon to 7pm Monday through Friday and during shows, and through the club's website. *Tel 202/393-0390. www.930.com. 815 V St. NW, at Vermont Ave. U St./Cardozo Metro. When there's a show, doors open Sun–Thurs 7:30pm, Fri–Sat 9pm; first act starts 45–75 minutes later. Ticket prices vary.*

THE INDEX

NIGHTLIFE

The Occidental (p. 157) DOWNTOWN Restaurant and bar two blocks from White House that looks like what you think a hangout for the politically powerful should look like. And they do hang out here. Pick the downstairs room for clubby atmosphere.... *Tel 202/783-1475. www.occidentaldc.com. 1475 Pennsylvania Ave. NW, between 14th and 15th sts. Metro Center Metro. Mon–Thurs 11:30am–3pm and 5–10pm; Fri–Sat 11:30am–3pm and 5–10:30pm; Sun 5–9:30pm. No cover.*

Old Ebbitt Grill (p. 157) DOWNTOWN White House staffers come to this 1983 version of a 150-year-old saloon that once served the presidents themselves.... *Tel 202/347-4800. www.ebbitt. com. 675 15th St. NW, between F and G sts. Metro Center Metro. Mon–Thurs 7:30am–2am; Fri 7:30am–3am; Sat 8:30am–3am; Sun 8:30am–2am. No cover.*

Omega DC (p. 161) DUPONT CIRCLE Double-decker, four-bar, gay institution with 60-inch video screen, pool tables, weeknight drink specials, DJs, VJs, and lots of men.... *Tel 202/223-4917. www.omegadc.com. 2122 P St. NW (rear entrance off Twining Court), between 21st and 22nd sts. Dupont Circle Metro. Mon–Thurs 4pm–2am; Fri 4pm–3am; Sat 7pm–3am; Sun 7pm–2am. Minimum $3 Wed when dancers perform.*

Phase One (p. 161) CAPITOL HILL Washington's oldest bar for lesbians.... *Tel 202/544-6831. 525 8th St. SE, between F and G sts. Eastern Market Metro. Thurs–Sun 7pm–2am; Fri–Sat till 3am. No cover.*

Platinum (p. 160) PENN QUARTER The young and the attractive like to dance in this equally attractive club in a grand old bank building. If you want in, you must "dress fashionable."... *Tel 202/393-3555. www.platinumclubdc.com. 915 F St. NW, between 9th and 10th sts. Gallery Place/Chinatown Metro. Thurs–Sat 10pm–3am; Sun 9pm–2:30am. Cover $10–$15.*

Remington's (p. 160) CAPITOL HILL Country-western gay bar with happy hours 4 to 8pm Monday through Friday.... *Tel 202/ 543-3113. www.remingtonswdc.com. 639 Pennsylvania Ave. SE, between 6th and 7th sts. Eastern Market Metro. Mon–Thurs 4pm–2am; Fri–Sat 4pm–3am; Sun 5pm–2am. Cover Fri–Sat nights $4, includes drink discount.*

Round Robin Bar (p. 157) DOWNTOWN Don't come here for a cocktail that was invented yesterday and will be out of style next week. The Round Robin's "Classic Cocktail Collection" features the mint julep, gin rickey, Old-Fashioned, Bloody Mary, Manhattan, Rob Roy, sidecar, and, of course, the gin-and-vermouth martini. *Tel 202/628-9100. 1401 Pennsylvania Ave. NW, at 14th St., in the Willard Inter-continental Washington. Metro Center Metro. Mon–Sat noon–11pm. No cover.*

Senators Grill (p. 163) CAPITOL HILL Spiffy hotel sports bar with TVs and memorabilia of old Washington Senators baseball team, TVs for watching the current Washington Nationals.... *Tel 202/638-1616. www.hionthehilldc.com/dining_senatorsgrill. php. 415 New Jersey Ave. NW, at D St., in the Holiday Inn on the Hill. Union Station Metro. Daily 6am–midnight, unless crowd won't let bartender close. No cover.*

Sky Terrace (p. 156) DOWNTOWN Great views of D.C. from this open-air bar/restaurant on top of the Hotel Washington.... *Tel 202/638-5900. www.hotelwashington.com/dining.php. 515 15th St. NW, at Pennsylvania Ave. Metro Center Metro. Daily Apr–Oct 11:30am–12:30am. No cover.*

The Tombs (p. 164) GEORGETOWN Landmark pub for Georgetown University students, faculty, and neighbors, with lots of beer on tap and very good food.... *Tel 202/337-6668. www.tombs.com. 1226 36th St. NW, at Prospect St. Take Georgetown Connection Rte. 2 shuttle bus from Dupont Circle or Rosslyn Metrorail Station. Mon–Thurs 11:30am–1:15am; Fri 11:30am–2:15am; Sat 11am–2:15am; Sun 9:30am–1:15am. No cover.*

Tune Inn (p. 157) CAPITOL HILL Plain old bar that's popular with nearby representatives and House staff. Cheap food and cheap beer.... *Tel 202/543-2725. 3311/2 Pennsylvania Ave. SE, between 3rd and 4th sts. Capitol S. Metro. Sun–Thurs 8am–2am; Fri–Sat 8am–3am. No cover.*

Zanzibar (p. 160) SOUTHWEST WATERFRONT Big dance club with picture windows, outdoor decks overlooking the Washington Channel.... *Tel 202/554-9100. www.zanzibar-otw.com. 700 Water St. SW, between 7th and 8th sts. Take a cab. Wed–Thurs 5pm–1am; Fri–Sat 5pm–3am; Sun 11am–4pm. Cover $10–$15 most nights.*

Zola (p. 165) PENN QUARTER Very popular, very attractive sleek, modern bar in bustling entertainment district.... *Tel 202/654-0999. www.zoladc.com. 800 F St. NW, at 8th St. Gallery Place–Chinatown Metro. Mon–Fri 11:30am–midnight; Sat 5pm–midnight; Sun 5–10pm. Closed Jan 1, Thanksgiving, Dec 25. No cover.*

THE INDEX

NIGHTLIFE

Basic Stuff

Congress may offer the best slapstick routine in town, but there are plenty of other places in which to be entertained in Washington. Various new or improved facilities—like the **Verizon Center** sports and concert arena (formerly titled the MCI Center and still nicknamed the Phone Booth) and the rapidly expanding performing- and visual-arts venues—have boosted Washington's entertainment quotient, high-, middle-, and lowbrow. The **John F. Kennedy Center for the Performing Arts** is the single biggest entertainment/cultural spot in town. With world-class concert hall, opera house, movie theater, and other facilities, the Kennedy Center provides a home to the **National Symphony Orchestra and Washington National Opera** (among others), and hosts scores of local and traveling performing groups. To elevate the cultural soul of the more budget-conscious, the center opened the **Millennium Stage** in the Grand Foyer, which puts on free concerts every day at 6pm.

Other cultural and entertainment venues are scattered around town. The Library of Congress, in addition to collecting books, presents films in its **Mary Pickford Theater.** Several theaters, both large and small, present works that range from blockbuster Broadway transplants to classical plays to the truly avant-garde. Rock stars and other pop-music headliners play the largest halls. D.C. boasts a serious audience for serious dance. With the move of the Montreal Expos to Washington in 2005 (renamed the **Washington Nationals**), the District now enjoys access to all big-time sports. And fair-weather visitors to Washington can enjoy outdoor performance spaces, some of which offer a significant number of free shows.

Sources

The *Washington Post*'s **Weekend** tabloid, which appears on Fridays, publishes up-to-date listings of entertainment events and reviews. Every day the *Post*'s "Style" section contains advertisements, stories, and reviews. The brawny alternative weekly **Washington City Paper** offers its own alternative lists, ads, and commentary, including shows that might not make the *Post*. The weekly **Washington Blade** highlights arts and entertainment of special interest to the gay community. Both weeklies are free and can be picked up in bars, restaurants, hotels, bookstores, libraries, and other public places.

ENTERTAINMENT

Getting Tickets

Ticketmaster may still be the greatest offend/ ticket-buyers with outrageous service charges, b that sell their own tickets have gotten into the act. You be able to save some money by buying tickets at the box on. or by phone or online from the theater. But be prepared to be socked with a service charge, even if you're printing the tickets out from your home computer or picking them up at the box office and relieving the theater of any delivery costs.

For bargains, go to **Ticket Place** (407 7th St. NW, between D and E sts.; Tel 202/842-5387, information only), which sells same-day (and some advance-sale) tickets for up to 40% off the face value. Go to the ticket booth Tuesday to Friday between 11am and 6pm or Saturday between 10am and 5pm. Some tickets are sold on the Internet (www.ticketplace.org) Tuesday through Friday from noon to 4pm. Because Ticket Place is closed Sunday and Monday, tickets for those days sometimes can be purchased Saturday.

Speaking of big-time ticket costs, if you want tickets to a sold-out event, such as impossible-to-buy Redskins tickets, for instance, try **Great Seats** (Tel 800/664-5056; www.greatseats. com), **Stagefront Tickets** (Tel 877/782-4337; www.stage front.com), **Ticket Connection** (Tel 800/468-8587; www.ticket connection.com), or **Top Centre** (Tel 800/673-8422; www.top centre.com). Also try classified ads in the *Washington Post* and on www.washingtonpost.com in the sports section.

The Lowdown

The play's the thing... Because it's so big and comprehensive, the **Kennedy Center** will keep popping up in this chapter. Top-notch plays and big-time musicals are staged regularly in the center's Eisenhower Theater and Opera House. Kid stuff, experimental work, festivals, and "Shear Madness" (an audience-participation comedy-mystery that's been performed here more than 7,000 times) play the smaller Terrace Theater and Theater Lab.

Within what passes for Washington's theater district, three historic theaters and one globally acclaimed company present a wide range of works from classic plays to blockbuster musicals. Opened in 1835, then rebuilt and refurbished several times, the **National Theatre** downtown claims that nearly every major American theater star who has toured has appeared here, from the beloved Helen Hayes to the despised John Wilkes Booth. Sister-brother act Shirley MacLaine and Warren Beatty once were, respectively, usher and stage doorman here. Nowadays you can take in the likes of *Spamalot, Mamma Mia!, Cats, Chicago,* and *42nd Street,* as well as more modest and adventurous offerings. Nearly a century younger than the National but with an equally rich history, the **Warner Theatre,** on the other side of 13th Street, opened in 1924 as a vaudeville and silent-movie house called the Earle. The death of vaudeville turned the Earle into a movies-only theater with a new name, the Warner, in 1945. The later decline of movies saw the Warner survive for a while as a porno joint. By the mid-1970s, however, the house regained its legitimacy as a concert hall, hosting, among others, the Rolling Stones. Following a 3-year renovation, it reopened in 1992 with a gala featuring Frank Sinatra and that ubiquitous Shirley MacLaine. Now it's a major venue for big-time concerts, plays, musicals, and dance. No D.C. house can top the history of **Ford's Theatre,** of course, but it's a history no place would want to claim. Ford's stage was dark from the night Lincoln was assassinated here in 1865 until it was restored and reopened as a fully functioning theater in 1969. American plays are a staple at this Penn Quarter venue. Dickens's *A Christmas Carol* has become a Christmas tradition. The critically acclaimed **Shakespeare Theatre,** also in Penn Quarter, presents works by the Bard and other classical playwrights, often setting them in contemporary times, taking them out of their original era in other ways, or otherwise tweaking the production, if not the script.

Arena Stage—boldly located south of downtown near Washington's Southwest Waterfront—was the first not-for-profit theater in the United States, the first regional theater to transfer a production to Broadway, the first regional theater invited by the State Department to tour behind the Iron Curtain, and the first regional theater to win a Tony. It prides itself on diversity, and that includes performing new and risky plays as well as reinterpreting standards that have established their popularity, including musicals. Arena promised its shows would go on throughout an expansion/renovation project scheduled for completion in 2008.

Studio Theatre presents everything from contemporary works by young artists to The Who's *Tommy* (in 2004). Having successfully converted an old automobile showroom into two fine, intimate performance spaces, Studio has embarked on further expansion and renovation in two adjoining buildings. Another company in construction mode was the **Woolly Mammoth Theatre Company,** which moved into new digs in Penn Quarter in mid-2005. Woolly searches out plays that "explore the edges of theatrical style and human experience." Washington's most interesting theater, the **Folger Theatre,** is found at the **Folger Shakespeare Library** on Capitol Hill. It's a replica of an Elizabethan theater. The Folger stages Shakespeare plays, of course, as well as works by other playwrights, and hosts poetry readings and music concerts.

Classical gas... The **National Symphony Orchestra** presents world-class concerts in the Kennedy Center Concert Hall and performs outside in summer at Virginia's **Wolf Trap Farm Park for the Performing Arts** and the **Carter Barron Amphitheater** in D.C.'s Rock Creek Park. With superstar tenor Placido Domingo as artistic director, the **Washington National Opera** mounts classic shows and pushes the edge with modern material. The 2006–07 season, for instance, included such standards as Puccini's *Madame Butterfly* and Wagner's *The Valkyrie*—as well as the North American premier of *Sophie's Choice,* Nicholas Maw's adaptation of the William Styron novel that was made into a hit movie starring Meryl Streep.

Men in tights... From October through May, the **Washington Ballet** pirouettes between the Kennedy Center and the Warner Theatre, with classic and contemporary works, including, every December, *The Nutcracker.* The Kennedy Center hosts visits by other outstanding companies, including the Kirov, the Royal, the Joffrey, the Bolshoi, and the American Ballet Theatre in the 2006–07 season alone. **Dance Place,** near Catholic University in Northeast D.C., puts on affordable performances by local and visiting troupes. Styles range through contemporary, postmodern, tap, ethnic, performance art, and special programs for children and families.

ENTERTAINMENT

Long-hair-free concert zones... Because of D.C.'s diversity, there's a market for nearly every kind of music, so eventually nearly every kind of music makes its way to Washington concert halls. The **Kennedy Center** occasionally books top jazz and pop acts and ready-for-prime-time comedians. When showbiz superstars tour, they often grace the grand stage of the **Warner Theatre.** Things have changed since 1939 when the Daughters of the American Revolution refused to let Marian Anderson sing at **DAR Constitution Hall** because she was black. Since then, black headliners such as Ray Charles, Bill Cosby, Patti LaBelle, and James Brown have trod that stage, as have rockers and other social misfits like Bill Maher, Aerosmith, Jimmy Buffet, George Carlin, and Frank Zappa. Anderson herself performed here before her death.

The **Lincoln Theatre**—originally a movie theater, vaudeville house, and nightclub that showcased the likes of Louis Armstrong—reopened in 1994 after a $9-million renovation. Now thriving in the heart of the U Street entertainment district, the Lincoln presents a broad variety of events—plays, dance, music, films—with diverse ethnic roots. As you might expect on a college campus, performances at George Washington University's **Lisner Auditorium** range from opera to rock, country, and pop.

Really big acts demand really big venues so they can draw really big crowds and walk away with really big paychecks. That's why Simon and Garfunkel's reunion tour stopped by MCI Center (now **Verizon Center**) in late 2003, and other superstars (Paul McCartney, Bruce Springsteen, Tim McGraw, Faith Hill, Dixie Chicks, Shakira, Mariah Carey, Luciano Pavarotti) fill in the calendar between sports events. The Rolling Stones—and gigantic festivals that can draw gigantic crowds—take a shot at filling 55,000-plus-seat **Robert F. Kennedy Memorial Stadium,** once the home of the Redskins, or **FedEx Field,** where more than 90,000 can watch the Redskins now.

Where the stars play under the stars... Just about every kind of entertainment shows up at **Wolf Trap Farm Park for the Performing Arts** over a typical Washington summer—from the National Symphony to Fiona Apple to film screenings. This national park sits on farmland about a half-hour out of town and puts on these shows in an open-sided, roofed pavilion with lawn seating for those willing to chance D.C.'s frequent summer storms. You're allowed to bring a picnic—including booze—although you can't take it under the roof. You also can buy food at the concession stands, order a ready-made picnic meal in advance and pick it up when you arrive, or make reservations at the sit-down Ovations Restaurant. At Ovations you can get a pretty good buffet for $30 ($11 for kids younger than 10) and meals that include salad and dessert for between $17 and $29. **Nissan Pavilion at Stone Ridge** is a similar, commercial venture even further out of D.C. in the Virginia countryside. It has about three times the seating of Wolf Trap and is famous for terrible traffic jams. Yet another open-sided theater with a lawn is the **Merriweather Post Pavilion,** between Washington and Baltimore.

The smallest of these venues, 4,250-seat **Carter Barron Amphitheater** in Rock Creek Park, offers the best cultural entertainment values in town. Two of Washington's premier performing-arts institutions—the **National Symphony** and the **Shakespeare Theatre**—play here several times for free each summer. It pays to pick up free tickets in advance to guarantee you can get in. Others offering free performances here include military bands and local groups. There are a few paid concerts each season as well. There's no roof here, so performances can be canceled in bad weather. Free **Military concerts are** also performed by armed-forces bands at the West front of the Capitol June through August. The Navy Band performs on Monday, Air Force on Tuesday, Marines on Wednesday, and Army on Friday. The concerts start at 8pm. The Marine Band also plays at 7pm Tuesday at the Iwo Jima Memorial.

Kid stuff... **Kennedy Center**'s Imagination Celebration presents plays, musicals, puppet shows, and other performances aimed at children, as young as 4 in some cases, while the **Millennium Stage** often features storytellers and ethnic dance ensembles. Get info by surfing to www.kennedy-center.org/programs/family, then clicking on "List of All Family-Friendly Events at the Kennedy Center." Also at Kennedy Center, the **National Symphony** presents a variety of programs aimed at children as young as 3 and their elders. Find the schedule at www.kennedy-center.org/nso/programs/family. During the "Petting Zoo," 1 hour before each Family Concert, kids can go up to the stage and handle instruments. After the 3pm Family Concerts, performers stay to answer children's questions and to tell stories about the life of the musician. Bring your favorite stuffed animal to the Teddy Bear Concerts. "Saturday Morning at the **National Theatre**" is devoted to using magic shows, pantomime, storytelling, puppets, music, and anything performers can think of to get kids hooked on live theater, from September into April. Children in kindergarten through sixth grade are the target audience for **Wolf Trap**'s "Theatre-in-the-Woods" family programs, which include music, dance, storytelling, puppetry, and plays. Every September the Arts Council of Fairfax County, Virginia, uses Wolf Trap as the site for a weekend-long "International Children's Festival."

The silver screen... Multiscreen movie theaters have become a boom industry in Washington. First-run films show in quantity at the **AMC Loews Georgetown, AMC Loews Wisconsin Avenue, Phoenix Theatres Union Station, AMC Mazza Gallerie,** and **Regal Gallery Place.** But the megaplexes don't limit themselves to Hollywood blockbusters. **Landmark's E Street Cinema** and the **AMC Loews Dupont** focus on independent, foreign, and documentary films.

The best movie house, with the largest screen, is the **Cineplex Odeon Uptown,** on upper Connecticut Avenue. It's not as ornate as those defunct movie palaces that it competed with and survived. But it is a large old theater with a great sound system and a balcony—absolutely the best place to watch cinematic marvels like the *Lord of the Rings* trilogy. Finally, there's the **Avalon,** in Upper Northwest. Born in 1923, closed, and stripped of its guts in 2001, the Avalon was saved by neighbors, movie buffs, and a sympathetic real estate developer who restored the theater and reopened it in 2003. Now the oldest motion-picture showplace in D.C., it serves up an eclectic blend of films.

The Library of Congress dips into its enormous film and TV-show collection for regular screenings in its **Mary Pickford Theater.** Similarly, the American Film Institute presents films and programs about films at the **Silver Theatre** in Silver Spring, Maryland, just north of the Washington border. Built in 1938, the Silver was saved and restored by the institute and the Montgomery County, Maryland, government. The main event of the Washington movie season is **Filmfest DC,** which, every spring, shows movies from around the world in theaters all around town.

ENTERTAINMENT

The sporting life... The NFL **Washington Redskins**—who proudly wear American sports' most controversial nickname (some call it downright irreverent)—are *the* toughest ticket in town. Don't even think about buying tickets through normal channels. See "Getting Tickets," above, for how you can give a broker a month's wages for a seat or two. Getting tickets to see the **Washington Wizards** play NBA basketball has been getting tougher as the team has begun winning again for the first time since the 1980s. The Wizards share **Verizon Center**—a wonderful sports arena—with the Women's NBA **Washington Mystics** and the National Hockey League **Washington Capitals,** two more dependable losers in the early 2000s. Things started looking up for the Mystics in 2006, however, and the Capitals' rebuilding project began showing promise with Alexander Ovechkin, the 2005–06 "Rookie of the Year." The Capitals do offer the best professional sports deal in town. Log on to their website for tickets in the nosebleed ("Eagles Nest") section for $10, plus a modest service fee. Sometimes you can grab four seats for $20—$5 a seat!

Washington's best professional teams recently both played soccer. The Washington Freedom won the Women's United Soccer Association championship in 2003, just before the league went belly up. D.C. soccer fans—and there are lots of them—keep hoping for a women's league rebirth. **D.C. United** dominated the early years of men's Major League Soccer—winning the first two championships in 1996 and 1997, then again in 1999. After falling on hard times in the early 2000s, the team came back to win the championship again in 2004 and to continue to play strong thereafter.

Regardless of record, the best recent news for Washington sports fans was the return of Major League Baseball. The Montreal Expos moved here in 2005, changed their name to the **Washington Nationals,** and went on to play far better than anyone could have hoped—contending for much of the season, and finishing at .500. The Nats play at 45-year-old **Robert F. Kennedy Memorial Stadium,** which doesn't offer the most-modern amenities but does have pretty good baseball sightlines from even the cheapest seats (bring your binoculars). Nats fans look forward to a brand-new, state-of-the-art ballpark on South Capitol Street before the end of the decade.

Map 10: Washington, D.C., Entertainment

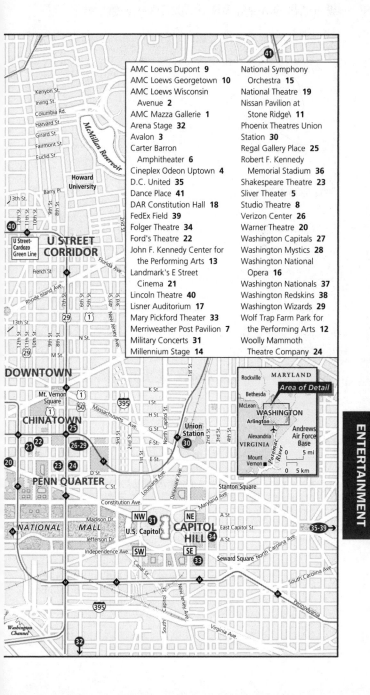

The Index

See Map 10 on the previous page for all entertainment listings.

AMC Loews Dupont (p. 184) DUPONT CIRCLE Five-screen multiplex that specializes in independent, foreign, and documentary films.... *Tel 800/326-3264. www.moviewatcher.com. 1350 19th St. NW, between Sunderland Place and P St. Dupont Circle Metro. Tickets $7–$9 adults.*

AMC Loews Georgetown (p. 184) GEORGETOWN First-run flicks on 14 screens under the Whitehurst Freeway near the Georgetown Waterfront. Pretend you're under the El in Chicago.... *Tel 800/326-3264. www.moviewatcher.com. 3111 K St. NW, between 31st St. and Wisconsin Ave. Take Georgetown Connection Rte. 1 from Foggy Bottom/GWU Metrorail station, or ride 30-series Metrobus. Tickets $7.50–$9.50 adults.*

AMC Loews Wisconsin Avenue (p. 184) UPPER NORTHWEST Another first-run multiplex.... *Tel 800/326-3264. www.movie watcher.com. 4000 Wisconsin Ave. NW, between Rodman and Upton sts. Take 30-series Metrobus. Tickets $7.25–$9.50 adults.*

AMC Mazza Gallerie (p. 184) UPPER NORTHWEST Plusher than your average first-run multiplex. You have to be 21 to enter two auditoriums—called the Mazza Club Cinema—where you pay a premium to eat and drink booze while sitting in super-comfortable chairs and watching the flick.... *Tel 202/537-9553. www. moviewatcher.com. 5300 Wisconsin Ave. NW, between Jennifer St. and Western Ave., in the Mazza Gallerie shopping mall. Friendship Heights Metro. Tickets $7.50–$13.*

Arena Stage (p. 180) SOUTHWEST WATERFRONT Prominent regional theater emphasizes diversity and risk but also reinterprets popular standards.... *Tel 202/488-3300. www.arena stage.org. 1101 6th St. SW, at Maine Ave. Waterfront Metro, but watch your step at night or take a cab. Ticket prices vary.*

Avalon (p. 184) UPPER NORTHWEST Roaring '20s r
oldest in D.C., saved from oblivion, restored, an
2003. Shows full range of films, from first-run
Tel 202/966-6000. www.theavalon.org. 5612 C
NW, at Northampton St. Take L2 Metrobus on Connec..
Tickets $7–$9.75 adults.

Carter Barron Amphitheater (p. 181) UPPER NORTHWEST Open-air theater in Rock Creek Park that hosts free summer performances by National Symphony, Shakespeare Theatre, and others. Free tickets for many performances available day of event at box office and other locations. Some paid performances. Call or check website for details.... Tel 202/426-0486. www.nps.gov/rocr/cbarron. 16th St. and Colorado Ave. NW. Take S4 Metrobus from 16th St. or grab a cab. Ticket prices vary.

Cineplex Odeon Uptown (p. 184) UPPER NORTHWEST Washington's best motion-picture showplace. Large theater with balcony, huge screen, excellent sound system, pick of the first-run flicks.... Tel 800/326-3264. www.moviewatcher.com. 3426 Connecticut Ave. NW, between Newark and Ordway sts. Cleveland Park Metro. Tickets $7.50–$9.50 adults.

Dance Place (p. 181) NORTHEAST School and performance space that explores contemporary, postmodern, tap, and ethnic styles as well as performance art.... Tel 202/269-1600. www.dance place.org. 3225 8th St. NE, between Kearney and Monroe sts. Brookland/CUA Metro or take cab. Ticket prices vary.

DAR Constitution Hall (p. 182) DOWNTOWN Large auditorium hosts a variety of programs.... Tel 202/628-4780. www.dar.org. 18th St. NW, between C and D sts. Farragut W. Metro. Ticket prices vary.

D.C. United (p. 185) EAST CAPITOL STREET Plays Major League Soccer games at Robert F. Kennedy Stadium and usually plays well.... Tel 202/587-5000. www.dcunited.com. Robert F. Kennedy Memorial Stadium, E. Capitol St. at 22nd St. Stadium/Armory Metro. Tickets $16–$40.

FedEx Field (p. 182) MARYLAND You probably won't score tickets to a Redskins game at this enormous football stadium, but maybe you'll be drawn to some huge concert or festival. Tel 301/276-6050. www.redskins.com/fedexfield. 1600 FedEx Way, Landover, MD. Walk 1 mile from Morgan Blvd. Metrorail station or take shuttle bus from Landover Metrorail station during events. Ticket prices vary.

:mfest DC (p. 184) Annual spring film festival with movies screened all over town.... *Tel 202/628-3456. www.filmfestdc.org.*

Folger Theatre (p. 181) CAPITOL HILL Elizabethan theater replica in Folger Shakespeare Library. Presents Shakespeare, plays by others, poetry readings, music concerts.... *Tel 202/544-7077. www.folger.edu/whatson.cfm?cid=. 201 E. Capitol St. SE, at 2nd St. Capitol S. Metro. Tickets $10–$40.*

Ford's Theatre (p. 180) PENN QUARTER Site of Lincoln's assassination functioning again as theater. Lincoln Museum in basement.... *Tel 202/347-4833. www.fordstheatre.org. 511 10th St. NW, between E and F sts. Metro Center Metro. Tickets $25–$55.*

John F. Kennedy Center for the Performing Arts (p. 179) FOGGY BOTTOM Washington's performing-arts hub. Home to National Symphony Orchestra, Washington National Opera, children's programs, traveling shows, restaurants, and guided tours. There are free performances at 6pm daily on Millennium Stage and outstanding views from the terrace.... *Tel 202/467-4600 (800/444-1324). www.kennedy-center.org. 2700 F St. NW, between New Hampshire Ave. and Rock Creek Pkwy. Free shuttle bus from Foggy Bottom/GWU Metrorail station every 15 minutes Mon–Fri 9:45am–midnight, Sat 10am–midnight, Sun noon–midnight, federal holidays 4pm–midnight. Tours Mon–Fri 10am–5pm, Sat–Sun 10am–1pm. Free admission; charge for performances varies.*

Landmark's E Street Cinema (p. 184) DOWNTOWN Multiplex shows independent, foreign, and documentary films.... *Tel 202/452-7672. www.landmarktheatres.com. E St. at 11th St. NW. Metro Center Metro. Tickets $6.75–$9.50 adults.*

Lincoln Theatre (p. 182) U STREET Diverse events presented in restored former movie theater and vaudeville house in the U Street nightlife neighborhood.... *Tel 202/328-6000. www.thelincolntheatre.org. 1215 U St. NW, between 12th and 13th sts. U St./Cardozo Metro. Ticket prices vary.*

Lisner Auditorium (p. 182) FOGGY BOTTOM Wide range of performances presented on George Washington University campus.... *Tel 202/994-6800. www.lisner.org. 730 21st St. NW, at H St. Foggy Bottom/GWU Metro. Ticket prices vary.*

Mary Pickford Theater (p. 184) CAPITOL HILL On third floor of Library of Congress Madison Building, this theater delves the infinite depths of the library's film and TV-show collection. Free reservations can be made Monday through Friday from 9am to 4pm up to 1 week before the show.... *Tel 202/707-5677. www. loc.gov/rr/mopic/pickford/pickford.html. Independence Ave. SE* *between 1st and 2nd sts. Capitol S. Metro. Screenings most Tues and Fri, many Thurs, usually 7pm. Free admission.*

Merriweather Post Pavilion (p. 183) MARYLAND Summer entertainment center with roofed open-air theater and open-to-all-the-elements lawn, about an hour north of downtown Washington.... *Tel 410/715-5550. www.merriweathermusic.com. 10475 Little Patuxent Pkwy., Columbia, MD. Ticket prices vary.*

Military Concerts (p. 183) CAPITOL HILL Army, Navy, Marine, and Air Force bands take turns performing at the West Front of the Capitol June through August. *Tel 202/895-5060. Capitol S. Metro. Mon–Wed and Fri 8pm. Free admission.*

Millennium Stage (p. 183) FOGGY BOTTOM The freebie performance space in Kennedy Center's Grand Foyer. You probably don't know most of these performers, but the occasional headliner does show up—Bobby McFerrin, Patti Smith, Norah Jones, the Pointer Sisters, Earl Scruggs, Asleep at the Wheel among them. Also occasional appearances by members of top D.C. groups such as the National Symphony and the Washington National Opera.... *Tel 202/467-4600 (800/444-1324). www.kennedy-center.org/programs/millennium. 2700 F St. NW, between New Hampshire Ave. and Rock Creek Pkwy. Free Kennedy Center shuttle bus from Foggy Bottom/GWU Metrorail station. Performances daily 6pm. Free admission.*

National Symphony Orchestra (p. 183) World-class orchestra performs at Kennedy Center, Carter Baron Amphitheater, and Wolf Trap.... *Tel 202/467-4600 (800/444-1324). www.kennedy-center.org/nso. Tickets $20–$80 at Kennedy Center; $18–$46 at Wolf Trap; free at Carter Baron.*

National Theatre (p. 179) DOWNTOWN America's top stars have performed here since 1835. Special Saturday kids' shows 9:30 and 11am.... *Tel 202/628-6161 (800/447-7400) (children's program information Tel 202/783-3372). www.nationaltheatre.org. 1321 Pennsylvania Ave. NW, at 13th St. Metro Center Metro. Ticket prices vary. Free Sat morning tickets distributed first-come, first-served half-hour before performance.*

Nissan Pavilion at Stone Ridge (p. 183) VIRGINIA Modernist megaspace—10,000 seats in pavilion, crawl space for 15,000 on lawn—in wilds of Prince William County. Presents stars of all kinds of popular music.... *Tel 703/754-6400. www.nissanpavilion.com. 7800 Cellar Door Dr., 1¼ miles off I-66, Bristow, VA, about an hour from downtown D.C.*

THE INDEX

ENTERTAINMENT

192

Phoenix Theatres Union Station (p. 184) CAPITOL HILL Another first-run movie complex.... *Tel 703/842-4455. 50 Massachusetts Ave. NE, in Union Station. Union Station Metro. Tickets $6.75–$8.75 adults.*

Regal Gallery Place (p. 184) PENN QUARTER Washington's newest first-run multiplex.... *Tel 800/326-3264. www.fandango. com. 701 7th St. NW, at G St. Gallery Place/Chinatown Metro. Tickets $7.50–$9.75 adults.*

Robert F. Kennedy Memorial Stadium (p. 182) EAST CAPITOL STREET Former home of Redskins football and Senators base-ball, current home of Nationals baseball, D.C. United soccer, and giant concerts.... *Tel 202/547-9077. E. Capitol St. at 22nd St. Stadium/Armory Metro.*

Shakespeare Theatre (p. 180) PENN QUARTER This highly praised company already was playing the Bard and others in a wonderful auditorium known as the Landsburgh Theatre. The troupe was to get a second, adjoining facility to play in during 2007.... *Tel 202/547-1122. www.shakespearetheatre.org. 450 7th St. NW, between D and E sts. Archives/Navy Memorial Metro. Tickets $14–$71.*

Silver Theatre (p. 184) MARYLAND American Film Institute shows films and presents educational programs about films in this restored 1938 theater.... *Tel 301/495-6720. www.afi.com/ silver. 8633 Colesville Rd., Silver Spring, MD, between Georgia Ave. and Fenton St. Silver Spring Metro. Tickets $6.75–$9.25 adults.*

Studio Theatre (p. 181) DUPONT CIRCLE The theater is renovated and growing. The company presents contemporary works.... *Tel 202/332-3300. www.studiotheatre.org. 1501 14th St. NW, at P St. Walk six blocks from Dupont Circle Metro or take cab. Ticket prices vary. Half-price for students on tickets available half-hour before curtain.*

Verizon Center (p. 182) PENN QUARTER Marvelous sports/con-cert arena with great sightlines from seats.... *Tel 202/661-5000. www.verizoncenter.com. 601 F St. NW, at 6th St. Gallery Place–Chinatown Metro. Ticket prices vary.*

Warner Theatre (p. 180) DOWNTOWN After a life presenting vaudeville, first-run movies, and even porn, the 80-year-old reju-venated Warner now thrives with popular concerts, plays, musi-cals, and dance.... *Tel 202/783-4000. www.warnertheatre.com. 513 13th St. NW, between E and F sts. Metro Center Metro. Ticket prices vary.*

THE INDEX

ENTERTAINMENT

Washington Ballet (p. 181) FOGGY BOTTOM Presents contemporary and classic works at both the Kennedy Center (p. 179) and the Warner Theatre (p. 180).... *Tel 202/362-3606. www. washingtonballet.org. Ticket prices vary.*

Washington Capitals (p. 185) PENN QUARTER National Hockey League team skates in Verizon Center. As long as Caps sell Eagles Nest tickets at four for $20, they offer the best bargain in professional sports.... *Tel 202/266-2200. www.washington caps.com. 601 F St. NW, at 6th St. Gallery Place–Chinatown Metro. Tickets $5–$225.*

Washington Mystics (p. 185) PENN QUARTER Women's National Basketball Association team has consistently led the league in attendance but not in games won.... *Tel 202/266-2200. www. wnba.com/mystics. 601 F St. NW, at 6th St., in Verizon Center. Gallery Place–Chinatown Metro. Tickets $10–$110.*

Washington National Opera (p. 181) FOGGY BOTTOM Artistic Director Placido Domingo lends superstar cachet to this troupe.... *Tel 202/295-2400 (800/876-7372). www.dc-opera.org. 2700 F St. NW, between New Hampshire Ave. and Rock Creek Pkwy., in Kennedy Center. Free Kennedy Center shuttle bus from Foggy Bottom/GWU Metrorail station. Tickets $45–$300.*

Washington Nationals (p. 185) EAST CAPITOL STREET D.C. sports fans rejoiced at the return of major league baseball in 2005. And it's the real, National League version, in which pitchers hit, batters field, and managers must manage. Upper-deck seats behind home plate offer a surprisingly good view for $16. Avoid the rear terrace seats.... *Tel 888/632-6287. http:// washington.nationals.mlb.com. E. Capitol St. at 22nd St., in Robert F. Kennedy Stadium. Stadium/Armory Metro. Tickets $7–$115.*

Washington Redskins (p. 185) MARYLAND D.C.'s always-sold-out pro football team. You can pay $2,500 to $4,150 for one premium season ticket, join the tens of thousands on the waiting list for regular season tickets, or contact a broker and pay hundreds of dollars for one ticket to one game.... *Tel 301/276-6050. www.redskins.com. 1600 FedEx Way, Landover, MD. Walk 1 mile from Morgan Blvd. Metrorail station or take shuttle bus from Landover Metrorail station during games.*

Washington Wizards (p. 185) PENN QUARTER Longtime National Basketball Association doormat has shown some promise in last couple years.... *Tel 202/661-5050. www.nba.com/wizards. 601 F St. NW, at 6th St., in Verizon Center. Gallery Place–Chinatown Metro. Tickets $35–$175.*

THE INDEX

ENTERTAINMENT

Wolf Trap Farm Park for the Performing Arts (p. 181) VIRGINIA
National park with open-air, roofed pavilion (called Filene Center)
and lawn seating, as well as smaller performance spaces, about
30 minutes from downtown D.C. on Dulles Toll Road. (Stay off
the parallel airport access highway or you can be fined.) Wide
range of entertainment, from National Symphony Orchestra to
rock and country stars, former stars, and programs for kids....
*Tel 703/255-1900 (ticket info Tel 703/255-1868, ticket pur-
chases Tel 703/255-9653). www.wolftrap.org. 1551 Trap Rd.,
Vienna, VA, at Dulles Toll Rd. (Va. Rte. 267) exit 15 (westbound
only). For Filene Center performances (except International Children's Festival and Summer Blastoff), Wolf Trap shuttle bus connects with West Falls Church Metrorail station every 20 minutes
from 2 hours before showtime till showtime, then returns after the
show. ($5 per person round-trip.)* **Note:** *Last Metrorail train
departs station for D.C. Sun–Thurs 11:32pm; Fri–Sat 1:32am.
Tickets $10–$70.*

Woolly Mammoth Theatre Company (p. 181) PENN QUARTER
Innovative, exploratory theater company in brand-new digs.
Theatergoers 25 and younger can get tickets for $10. Anyone
can buy $10 tickets, when available, 15 minutes before the
show.... *Tel 202/393-3939. www.woollymammoth.net. 641 D St.
NW, between 6th and 7th sts. Archives/Navy Memorial Metro.
Tickets usually $20–$48 adults.*

HOTLINES & OTHER BASICS

Airports... **Ronald Reagan Washington National Airport** (DCA; Tel 703/417-8000; www.metwashairports.com/ national) is Washington's favorite airport, scenically located just across the Potomac River from Washington in suburban Virginia. Locals still call it "National," even though the Republican-controlled Congress insisted on renaming it after their No. 1 hero in 1998. (Yes, those same Republicans who constantly rail against the federal government and preach the virtue of states' rights and local control.) You now can catch some coast-to-coast nonstops here, but you have to go elsewhere for nonstop international flights (other than to Canada and the Caribbean). National operates under anti-noise regulations that severely restrict flights between 10pm and 7am. National opened a spectacular new terminal in 1997, which turned this place into a marvelously attractive and efficient airport.

Taxi fares from National to downtown D.C. are about $11 to $12 for the 15-minute (traffic willing) ride. (See "Taxis," below, for more details.) **SuperShuttle** (Tel 202/ 296-6662, 800/258-3826; www.supershuttle.com) provides door-to-door shared van service to downtown for about $13 for one passenger, $8 for each additional passenger.

Metrorail (Tel 202/637-7000; www.wmata.com) Yellow and Blue Line trains connect National with downtown D.C. in less than 20 minutes for about $1.35 to $1.65.

Washington Dulles International Airport (IAD; Tel 703/572-2700; www.metwashairports.com/dulles) is located in the rapidly developing Virginia countryside 26 miles and, in the absence of bad traffic, about 45 minutes west of downtown D.C. Dulles, with its sleek Eero Saarinen–designed terminal, has both short- and long-haul domestic flights and international service. This airport is constantly growing and renovating and is much harder to get around than National. You have to take buslike "mobile lounges" to get from the main terminal to the midfield terminals where most planes pull up. Eventually, underground trains will connect the terminals. The first stage, linking the main terminal to concourses B and C, is scheduled for completion in 2009.

SuperShuttle (Tel 202/296-6662, 800/258-3826; www.supershuttle.com) provides door-to-door shared van service to downtown D.C. for about $22 for the first passenger and $10 for each additional rider. **Washington Flyer** (Tel 703/661-6655) operates exclusive taxi service from Dulles, but you can use any cab you want to travel to the airport. Cab fare to downtown averages $54. **Washington Flyer buses** (Tel 888/927-4359; www.washfly.com) will take you from Dulles to the West Falls Church Metrorail station in 25 minutes for $9 one-way and $16 roundtrip. From there, the 22-minute train ride to Metro Center costs $1.85 to $2.65 depending on the time of day. The best bargain is the 5A **Metrobus** express (Tel 202/637-7000; timetable at www.wmata.com/timetables/dc/5a.pdf) between Dulles and the L'Enfant Plaza Metrorail station just south of the Mall. It takes about 50 minutes and costs just $3.

Baltimore Washington International Thurgood Marshall Airport (BWI; Tel 800/435-9294; www.bwi airport.com) is an even bigger mouthful than the official name for National. But at least the locals were the ones who decided to add the name of the Baltimore-born Supreme Court justice and civil rights legend to BWI's original moniker. This airport is a 32-mile, 45-to-60-minute drive from downtown D.C. and provides national and international service and often offers better fares than

National or Dulles. A **taxi** to downtown D.C. will cost about $62. You can get door-to-door shared van service to downtown D.C. on the **SuperShuttle** (Tel 800/258-3826; www.supershuttle.com) for $31 for the first passenger and $11 for each additional rider.

Free shuttle buses connect the terminal to the **BWI Railroad Station** (Tel 410/672-6169) where **Amtrak** (Tel 800/872-7245; www.amtrak.com) and **Maryland Rail Commuter,** or MARC (Tel 800/325-7245; www.mta maryland.com), trains depart for Washington's Union Station. MARC's Penn Line, which runs Monday to Friday only, takes 30 to 40 minutes and costs $6 one-way. The fares on Amtrak, which runs all the time, range from $11 to $37, depending on time and class of service, and the trip takes 25 to 35 minutes. As with National, the cheapest way to get to and from BWI is by **Metrobus.** The B30 bus (Tel 202/637-7000; timetable at www.wmata.com/time tables/md/b30.pdf) costs $3 and takes about 35 minutes to travel between the airport and the Greenbelt Metrorail Station. The Metrorail ride from there to Penn Quarter takes about 25 minutes and costs between $2.35 and $3.05.

Babysitters... Many hotels will secure a bonded sitter for you. Ask the concierge or at the front desk. **White House Nannies** (Tel 301/652-8088, 800/266-9024; www.white housenannies.com) sends sitters to hotels on short notice. Reserving early saves you money.

Buses... Greyhound (Tel 800/231-2222; www.greyhound. com) offers national service. **Peter Pan** (Tel 800/237-8747; www.peterpanbus.com) serves the Northeast. Both bus lines use the terminal at 1005 1st St. NE, at K Street, one extremely long block from Union Station's rear parking garage entrance.

Metrobus operates to all areas of the city and close-in suburbs, with many routes providing 24-hour service. The fare is $1.25 with free bus-to-bus transfers. Transferring from Metrorail to Metrobus costs 35¢. Get the transfer from a machine in the station. There is no bus-to-rail transfer discount. Check out the Metro Information Center (Tel 202/637-7000; www.wmata.com).

For $1 (exact change) you can ride the bright red **Circulator** bus around downtown and many tourist spots: they run every 5 to 10 minutes between the Convention Center and the Southwest Waterfront, between Union Station and Georgetown, and around the National Mall. The Mall route operates from 9:30am to 6pm daily, the others 7am to 9pm (Tel 202/962-1423; www.dccirculator.com).

Car rentals... Major rental-car companies are represented at all three airports, and several are at Union Station. Call **Alamo** (Tel 800/462-5266; www.alamo.com), **Avis** (Tel 800/331-1212; www.avis.com), **Budget** (Tel 800/527-0700; www.budget.com), **Dollar** (Tel 800/800-3665; www.dollar.com), **Enterprise** (Tel 800/261-7331; www.enterprise.com), **Hertz** (Tel 800/654-3131; www.hertz.com), **National** (Tel 800/227-7368; www.nationalcar.com), or **Thrifty** (Tel 800/847-4389; www.thrifty.com).

Convention center... The new **Washington Convention Center** (Tel 202/249-3000, 800/368-9000; www.dcconvention.com) sits between Mt. Vernon Square and 7th, 9th, and N streets, at the Mt. Vernon Square Metrorail station.

Doctors and dentists... Ask your hotel's concierge or the front desk for the name of a physician who treats hotel guests. Or try the physician referral services at **George Washington University Hospital** (Tel 888/449-3627), **Washington Hospital Center** (Tel 202/877-3627), or **Georgetown University Hospital** (Tel 202/342-2400). In a dental emergency, call the **District of Columbia Dental Society Referral Service** (Tel 202/547-7615).

Driving in D.C.... Don't. Trust me.

Emergencies... For **police, fire department,** and **ambulance service,** call Tel 911. For the **Poison Center,** call Tel 202/625-3333. Twenty-four-hour hospital emergency rooms are at **George Washington University Hospital** downtown, 900 23rd St. NW, at I Street (Tel 202/715-4911); **Georgetown University Hospital** in Georgetown, 3800 Reservoir Rd. NW, at 38th Street (Tel 202/444-2119); and **Sibley Memorial Hospital** in Upper Northwest, 5255 Loughboro Rd. NW, between Macarthur Boulevard and Dalecarla Parkway (Tel 202/537-4080).

Gay and lesbian resources... Whitman-Walker Clinic
(Tel 202/797-3500; www.wwc.org) supplies information
and various medical services. **Dignity/Washington** (Tel 202/
546-2235; www.dignitywashington.org) is a Catholic support group.

Newspapers and magazines... The *Washington Post*
(35¢ daily, $1.50 Sun; Tel 202/334-6000; www.washington
post.com) is one of the world's great daily newspapers,
although it sometimes seems better at covering the nation
and the world than the city in which it is located. Its online
"City Guide" can be accessed from the top of its website's
home page. The *Washington Times* (25¢ daily, $1.50 Sun;
Tel 202/636-3000; www.washingtontimes.com) is a conservative daily published by the Unification Church
(Moonies). *Washington City Paper* (free; Tel 202/332-
2100; www.washingtoncitypaper.com) is D.C.'s leading
weekly alternative tabloid with invaluable listings of local
events. Founded in 1969, the weekly *Washington Blade*
(free; Tel 202/797-7000; www.washblade.com) is one of
the nation's pioneering gay-oriented publications. *Washingtonian* ($3.95; Tel 202/296-3600; www.washingtonian.
com) is one of the country's better monthly city magazines.
It lists events, reviews restaurants, and compiles best-of
lists based on its critics' and readers' opinions. At its website home page, you'll find links to "Restaurants & Dining," "Arts & Fun," "Visitors Guide," and other useful
topics.

Parking... If you heed the "Driving in D.C." item above, this
will not concern you. If you ignored it, you've set yourself
up for quite a challenge. Metered parking is available on
streets throughout the city, but you're restricted to a few-
hours stay, you'll need a Santa's sack of quarters to keep the
meters happy, and empty spaces are hard to find. The
Washington Post reported that 30% of D.C. traffic at peak
times consists of vehicles looking for parking spaces. Free
parking is available on and around the Mall after 10am
weekdays and all day Saturday and Sunday, but open spots
are scarce and you can only stay 2 or 3 hours. It may be
possible to park in a nearby residential neighborhood—
Capitol Hill, for example—and walk a few blocks to Mall
attractions. But generally, if the neighborhood is close
enough and safe enough, only cars with resident decals are

allowed to park for more than an hour or two. Follow the sign instructions.

That leaves paid parking lots and garages, which are plentiful but expensive. Lots in central D.C. typically charge $4 per hour up to $15 or more a day, often with "early-bird" discounts before 8 or 8:30am. Closing times vary.

Parking illegally is a big mistake in D.C. Parking-enforcement officers are the District's most efficient employees.

Radio stations... Some of Washington's top AM radio stations are WMAL, 630, news/talk/entertainment; WAVA, 780, Christian/conservative talk; WTEM, 980, sports; WUST, 1120, ethnic/international; WWRC, 1260, liberal talk; WYCB, 1340, gospel; WOL, 1450, African-American talk; WTWP, 1500, Washington Post radio; WPGC, 1580, gospel. Among the top FM stations are WAMU, 88.5, NPR; WPFW, 89.3, Pacifica; WCSP, 90.1, C-SPAN; WETA, 90.9, NPR; WKYS, 93.9, hip-hop/R&B; WARW, 94.7, classic rock; WPGC-FM, 95.5, urban contemporary; WHUR, 96.3, adult urban contemporary and classic; WASH, 97.1, adult light rock; WMZQ, 98.7, country; WHFS, 99.1, Spanish adult contemporary; WBIG, 100.3, classic rock; WWDC, 101.1, rock/alternative rock; WMMJ, 102.3, urban adult contemporary; WTOP, 103.5, news/sports/traffic/weather; WGMS, 104, classical; WAVA, 105.1, Christian/conservative talk; WJZW, 105.9, smooth jazz/easy listening; WJFK, 106.7, talk; WTPW, 107.7, *Washington Post* radio.

Subways... **Metrorail** (Tel 202/637-7000; www.wmata.com) connects most Washington attractions, hotel clusters, outlying D.C. neighborhoods, and Virginia/Maryland suburbs that tourists are likely to visit. Metrorail—Metro for short—does not serve Georgetown or Adams Morgan directly, but there are rail-to-bus links that do. Spotless, safe, and efficient, it's a system where rules against graffiti, eating, and drinking are not only enforced but respected. People are arrested—*Note: are arrested*—for eating a potato chip or continuing to chew after entering a Metro station.

Five color-coded lines—Red, Blue, Orange, Green, and Yellow—operate Monday to Thursday 5am to midnight, Friday 5am to 3am; Saturday 7am to 3am, and Sunday 7am to midnight. Fares range from $1.35 to $3.90 depending on length of trip, time of day, and day of the week. The lowest fare covers trips between most tourist sites. Up to two children younger than 5 ride free with each paying adult.

Passengers must purchase encoded fare cards that let you through the automated gates and to the trains. Fare-card vending machines that accept everything from nickels to $20 bills and credit cards are in every station. (*Note:* They give a maximum $5 in change and it's all in coins.) Invest in fare-card futures if you plan to use Metro a lot. Putting $10 or $20 on your card will save you the time and frustration of having to purchase a new card for each trip, an especially troublesome task during rush hour. For $6.50, you can buy a 1-day pass that allows unlimited travel after 9:30am weekdays or all day Saturday, Sunday, and federal holidays. The 7-day short-trip pass, for $22, offers a week's worth of riding most places tourists go. An unlimited 7-day pass costs $33.

Taxes... The D.C. general sales tax is 5.75%, restaurant tax 10%, hotel tax 14.5%. Maryland's sales and restaurant taxes are 5%. An additional 1% to 10% lodging and amusement tax may be imposed by localities. Virginia's general sales tax is 4.5%.

Taxis... Unlike taxis almost everywhere else, D.C.'s don't have meters. For years, D.C. cabs have operated according to a bewildering zone system. Drivers compute fares according to the number of subzone boundaries the cab crosses in the course of a trip. The current fares start at $6.50. Crossing into another subzone makes the fare $8.80, and it continues to increase as more subzones are entered. Trips outside the district are charged by distance—$3.25 for the first ½ mile, 90¢ for each additional ½ mile. There also are surcharges of $1.50 for each additional passenger 6 and older, $1 for trips during the 7-to-9:30am or 4-to-6:30pm weekday rush hours, 50¢ to $2 for luggage handled by the driver depending on its size, and $2 if you telephone for a cab instead of hailing it on the street. There's a $1.75 surcharge for single passengers at National Airport and a $2.50 surcharge when the DC Taxicab Commission declares a snow emergency.

Beware: It may cost more to ride a couple blocks across a subzone border than it would to travel for many blocks within one subzone. If you know where the boundary line is, get out of the cab before you reach it. Taxis have Zone Maps; for a better map, with fare calculator, go to www.dctaxi.dc.gov/dctaxi and click "Taxicab Zone Maps."

Other D.C. taxi quirks: It's perfectly legit for drivers to pick up additional passengers without the consent of the original passenger, as long as the original passenger doesn't have to go more than five blocks out of the way. The driver needs the original passenger's consent if the subsequent passenger has a pet or other animal (other than a Seeing Eye dog). Each passenger pays full fare for his or her trip.

Washington cabbies cruise major government/business/tourist areas and usually are easy to find during the day and early evening. Off-hours and off-the-beaten-track, cabs can be nearly impossible to hail. Try outside a major hotel. Or pay that $2 surcharge to summon a taxi by phone. Try **Diamond Cab** (Tel 202/387-6200) or **Yellow Cab** (Tel 202/544-1212).

Tipping... Tipping is a fact of life in Washington. Keep singles on hand for all the porters, doormen, maids, and checkroom attendants you'll encounter. The tip for the concierge is trickier: nothing for basic directions or information, but at least $5 and possibly much more (depending on degree of difficulty) for making restaurant reservations, obtaining hard-to-come-by tickets, or performing some other service. Restaurant waiters and bartenders get 15% to 20% of the bill, as do taxi and limo drivers.

Trains... Washington's **Union Station** is the southern terminus of **Amtrak**'s (Tel 800/872-7245; www.amtrak.com) frequent Northeast Corridor service and has links to less frequent and slower trains throughout the country. There's a Metrorail Red Line station on the lower level and a gigantic food court, restaurants, shops, and a movie theater.

Travelers with disabilities... Washington is a good city for people with disabilities, partly because it wants to prove it can obey laws (notably the Americans with Disabilities Act) as well as pass them. The **White House** has a special entrance for the disabled; the **Lincoln and Jefferson memorials** and the **Washington Monument** have elevators for disabled visitors. In addition to accessible entrances, the **Capitol** and other congressional office buildings offer other services to the disabled—wheelchair loans and interpreters for the deaf or hard of hearing, for example (Tel 202/224-4048; www.aoc.gov/cc/visit/accessibility.cfm). Handicapped parking is available along the streets, and most museums are designed to comply with federal regulations regarding entrance ramps, elevator service, accessible restrooms, and water fountains. The **Smithsonian Institution** distributes a free brochure, *Smithsonian Access,* detailing accessibility features, parking, special entrances, and special tours available at all Smithsonian facilities, including the National Zoo. Pick up a brochure at any Smithsonian information desk, or contact the **Smithsonian Information Center** (Tel 202/633-1000; www.si.edu/visit) or the accessibility program (Tel 202/786-2942; www.si.edu/visit/visitors_with_disabilities.htm). Difficulties are most likely to be encountered at old, historical properties.

TV stations... Channel 4 (WRC) is the NBC affiliate; Channel 5 (WTTG) is Fox; Channel 7 (WJLA), ABC; Channel 9 (WUSA), CBS; Channel 20 (WDCA), MNTV; Channel 22 (WMPT), Maryland Public Television; Channel 26 (WETA), D.C. Public Television; Channel 32 (WHUT), Howard University Public Television; Channel 50 (WBDC), CW. NewsChannel 8 is Washington's local version of CNN—round-the-clock news, except when they're running an infomercial or the occasional sports event. Strangely, it's on Channel 28 on the Comcast cable system and 48 on RCN.

Visitor information... Washington, D.C. **Convention and Tourism Corporation:** Tel 202/789-7000; www.washington.org; 901 7th St. NW, Suite 400, Washington, DC 20001. **D.C. Chamber of Commerce:** Tel 202/347-7201; www.dcchamber.org; 1213 K St. NW, Washington, DC 20005. **Visitor Information Center:** Tel 866/324-7386; www.dcvisit.com; 1300 Pennsylvania Ave. NW, Washington, DC 20004 (at 13th St., in the Ronald Reagan Building and International Trade Center).

What's happening... The **Smithsonian Information Line** (Tel 202/633-1000) provides recorded information about the Smithsonian museums. **Kennedy Center Performance Information** (Tel 202/467-4600) provides information about performances and lets you charge tickets.

GENERAL INDEX

210

Accommodations

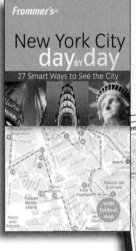

Explore over 3,500 destinations.

TOKYO 7766 miles

LONDON 3818 miles

TORONTO 4682 miles

SYDNEY 5087 miles

NEW YORK 4947 miles

LOS ANGELES 2556 miles

HONG KONG 5638 miles

Frommers.com makes it easy.

Find a destination. ✓ Book a trip. ✓ Get hot travel deals.
Buy a guidebook. ✓ Enter to win vacations. ✓ Listen to podcasts.
Check out the latest travel news. ✓ Share trip photos and memories.
And much more.

FROMMER'S® CRUISE GUIDES

Alaska Cruises & Ports of Call | Cruises & Ports of Call | European Cruises & Ports of Call

FROMMER'S® NATIONAL PARK GUIDES

Algonquin Provincial Park | National Parks of the American West | Yosemite and Sequoia & Kings
Banff & Jasper | Rocky Mountain | Canyon
Grand Canyon | Yellowstone & Grand Teton | Zion & Bryce Canyon

FROMMER'S® MEMORABLE WALKS

London | Paris | San Francisco
New York | Rome

FROMMER'S® WITH KIDS GUIDES

Chicago | National Parks | Toronto
Hawaii | New York City | Walt Disney World® & Orlando
Las Vegas | San Francisco | Washington, D.C.
London

SUZY GERSHMAN'S BORN TO SHOP GUIDES

France | London | Paris
Hong Kong, Shanghai & Beijing | New York | San Francisco
Italy

FROMMER'S® IRREVERENT GUIDES

Amsterdam | London | Rome
Boston | Los Angeles | San Francisco
Chicago | Manhattan | Walt Disney World®
Las Vegas | Paris | Washington, D.C.

FROMMER'S® BEST-LOVED DRIVING TOURS

Austria | Germany | Northern Italy
Britain | Ireland | Scotland
California | Italy | Spain
France | New England | Tuscany & Umbria

THE UNOFFICIAL GUIDES®

Adventure Travel in Alaska | Hawaii | Paris
Beyond Disney | Ireland | San Francisco
California with Kids | Las Vegas | South Florida including Miami &
Central Italy | London | the Keys
Chicago | Maui | Walt Disney World®
Cruises | Mexico's Best Beach Resorts | Walt Disney World® for
Disneyland® | Mini Mickey | Grown-ups
England | New Orleans | Walt Disney World® with Kids
Florida | New York City | Washington, D.C.
Florida with Kids

SPECIAL-INTEREST TITLES

Athens Past & Present
Best Places to Raise Your Family
Cities Ranked & Rated
500 Places to Take Your Kids Before They Grow Up
Frommer's Best Day Trips from London
Frommer's Best RV & Tent Campgrounds
  in the U.S.A.

Frommer's Exploring America by RV
Frommer's NYC Free & Dirt Cheap
Frommer's Road Atlas Europe
Frommer's Road Atlas Ireland
Great Escapes From NYC Without Wheels
Retirement Places Rated

FROMMER'S® PHRASEFINDER DICTIONARY GUIDES

French | Italian | Spanish